ORPHANS
OF
THE HEART

ORPHANS
OF
THE HEART

Lucille Iremonger

SECKER & WARBURG

Distributed by David & Charles, Inc.
North Pomfret, Vermont 05053

First published in England 1984 by
Martin Secker & Warburg Limited
54 Poland Street, London W1V 3DF

Copyright © Lucille Iremonger 1984

British Library Cataloguing in Publication Data

Iremonger, Lucille
  Orphans of the heart.
  1. Personality   2. Child psychology
  I. Title
  155.2'34   BF698

  ISBN   0–436–21803–8

Typeset by Inforum Ltd, Portsmouth
Printed and bound in Great Britain by
Biddles Ltd, Guildford and King's Lynn

"The world is full of orphans: firstly, those
Who are so in the strict sense of the phrase;
But many a lonely tree the loftier grows
Than others crowded in the Forest's maze –
The next are such as are not doomed to lose
Their tender parents, in their budding days,
But, merely, their parental tenderness,
Which leaves them orphans of the heart no less."

Byron Don Juan, Canto XVII

CONTENTS

vii

ACKNOWLEDGMENTS

I owe much to those who have so generously accepted my theory, which can be briefly described as "the Phaeton complex". My dept to the famous French psychiatrist, the late Maryse Choisy, is immense. I offer my thanks to many others, to Professor Hugh Barrington of the University of Newcastle-upon-Tyne in particular.

Five years after *The Fiery Chariot* was published, the distinguished Dr Pierre Rentchnick, editor of *Médecine et Hygiène*, published in Geneva, brought out a pamphlet called *Les Orphelins mènent le monde, une nouvelle théorie sur la genèse de la volonté de puissance politique*. (Orphans lead the world, a new theory about the will to political power). Completely independently, he had come to the same conclusions as I had done, and he offered the world the result of his conclusions. He, however, took his orphans and bastards to the age of twenty, while I prefer to regard childhood as generally ending at around fifteen at the latest. He also confined his orphans and bastards to world leaders, as I had done mine to Prime Ministers. In this book I shall be taking them from various other fields as well.

As always, I thank my husband for his never-failing help and support. I also offer very special thanks indeed to my daughter, Mrs Pennant Huskinson, who, despite being a very active barrister, wife and mother, has produced an endless supply of Phaetons for my lists. Without her keen eye those lists would have been much slighter than they are.

The author and publishers acknowledge permission to reprint extracts from the following publications:

The Primal Scream, Copyright © 1970 by Arthur Janov, first published 1973 Abacus by Sphere Books Ltd; also reprinted by permission of G.P. Putnam's Sons.

Children Under Stress by Sula Wolff (Penguin Books, Second edition 1981) pp. 90, 96. Copyright © Sula Wolff, 1969, 1973, 1981. Reprinted by permission of Penguin Books Ltd.

Fatherless Families by Margaret Wynn, reprinted by permission of Michael Joseph.

Augustus John by Michael Holroyd, reprinted by permission of William Heinemann Ltd. and Holt Rinehart & Winston. Copyright © Michael Holroyd 1974.

The Paderewski Memoirs by Ignace Jan Paderewski and Mary Lawton, published by Collins Publishers, reprinted by permission of the Jagellonian University, Cracow.

The Manson Murders, An Investigation into Motive by Vincent Bugliosi with Curt Gentry, reprinted by permission of W.W. Norton & Company.

The Path to Leadership by Bernard Montgomery, published by Collins Publishers, reprinted by permission of The Viscount Montgomery of Alamein, CBE.

Montgomery of Alamein by Alun Chalfont, reprinted by permission of Weidenfeld & Nicolson.

LUCILLE IREMONGER

CHAPTER 1

In 1970 a book of mine called *The Fiery Chariot* was published.

I had been asked to write a book about Prime Ministers, with special reference to their personal lives, and the choice of those to be treated was entirely mine. I proceeded to read a wide variety of books, in order to make that choice. As I read, I noticed that a particular factor cropped up over and over again. Moreover, I thought that I also perceived a certain broad pattern to their lives, not entirely accounted for by these men's setting themselves to, and attaining, a common objective.

The factor which occurred so frequently that I began to wonder whether it was not of more than passing significance was the loss of a parent in childhood or early adolescence. Out of twenty-four consecutive Prime Ministers, I saw, sixteen had lost a parent, or parents, in childhood – ten had lost a father, and five a mother; and Lords Liverpool and Aberdeen had lost both parents. There was yet another, Ramsay MacDonald, who was actually a bastard.

Next, I looked for the characteristics common to all these childhood-bereaved Prime Ministers. It was clear that these men shared common characteristics. They were abnormally sensitive, reserved and isolated; had a propensity to depression; demonstrated the most powerful drives for attention and for affection; benefited in childhood from the devotion of an outstanding and self-confident mentor; showed extreme religious concern, in one form or another; grieved extravagantly for their dead; were often reckless; suffered from an insatiable ambition; were superstitious; and had an intense devotion to their own children. A further, amusing, reaction, after the advent of Sir Walter Scott, was a predilection for his books. There was also an interesting fascination with storms, in many cases.

My search led me direct to that great French psychiatrist, Maryse Choisy, who had dared successfully to take issue with Freud, the master at whose feet she had once worshipped, and who had written the remarkable *Le Complexe de Phaéton*, published by Psyché, in 1950. Maryse Choisy had asked a question startling in its simplicity, and far-reaching in its implications. Freud had concerned himself with children who had living parents. What of those who had none? For Maryse Choisy spoke from considerable knowledge of bastard orphans who had been thrown on the charity of the State. If the super-ego, or conscience, was born of the Oedipus complex, which led the infant son to wish for his father's death, no less, what if there was no rival parent-figure? Was there then, I asked myself, no Oedipus complex, no conscience, no super-ego, no moral sense to repress murderous instincts in the infant?

Maryse Choisy, however, had found among her bastard orphans quite the contrary. With them there was present a decided super-ego, or conscience, or controlling sense of right and wrong, indeed, one often crueller and more severe than, as she put it, the harshest of fathers. Sometimes this took the form of inner voices, which called on the child to exercise restraint, and often made him turn his back on the common-place pleasures and relaxations in life in order to remain, as he saw it, pure, for some lofty purpose. And among these extremely narcissistic creatures there was not only this exaggerated conscience, but also a very fluid boundary line between the real and the imaginary world. Their demanding consciences were not directed to the realities of life as most people know it, but to their own fantastic worlds. This Maryse Choisy considered the result of the bastard's never having to adjust to the needs of the family in a realistic way. He remained for ever in the state of infancy, where thought and action are the same. The infant, weak and powerless in fact, believes himself to be strong and all-powerful, and when he is filled with a black rage against his father-rival, who is spoiling his cosy, authoritarian and exclusive relationship with his mother, he wishes him dead. If thoughts could kill, his father *would* be dead. In a normal family, the infant soon has it brought home to him that thoughts cannot kill, and that, anyway, the consensus of opinion is that they should not kill, and certainly not in this situation. So his weakness, the growing ambivalence of his relationship with his father, and his own mother's express disapproval, among other pressures, bring him to a sense of the desirable and the possible; and with this realisation comes a lively sense of guilt at his own wicked thoughts. Hence the super-ego or conscience, from the prickings of which most of us learn to flinch, and which we, most of us, more or less, obey.

The bastard, says Maryse Choisy, knows no such conflicts, and no such guilt. With him, his earliest conviction that to will is to achieve – 'I want, and it happens' – is not disturbed. In fact, such thought-processes are never connected, from their beginnings, with the sin of parricide, and therefore strongly repressed. (The original sin, the eating of the forbidden fruit of the tree of knowledge of good and evil, she points out, is the sin of disobedience to the father.) Never checked, the bastard's infantile omnipotence of thought persists. He believes, very noticeably, in magic and the supernatural. Wizards and wonder-workers, and the performers of miracles, from Merlin to Moses and down to village sorcerers, so often sprang from these parentless people, who were themselves often miraculously rescued as babies from the water, and subsequently developed to exercise extraordinary power by their particular "magical" gifts. If wishes were horses, beggars would ride . . . wishes *are* horses with them, she implies, and sometimes, because they think so, and convince others, they do ride.

(In an interesting passage she refers to one of their major, prevalent fantasies, that of marvellous birth. It is a common enough piece of fantasy-comfort with ordinary, unhappy children to console themselves with the thought that they are really the offspring of kings and queens, and come only by some unlucky chance into the power of their dull, low parents. The bastard's fantasy can go further. With him there is a god for a father, conception perhaps by remote impregnation, and virgin birth, often in an atmospheric storm, with thunder and lightning. His fantasy persists much longer than the ordinary unhappy child's. It is unshakeable, even in the face of strong denials. More or less conscious, more or less displaced, it is present with most bastards.)

So Maryse Choisy marvelled at the instinctive re-creation of

3

the old Phaeton myth by even the most ineducable infant waifs for their own purposes. "Already I asked myself," she wrote, "if the myth of Merlin the Magician was not an archetype of the collective unconscious . . . How could the little illiterate boy have found out all by himself the Merlin legend, the Phaeton myth?" And, going to Ovid's verses, recapitulating the Phaeton myth, she claimed that she found there summarised not only the bastard's instinctive fantasy, but the features which linked the cases which she had herself investigated and published.

To her, the sun, Phaeton's father, represented two things – the all–seeing, censorious eye of the outside world; and the warmth denied to those who have not known the love of a mother or father. It is a strange warmth, however. It lights up dark places; but it also burns. It gives life, but it also destroys.

The bastard child, suffering from a feeling of impurity at his impure birth, projects his aggressiveness and his frustrated love on to his unknown father. Phaeton, suffering from this same inferiority, seeks to compensate by a startling feat. For when Phaeton asked his mother who his father was, and she told him, he went to Apollo to seek proof. Apollo promised to give him anything he asked; and Phaeton, to Apollo's horror and terror, demanded nothing less than to be allowed to drive his father's chariot, the sun. Inevitably, he had selected a feat beyond his powers, and which was bound to lead him to disaster. For when one chooses a task beyond one's powers, it is because the unconscious has already planned its failure.

Sors tua mortalis, non est mortale quod optas.
(Thy lot is mortal, not for mortals is what thou askest.)

So spoke his father, the sun, but to no avail.

Consciously Phaeton needed and wanted to be recognised, but, it seems, when one has not been recognised as an infant one cannot tolerate being so later on. If love, in fact, is denied to an infant, he cannot accept it later, though his need for it is almost insatiable. The process is unconscious, but inescapable.

Phaeton was driven. He needed desperately to soar, to be seen flying high. But the drama was all played out in advance, and his ride had to end in a fall. Compulsively he sought the bitter end. He *must* be recognised by his father, even more than by a mere acknowledgment. He *must* demand the ultimate recognition. He *must* take the seat in the chariot which only his

4

father, and not even Jupiter himself, the king of the gods, was allowed to occupy. He *must* be seen to be the son of his father in every particular. Only, he is not a god like his father. At best his mother, one of the Oceanides, was only an inferior deity, if not actually as low as a mortal. From the moment when he sat in the chariot, that is to say, from the moment when he had dared to take the place which his father had not, in fact, acknowledged to be his rightful one, he turned pale from fear, he did not know to which side to draw the reins, or which direction to take, and he could not control the horses.

Ipse pavet. Nec qua comminas flectat hebendas,
Nec suit qua sit iter; nec, si suit, imperet illis.
(Panic-stricken, he knows not how to handle the reins entrusted to him, nor which way to go; nor, if he knew, would he be able to control the horses.)

So it ended in death for Phaeton, and devastation of a large part of the earth by fire.

Are not these bastards Phaetons? So Maryse Choisy asks. All the components of the myth are there in their lives. Because of their "birth blow" nothing they do succeeds. Guilt-ridden, and ashamed at being alive, they merely exist, barely integrated, never properly belonging to family, group or community, strangers on the face of the earth. They cannot mix except uneasily, so fundamentally ill-adapted are they to ordinary life. The anguish of living never leaves them. They have no place in the accepted order of things; do not belong; do not even accept themselves, since they are not accepted.

And, she adds, when natural children over-compensate for their feelings of inferiority they do so in the spectacular Phaeton style. Vertigo seizes them. They let go of the reins of the horses – their unleashed instincts. They cannot take the place of the father who has not recognised them. And Phaeton ends in the fire, with the result described by Ovid in what she notes as a particularly apposite description of the drying up of feeling in the deprivation of love – sandy plains taking the place of the maternal element, the sea. (Phaeton's mother, we observed in passing, was a sea-nymph, daughter of the ocean. It looks as if Ovid, all those centuries ago, in retelling the old Greek myth, had used with uncanny precision the same symbolism.)

The deprivation of love. That was the phrase I found most

interesting in the whole thesis, the phrase that was to open the door to conclusions of my own. But Maryse Choisy had more to say.

Why then, she asked, are these bastards propelled to self-destruction? And she answered, because between man and man there are only the bonds of feeling; and those bonds are two, and two alone, love and hate. To an illegitimate child who has not known love, the only possible relationship with the world is hate. Put another way, he is "fixated at the sado-anal phase, since the lack of a love object and an Oedipal situation have closed the gateway to the genital-oblatif phase". Taking her word for that, we also accept her assurance that that is why the Phaeton complex is more difficult to dissolve than the Oedipal one – an overdose of love is pretty easy to sublimate, but an overdose of hate poses insoluble problems. No mother has ever taught a bastard to love, she asserts, and that is the greatest tragedy which can happen to a human being.

What happens to all this hatred? It shows itself in two distinctive ways: against the world, and against itself. It takes the form of rebellion and refusal of the social pact, in the first instance, often creating delinquents, and, in the second, a determined seeking of self-destruction in one way or another.

And so on.

Well, it was all very interesting. And whatever one's feelings at being taken on such a hair-raising ride, borne onwards more vertiginously than Phaeton himself on the back of assumptions natural to the writer, and unfamiliar, if not positively inimical, to oneself – such as the concepts of an unloved infant's being for ever unable to accept love, and of there only being two possible bonds of feeling between man and man, love and hatred – one had to recognise that this author spoke from actual experience, and with the authority of one who had addressed a trained mind to the phenomenon of bastardy and its effects on the human personality.

Moreover, although Maryse Choisy's theories had been published in 1950, and it was in 1969 that I was examining them for the first time, they did not seem to be out of tune with current thought. As I considered them a book appeared, *Children Under Stress,* by Dr Sula Wolff, doubly qualified by years of clinical work in paediatrics and child psychiatry, and by long research into child development and the behaviour disorders of childhood. Her own researches, her publishers claimed, had added significantly to our knowledge of those factors which may lead to emotional disturbance in the early years, and had helped us to recognise that disturbance where it showed itself. She had drawn on all the best-authenticated papers in Britain and America, as well as on the European contributions in her field. Her own review of childhood psychiatric disturbances and their causes was backed by the solid findings of research. It was valuable, therefore, to discover that those findings did not by any means run counter to Maryse Choisy's.

The general Phaeton pattern fitted my Prime Ministers' pattern remarkably well in important respects. However, there was that salient difference. My Prime Ministers were not all bastards. Only one was actually, acknowledgeably so, and two or three others had been rumoured to be so.

But that phrase "deprivation of love", which had immediately struck a chord with me, fitted well with the course my reasoning was taking, almost of its own accord, and with a kind of inevitability.

There were, after all, more ways of being deprived of a parent than the crude one of being born a bastard. A child who loses a lawful father by death, it might be maintained, is, surely, no less deprived than the one who never knew his father, and could even be more so. Perhaps it was not only the master, Freud, who had too strictly limited himself. Might not Maryse Choisy herself, in the very act of bounding freely forward beyond his limits, have stopped short too soon? Had she not herself too narrowly confined her own conclusions to bastards deprived of parents by their illegitimacy, when they could have been applied, to some extent at least, to all children deprived of a parent, whether by death, or absence, or bastardy, or rejection, or any other cause? And if the field were so extended, how many more of my Prime Ministers became candidates for the role of Phaeton, which seemed to fit them so well!

The wheel had come full circle. First, almost casually, I had strolled along the path which had begun with my discovery that so many Prime Ministers had lost a parent in childhood, and had led to the conclusion that traumatic loss was probably deprivation of love rather than the fact of an actual bereavement.

7

Next, whimsically engaged by Maryse Choisy, I had followed the path which led from bastards, and their common manifestation of certain characteristics and life-patterns, and had come once again to the conclusion that it might be the loss of parental love, and not loss of that love in a particular and limited way, which had affected the victims so severely.

The paths had converged. It was, I suspected, deprivation of love, not the absence of a parent from any particular cause, such as bastardy or death, which lay at the root of such destinies. That deprivation of love might be as apparently negligible as lack of warmth from a living parent, or so apparently extreme as the refusal of recognition by the father of a bastard, and on each child the impact would vary according to his own genes, his own temperament, his own fibre, and his own environment. But all who shared the common, tragic loss of parental love in childhood would be powerfully affected, for it is a terrible blow.

So I accepted that deprivation of love might be equated not only with bastardy and bereavement but also with parental rejection. Once that door was opened, other Prime Ministers, who had at first seemed excluded because they had not lost a father or a mother prematurely, immediately came through it to join the ranks of the potential candidates for the Phaeton pattern. Who among those seven exceptions, Grey, Derby, Palmerston, Disraeli, Gladstone, Campbell-Bannerman and Baldwin – Melbourne, possibly, also – might not have suffered from lack of love in their childhoods? I was not dealing with any Prime Ministers after Neville Chamberlain. But Winston Churchill's own son had recently shown the world, in his biography of his father, that Churchill, who had lost neither parent in childhood, and who had demonstrated an almost obsessive determination to create a contrary impression during his life-time, had suffered massive childhood rejection from both parents, apparently enough to create a giant among giants, a Phaeton of Phaetons.

So there it was: the pattern complete. It was not bastardy, I was inclined to believe, and not even the death of a parent alone, but deprivation of love in childhood which set up the drives in certain gifted children which were to take them to the heights of endeavour and achievement. (In the case of my subjects this happened to be politics, the most obvious way to the top since gaining a throne by force of arms went out of fashion.) If Maryse Choisy were right in her contentions, then their drives would as surely lead them on to catastrophic disaster. These were the Phaetons, the seekers after attention, acclaim and adoration, in order to fill the unfillable void of their loveless years, these the unconscious engineers of their own fell destinies. Well, we would see.

I decided that the Prime Ministers I would choose to treat from among my original two dozen would be the fifteen bereaved in childhood and the one bastard about whose illegitimate status there could be no dispute. All these would have been deprived of the love of a parent. As I wrote of their lives and careers I would consciously seek for evidence, but only convincing evidence, of the recurring Phaeton characteristics noted by Maryse Choisy – abnormal sensitivity; solitariness and maladjustment; chronic depression; aggressiveness, and its obverse, neurotic timidity; omnipotence, a belief in their own genius or "magic powers", and a determination to train themselves to fulfil them, often in austere ways; excessive concern with religion, that is, preoccupation with a god as father; the compulsive need for love in its various forms; recklessness and self-destructiveness – and even such trivial ones as a fascinated interest in fire and natural cataclysms, also remarked by Maryse Choisy, which seemed to provide some form of release for their tense and troubled temperaments. I would also keep a look-out for the features of the pattern which I had myself observed, whether they overlapped hers or not – such as lack of love in the early years; abnormal sensitivity; reserve; isolation; disproportionate grief for their dead; ultra-normal drives for attention and affection; subjugation to the inspirational teaching and unbending discipline of a stern but transparently admiring mentor; marked interest in religion, in one form or another; passionate need for an ecstatic and total relationship with one self-immolatory and adoring woman, often involving a ceaseless, tormented and fruitless search in the courts of love; and suicidal, astounding recklessness, there and elsewhere. I would not be too solemn to look for the little, apparently trivial, resemblances, which might, who knew, cast light in the darker corners of these strange characters. What did these men eat, drink, read, listen to, look at, and do in their hours of relaxation? What were they like in their families? Did they laugh easily, or much? What was their taste in humour?

Strangely, it was many months after I had embarked on the book that I suddenly realised that I happened to be, myself, most unusually, the child of parents, both of whom had suffered parental loss in early childhood, and one of whom had lost both parents by adolescence. If there were reactions on personality and life-patterns which were caused by childhood bereavement, then I had for many years been in a position to observe them minutely and intimately.

So *The Fiery Chariot* was written, and published, with chapters on Spencer Perceval, Liverpool, Canning, Goderich, Wellington, Peel, Russell, Aberdeen, Salisbury, Rosebery, Balfour, Lloyd George, Asquith, Bonar Law, Ramsay Mac-Donald, and Neville Chamberlain. In all these men the Phaeton characteristics were clearly evident. Now I take the Phaeton theory outside the world of politics and into the world beyond.

Two interesting things happened after the publication of *The Fiery Chariot*. First John Lennon – the late "Beatle", whose death led to a mourning that would seem exaggerated for a national hero or a monarch – sent me a volume called *The Primal Scream*, written by Arthur Janov, Ph.D. Like Marilyn Monroe, John Lennon, a bastard, had been rejected by his father. Further, John Lennon's mother had died when he was fourteen. He was, indeed, a Phaeton of Phaetons. He had been brought up by an aunt, his Aunt Mimi, his mother giving him little more love than his father. That aunt thoroughly disapproved of his embarking on his pop-singing career, and showed it in no uncertain terms when she discovered him in Brian Epstein's group, instead of going to Art College, as she had believed. She little knew that that career would bring him a huge fortune.

Lennon had apparently recognised himself in my book, and had underlined certain passages in *The Primal Scream* which he considered relevant. One ran: "Why is it that early neuroses cannot be undone by loving parents, teachers? A number of patients did have new stepmothers and stepfathers in their teens, with whom they got along very well, who were often warm and kind, and still these individuals needed therapy later. Those kind stepmothers and stepfathers *never* undid lifelong stuttering, tics, allergies etc. Speech therapists did not undo speech disorders. Leaving home in the late teens, finding decent loving boy-friends and girl-friends did not

10

undo tension and long-lasting symptoms such as psoriasis. . . . If kindness and love and interest could undo neurosis, certainly psychotherapy as practised by warm therapists should have been able to reverse many neuroses, which I think is not the case."

So his Aunt Mimi had not made up for the loss of his father, and of his mother – or for his bastardy.

Again, Lennon marked: "The patient is an ally in Primal Therapy. His pain has waited a long time, and it usually wants to surface. His compulsive behaviour seems to have been an unconscious search for the right connection, so that it could get out when the opportunity presented, it cannot be stopped, and I think that this accounts for our success with a wide variety of neurotic types."

And, finally, he marked: "The end of neurosis is very much like its beginning . . . Here is the end of neurosis in the words of one patient: 'I don't know what I expected out of all this. I suppose I wanted something dramatic to even the score for all those years of misery. Maybe I expected to become my neurotic fantasy – that someone special who would finally be loved and appreciated.' "

The other interesting thing that happened concerned the distinguished Maryse Choisy. I naturally sent her a copy of *The Fiery Chariot*, but not without trepidation, since I was a complete outsider to her close-knit world of psychiatry, with no training, and no credentials, daring to venture into a highly specialised field. With great generosity she replied, "Thank you so much for your *Fiery Chariot*. It is a very great book. Both your documentation and your psychological analysis are a success."

Heartened by such generosity from one of the greatest distinction in her chosen field, I now present the results of my extending that theory into other fields.

CHRONOLOGICAL LIST OF
BRITISH PRIME MINISTERS WHO LOST A
PARENT IN CHILDHOOD

Earl of Wilmington, father died when he was 7 or 8.
Henry Pelham, mother died when he was 5.
Duke of Newcastle, mother died when he was 7.
Earl of Bute, father died when he was 10.
George Grenville, father died when he was 14.
Duke of Grafton, father died when he was 6.
Lord North, mother died when he was 2.
Earl of Shelburne, orphaned, and grandfather died when he was 4.
Lord Grenville, father died when he was 11.
Spencer Perceval, father died when he was 8.
Earl of Liverpool, mother died when he was 1, father when he was 12.
George Canning, father died when he was 1.
Viscount Goderich, father died when he was 4.
Duke of Wellington, father died when he was 12.
Viscount Melbourne, putative bastard.
Sir Robert Peel, father died when he was 15.
Lord John Russell, mother died when he was 9.
Earl of Aberdeen, father died when he was 7, mother when he was 11.
Marquess of Salisbury, mother died when he was 9.
Earl of Rosebery, father died when he was 3.
A.J. Balfour, father died when he was 7.
H.H. Asquith, father died when he was 8.
Lloyd George, father died when he was 2.
Bonar Law, mother died when he was 2.
Ramsay MacDonald, bastard.

Neville Chamberlain, mother died when he was 6.
James Callaghan, father died when he was 9.

CHAPTER 2

What did it mean to a child to lose a parent? What could one learn of childhood bereavement?

The most dramatic thing that I discovered was that one who has been bereaved as a child reacts abnormally to bereavement ever afterwards. He will show panic at the thought of death, or any threat of it, such as illness, and will demonstrate grief at subsequent bereavement which is extreme by any standards.

Next, it is, it seems, far more damaging for a boy to lose his father than to lose his mother. A survey made in Minnesota among adolescent children from different kinds of homes brought this out very strongly. The survey dealt with delinquency; and delinquency was highest among children who had lost parents through separation or divorce. But boys whose fathers had died, and girls whose mothers had died, showed the second highest delinquency rates.

It also transpired that the highest delinquency rates were among boys living with their mothers only, or with neither parent. For girls the highest rates occurred among those living with fathers only, or with neither parent, or with step-parents. Whatever the social class, the rates held true. The conclusion was inescapable. An important cause of delinquency was loss of the parent of the same sex. The explanation advanced was lack of a parental model with whom the child could identify.

The survey only related one specific manifestation of disturbance, delinquency, to particular types of family background. (Dr Sula Wolff, however, takes it further. In her authoritative *Children Under Stress* p. 90, she says, "Many groups of psychiatric patients have been compared with non-

14

patients . . . There is evidence that patients with personality disorders, patients who have attempted suicide, and delinquents more often have a background of family disruption than controls." And such "family disruption" does, of course, almost invariably, follow loss of a parent through death or any other cause.) It would be strange, however, if its revelations, and the findings of others, were without relevance to our own observations of children suffering from the same stresses, and, while perhaps not actually becoming delinquent or otherwise unviable – with the exceptions in one chapter of this book – showing symptoms of disturbance. Bereavement and bastardy can produce delinquents and Prime Ministers, and famous authors, artists, poets and the rest. Why does, we may ask, one child become a delinquent, and another a Prime Minister? (And, in Arthur Balfour's family, two brothers indeed reacted thus differently.) How much credit should that ever-recurring mentor take to himself, how much the surviving parent, the support of religion, the inherited genes, and how much mere chance, in each case?

Such speculations are fascinating, and infinite. But what, less generally, and more specifically, in the light of such knowledge as we have today, can we conclude that parental loss means?

That it means a great deal to any child to lose a parent is undisputed. Gone are the days when the comforting assurance that a child was "too young to understand" was taken as valid. Naturally, once more, statistics do not come from the less extreme cases of disturbance, those which never reach a consulting room; but that such bereavement can actually be the cause of psychological disturbance is established beyond question now.

Dr Michael Rutter broke new ground. He was the first to examine systematically the relationship between bereavement and psychiatric disturbance in children. In order to do this, he compared children who had been referred to the Child Psychiatry Department of the world-famous Maudsley Hospital with a control group of other, normal, children. Where should he find his normal children? He drew on two sources: the first, children attending paediatric clinics, because presumably such illnesses as took them there, even if purely physical, might have had some repercussions on their mental health, and children attending dental clinics. It would be hard to find a more normal cross-section than the latter. Dr Rutter then matched these children with their opposite numbers for age, sex, and even for the class of work their fathers did.

His findings were startling. More than twice as many children attending the child psychiatric clinic had lost a parent by death than had those who were attending a paediatric department for their health. Even more noteworthy, nearly six times as many psychiatrically disturbed children had been bereaved than had the "normal" children who were attending dental clinics. No one could doubt from these figures that losing a parent can have the most devastating effect on a child. Of those most affected emotionally, the luckier ones may become ill – or, possibly, I suppose, one might interpret this particular set of statistics as meaning that those with a tendency to illness, psychosomatic or otherwise, have it increased. The less fortunate ones may suffer a blow which leads to unbalancing them, perhaps for life.

(The proportion of disturbed children who had lost a parent was, in fact, small, only one in twelve; but that was not surprising. What was, was that bereavement, which might be considered a normal, if unusual, fact of life, should bring so many children into such medical care at all.)

The differences between the disturbed children and the others was most marked when the parent had died when the child was in its third or fourth year. Dr Rutter's suggestion was that the loss of a parent at the age of three or four was especially damaging, because it was at that time that parents were most needed as models, a vitally important factor in development.

Another finding of Dr Rutter's of great relevance was that psychiatric illness in these children rarely began soon after the parent's death. With nearly a third of them, five years or more had gone by before symptoms appeared in the child severe enough to prompt adults to take action, and seek advice and help for them. When a child was bereaved at three or four years, it was not until puberty that he was brought in for attention. The only group of children whose illness began within six months of their loss was one composed mainly of adolescent boys. They suffered from depressive illnesses, resembling grief in adults, or behaved anti-socially.

Except at adolescence, Dr Rutter concluded, on rehearsing the details of these researches, the long-term consequences of parental loss are more important than the experience of the death itself; and even those long-term consequences most frequently come to the surface in late childhood and adolescence. Those words we in our search should read, mark and soberly digest.

Studies such as Dr Rutter's and Dr Wolff's throw interesting sidelights, too, on the causes of disturbances in bereaved children. They are not always the ones which we in our sentimentality might consider obvious. It is not only, and merely, the sense of loss for a beloved parent, real though that may be, which can lead to tragic upheavals. Children are egotists and solipsists, and the more practical results of a death can be the cause of a good deal of the damage.

Material effects of a bereavement affect the children, often directly and blatantly, as they percolate into their consciousness, and give them a feeling of inferiority. This applies, of course, most in families where widows are left without much money, and where they suffer stringent financial hardship, and the change in circumstances becomes immediately, obviously, and painfully, apparent – even, perhaps, involving the breakup of a home and travel to another, possibly even dependence on charity. The children feel these altered conditions acutely. Their clothes, perhaps, from them on, will not be as smart, their toys as plentiful, new and expensive as those of their friends, or their food as pleasant. They may even have to wear cast-offs. Treats will be few and far between, paltry, different from other children's, and, in short, not very thrilling. "No child likes to feel different from his peers," as Dr Wolff says, and as we all know. Still less does he like to feel inferior to them. A bereaved family of children will wilt under the pity others feel for them, and see their living parent, too, smarting under it. The children experience a loss of self-esteem, the more bitter when pride goes hand in hand with the new poverty.

Then, although the contrasts may be sharpest in the so-called "lower class" and "lower middle class" families, where the borderline between being "respectable" and not is so thin a one, they none the less exist in families which are still apparently well-to-do after bereavement, if less so than before. It is commonly accepted, certainly so in the courts, that any departure from the standard of life to which you are accustomed constitutes hardship; and this is based on sound psychological grounds. So the deprivation of what might seem to be luxuries to some families is the loss of necessities to others; and the children can suffer as sharply from such alterations in their way of life as their less well-off cousins in more straitened circumstances. (Wellington's having to leave Eton early because there was so little money after his father's debt-laden demise was a good example of this.)

It is not, however, only in these materialistic matters, like changes in food, clothing, shelter, and treats, that the child, and even a very young child, can be profoundly affected by the practical results of bereavement. The widowed mother often withdraws emotionally from her child. At first, naturally, this is because she is drowned in grief. Later, however, the child still finds her changed. Even if she is not compelled to go out and work to support her family she may, in another way, leave them, spiritually depriving them of her love. She has to play the man's part, call on qualities never before drawn on by her, dormant, or, maybe, even unnatural to her – and they are the colder, rougher, so-called masculine qualities, such as the ability to organise, administer, economise, dominate, plan and command. The child, dismayed, sees his gentle, cosily available and playful mother, who has until then been exclusively occupied with the tender tasks of being a young wife and mother, transformed into a sterner, more autocratic and peremptory, and less attractive, figure, who calls on him to brace up, grow up, look after his brothers and sisters, and help her. And where the widow soon remarries, that brings its own inevitable stresses, especially where there are stepbrothers and stepsisters.

What if the widower remarries? The supplying of a substitute mother at precisely the right moment by a widower father, and her ability to set up a relationship with the bereaved child as successful as the one he had enjoyed with his own mother, must be something of a miracle, a combination of miraculous good timing, good judgment, good-heartedness and good fortune, and of correspondingly rare occurrence.

Neither poverty nor the unavoidable new restrictions on the family life seem to be so extensively damaging if the children love and are happy with their one remaining parent, and the home remains intact. The strains are of course immeasurably greater where that love and happiness do not exist; and they can become almost intolerable where there is, as well, a break-up of one form or another, even to the (apparently minor, but really major) extent of being sent away to a school which is not enjoyed.

Even where love, happiness and some form of security at home exist, what does seem to matter very much is the gap in the children's accurate knowledge of, simply, how fathers and mothers behave towards each other and their children within the family circle. At first sight this may not seem a lack which could have quite such destructive effects as are claimed for it. But it can lame a child for life.

In short, it would be impossible to exaggerate the importance of these early disasters in these children's lives; and especially when occurring during the age-span from two to six. It is at that stage that children most notably model themselves on their parents, girls on their mothers, boys on their fathers. Girls and boys can visualise their future only in terms of their growing up to be like their mothers and fathers. The very core of our personalities, the hearts of our beings, the parts we think of as "us", permanently, throughout our lives, whatever else may change about us, are mainly built up around these identifications made in childhood. To that extent we *are* our fathers and our mothers. When a parent is missing, from whatever cause, during these critical years, this vital development of personality is impaired. The task of "identity formation", or "knowing who you are", is, then, an almost impossibly difficult one to achieve in adolescence. For girls, the loss of a mother between two and four years of age, as Dr Rutter showed, is particularly damaging. But boys who have lost their fathers at that stage are more liable than girls (in the same situation) to have difficulties in their own sexual and marital adjustments in later life.

On that particular aspect another work, *Fatherless Families*, by Margaret Wynn, gave relevant information, and bewailed our lack of knowledge. For even today, although we know a good deal about the results of maternal deprivation, it pointed out, we are still on the outskirts where those of fatherlessness are concerned. "The whole consequences to children of fatherlessness are not fully understood," the author wrote. "There is evidence, for example, that childhood bereavement by loss of a father is a factor in adult depressive illness. There is also evidence that loss of a father while under the age of two is a factor in other mental illness. The graver psychological consequences of fatherlessness can be avoided, though further research is needed to make clear just how they *can* be avoided. Serious mental illness lasting into adult years is less common than the simple unhappiness of his mother, and often resulting in unsatisfactory performance at school, inability to settle in a job, and even in unhappiness in marriage." But, as the author states elsewhere, there has never been a review of the effect of paternal deprivation on mental health which can in any way be compared with that famous one of Dr Bowlby and his colleagues on the effect of maternal deprivation.

Remembering what a life-belt in trouble a satisfactory parental substitute can be for a child, I found the reactions of the experts to this situation to be surprisingly unoptimistic and lukewarm. Often when a parent has been lost, other people served as models for identification for bereaved children; but to Sula Wolff at any rate, such people are never known as intimately as a real father and mother, and to this extent they are less satisfactory. Yet could any substitute father have been closer to his sister's son than Lloyd George's Uncle Lloyd? I doubt it.

Knowledge in this field is also, however, very limited. It is important to realise that we have no knowledge as to what proportion of bereaved children are, in fact, disturbed. We know only that among those children who have become psychiatrically disturbed, more have been bereaved than among normal children. That is a different matter. Perhaps only a small proportion of children who lose a father or mother do become actually disturbed. We cannot know what are the precise extents of the psychological hazards of parental death for children unless and until a special study of bereaved children in the community is undertaken.

I would welcome the special study. But perhaps it is not of absolutely vital relevance to this, my own modest contemplation of certain well-known bereaved children from the past. None of these children reached the psychiatrists's couch, or its contemporary equivalent, except, eventually, Charles Manson. It will be enough for our purposes to examine what we know of their lives, in order to look for signs, not only of my pattern, and the orthodox Phaeton pattern, but of lesser, if not minor, disturbance. Whether or not they were disturbed in the full psychiatric meaning of that term, in layman's language they were affected by their unhappy childhood circumstances, possibly for the whole of their turbulent and tormented lives.

MAJOR HISTORICAL FIGURES

Kemal Atatürk, father died when he was 9.
Attila, father died when he was 10.
Augustus, father died when he was 4.
Ayatollah Khomeini, father died when he was 3.
David Ben-Gurion, mother died when he was 11.
Simon Bolivar, father died when he was 3, mother died when he was 9.
Cesare Borgia, bastard, and his father died when he was 1.
Buddha, mother died when he was 7.
Julius Caesar, mother died at his birth.
Caligula, father died when he was 7.
Cato, mother died when he was 3.
Chiang Kai-Chek, father died when he was 10.
Claudius, father died when he was 3.
Constantine, father died when he was 10.
Georges Jacques Danton, father died when he was 3.
Charles Darwin, mother died when he was 8.
King David, father died when he was 12.
René Descartes, mother died when he was 1.
Eamon De Valera, father died when he was 9.
Queen Elizabeth the First, father died when she was 14, mother when she was 3.
Erasmus, bastard.
Mahatma Gandhi, father died when he was 15.
Genghis Khan, father died when he was 12.
François Guizot, father died when he was 7.
Hadrian, father died when he was 9.
Haile Selassie, father died when he was 14.

Alexander Hamilton, founding father of the USA, bastard.

Adolf Hitler, father died when he was 13.

Ho Chi Minh, mother died when he was 10.

Herbert Hoover, father died when he was 6.

Hua Guo-Feng, father died when he was 6.

Ivan the Terrible, father died when he was 3.

"Stonewall" Jackson, mother died when he was 14.

Thomas Jefferson, father died when he was 14.

Pope John Paul II (Karol Wojtyla, the first Polish Pope), mother died when he was 8.

Nikita Kruschev, father died when he was 13.

Marquis de Lafayette, father died before he was born, mother died when he was 13.

Lenin (Vladimir Ilich Ulyanov), father died when he was 15.

Abraham Lincoln, probably a bastard, and his mother died when he was 4. ("I don't know who my grandfather was. I am much more concerned to know what his grandson will be.")

St Ignatius Loyola, mother died when he was 5, father died when he was 15.

Catherine de Medici, both father and mother died before she was 1.

Mohammed, father died before his birth, mother died in his infancy.

Napoleon Bonaparte, believed himself to be a bastard, and that his father was a womaniser who was seldom at home. His legal father died when he was 15, in any case.

Gamal Abdel Nasser, mother died when he was 8.

Nero, father died when he was 3.

Isaac Newton, born after his father's death.

Blaise Pascal, mother died when he was 3.

Eva Peron, bastard, and her father died when she was 7.

Peter the Great, father died when he was 4.

Richelieu, father died when he was 5.

Robespierre, mother died when he was 10, father died when he was about 11.

Jean Jacques Rousseau, mother died when he was 1.

Saint-Just, father died when he was 10.

Joseph Stalin, father died when he was 11.

Tiberius, father died when he was 9.

Timon of Athens, father died when he was 11.

Vespasian, father died when he was 5.

Queen Victoria, father died when she was 8 months.
George Washington, father died when he was 11.
William the Conqueror, bastard, and his father died when he
   was 8.
William of Orange, father died before he was 1.

CHAPTER 3

Adolf Hitler (1889 – 1945)

Adolf Hitler lost his father, whom he had hated, when he was thirteen.

What did this man, who would bring so much misery to so many, and most of all to the Jewish race, look like? In height he was rather below the average; he had wide hips, narrow shoulders, and flabby muscles; his legs were short, thin and spindly, and later on he was careful to hide them in heavy boots or long trousers; he had a large torso, but was so hollow-chested that when he came to power he had to have his uniforms padded; his mouth was full of brown, rotten, teeth; he had long, dirty fingernails; and a tic on his face which caused the corner of his lip to curl upwards. More, he had a mincing, ladylike gait, and cocked his right shoulder upwards after every few steps, snapping up his left leg as he did so. In his early years, when he wore the Bavarian mountain costume of leather shorts, with a white shirt and suspenders – none too clean, incidentally – he presented an even more grotesque appearance. He had a pointed beard, and his dark brown hair was parted down the middle and pasted down flat on his head with oil. Not exactly the picture of someone one would expect to rise to be the dictator of a great and powerful nation.

Hitler had many psychological hang-ups too. He was beset by the fear of horses, microbes, and moonlight; he sucked his little finger in moments of agitation; he longed to create, but he also lusted to destroy; he ordered the massacre of millions of innocents, but worried about the most humane way to cook

24

lobsters; he saw himself as a kind of Messiah, and often spoke of himself in the very words of Jesus, but also called himself a *Scheisskerl* (a shithead); and he kept three favourite riding whips with which he would strike his hand or his thigh, given him by three women of the age of his mother. Most noticeable of all, he had an obsession with wolves. At the start of his political career he called himself, as a cover name, Herr Wolf. His favourite dogs, and the only ones he allowed himself to be photographed with, were Alsatians – in German *Wolfshunde*; he called his headquarters in France *Wolfsschlucht* (Wolf's Gulche); and in the Ukraine his headquarters was *Werwolf*, and in East Prussia *Wolfschanze* (Wolf's Lair), Hitler explaining to his servant, "I am the wolf, and this is my lair." After the *Anschluss* with Austria in 1938, he asked his sister Paula to change her name to Frau Wolf. The name of the secretary he kept for twenty years was Johanna Wolf. His favourite tune, which he often whistled, came from his favourite Walt Disney movie, and was "Who's Afraid of the Big Bad Wolf?"

He played childish guessing games, seeing how fast he could get dressed, or how quickly his valet could tie his tie for him.

His favourite doodle was of severed heads. When he was asked where he would like to go on first landing in England he replied without hesitation that he wanted most to see the place where Henry VIII had chopped off the heads of his wives. When he tossed a coin he never chose heads to win. His definition of politics was, "Politics is like a whore, if you love her unsuccessfully she bites your head off." He was infatuated with the head of the Medusa, once remarking that in Von Stuck's painting the flashing eyes that turned men to stone and impotence reminded him of the eyes of his mother. He was reputed to have taken great pleasure in having young women urinate and defecate on his head – in psychological language, this "showed the mixture of intense anal interest and grovelling submission which betokens a more than usually disturbed anal neurotic".

The ambition of a man who could rise from living in the utmost poverty in Vienna, often surviving on soup and bread distributed by the Church, dressing in an old trenchcoat or a cheap raincoat, to be the dictator of a great nation, was formidable. There were times, indeed, when he was homeless, living as a tramp, sleeping in parks and doorways, taking refuge under the arches of the rotunda of an amusement centre when it rained, and using his jacket as a pillow, his garments bug-infested. Even in those days, everyone who knew him was struck by the extraordinary combination of ambition, envy and indolence of which his nature was composed. Always desperately anxious to impress, he was full of ideas for making fame and fortune, from water-divining to designing an aeroplane. Even when living in poverty in Meidling in 1909, hanging round night-shelters, subsisting on bread and soup alone, he would shout and wave his arms until the others in the room cursed him for disturbing them, or the porter came to stop the noise. Sometimes they laughed at him, but at others they were impressed.

From his youth Hitler was ascetic. In Vienna he lived for days on end on milk and bread and butter only. He neither smoked nor drank. As Führer this asceticism became even greater. Göring, fat and self-indulgent, was miserable at Hitler's table. The food was of the simplest, as Albert Speer recalls in his memoirs – a soup, no appetiser, meat with vegetables and potatoes, and a sweet. To drink there was only a choice between mineral water, ordinary Berlin bottled beer, or a cheap wine. Hitler was served his vegetarian food and drank Fachinger mineral water, and those of his guests who wished could imitate him, but few did. He even disapproved of such harmless delicacies as lobster, and wanted to have such luxuries forbidden in Germany. As he grew older his asceticism grew even more pronounced. He was indifferent to the clothes he wore, ate very little, never touched meat, and, of course, still neither smoked nor drank. His luxuries consisted of being driven fast in a powerful car, eating cream cakes and sweets, and having flowers in his rooms. He not only kept a special vegetarian cook to prepare his meals for him, but held that eating meat or any cooked food was a pernicious habit which had led to the decay of past civilisations. The world of the future, he maintained, would be vegetarian. He never even drank coffee or tea.

Hitler had a decided interest in magic and the supernatural, spending hours as a young man in the library, reading about occultism, hypnotism, astrology and yoga. He was greatly impressed when, in September 1923, he received a letter from Frau Elsbeth Ebertin, a member of his movement, saying that a man of action born on 20th April 1889 could expose himself to personal danger by excessively incautious action, and very likely trigger off an uncontrollable crisis. This man, she said, was to be taken very seriously indeed, and was destined to play what she called "a Führer role" in future, and to sacrifice himself for the German nation.

Indeed, Hitler was a great believer, in his early days, in astrology, and was in constant touch with astrologers, who advised him concerning his course of action. Later, it is true, he forbade the practice of fortune-telling and star-reading in Germany. But in his early days, in 1921 and 1922, he was in touch with a circle which believed enthusiastically in the portents of the stars.

He was, in fact, convinced that he had been sent to Germany by Providence, and that he had a particular mission to perform; had, indeed, been chosen to redeem the German people, and to reshape Europe. His conviction was largely responsible for the effect that he had on the German people. He believed in an inner voice which communicated to him the steps he was to take, a guide which led him on his course with the precision and security of a sleep-walker. "I carry out the commands," he said, "that Providence has laid upon me"; and, "No power on earth can shake the German Reich now, Divine Providence has willed it that I carry through the fulfilment of the Germanic task"; and, "But if the Voice speaks, then I know the time has come to act."

Believing firmly that he was under divine protection, Hitler often told a story of how he was eating his dinner in a trench with several of his comrades when suddenly, as he put it, a voice seemed to be saying to him, "Get up and go over there!" He obeyed. Then a stray shell burst over the group in which he had been sitting, and every member of it was killed.

His conviction of his great destiny was a support to him even when he lay, blinded, in hospital in Pasewalk, and he said, "When I was confined to bed, the idea came to me that I would liberate Germany, that I would make it great. I knew immediately that it would be realised." As a diplomat said, Hitler's logic and sense of reality had impressed him at first, but as time went on he appeared to become more and more unreasonable, and more and more convinced of his own infallibility and greatness.

His ambition was insensate, even from his youth, and, as he said himself, when giving testimony at the trial which followed the unsuccessful Beer Hall *Putsch* of 1923, he was not interested in being merely a minister, he wanted to be "the annihilator of Marxism". He added, "I shall solve the task, and when I solve it, then to me the ministerial title would be a trivial matter." He wanted much, much more; and he got it.

Soon, indeed, he began to think of himself as the Messiah, who was to lead Germany to glory, referring more and more frequently to the Bible, and giving the movement a religious atmosphere. He actually began to compare himself with Christ.

"When I came to Berlin a few weeks ago," he said, "and looked at the traffic on the Kurfürstendamm, the luxury, the perversion, the iniquity of the wanton display, and the Jewish materialism disgusted me so thoroughly that I was almost beside myself. I nearly imagined myself to be Jesus Christ when He came to His Father's temple and found it taken by the money-changers. I can well imagine how He felt when He seized a whip and scourged them out." And he swung his whip violently about as he ranted. He identified with the angry Jesus Christ lashing out, and he said, "My feeling as a Christian points me to my Lord and Saviour as a fighter. It points me to the man who once in loneliness, surrounded by only a few followers, recognised these Jews for what they were and summoned men to fight against them, and who, God's truth! was greatest not as a sufferer but as a fighter. In boundless love, as a Christian and a man, I read through the passage which tells us how the Lord rose at last in His might and seized the scourge to drive out of the Temple the brood of vipers and adders. How terrific was the fight for the world against the Jewish poison."

In the end, in his eyes, Christianity became a religion fit only for slaves, and he detested its ethics. To him its teaching was a rebellion against the natural law of selection by struggle and the survival of the fittest, leading to the systematic cultivation of the human failure. Once the war was over, he was, he said, determined to root out and destroy the influence of the Christian churches. He was equally impatient of pagan rites, against the worship of Wotan, determined that his movement would never acquire a religious character and institute a form of worship – a thought which filled him with horror. He was, eventually, a rationalist and a materialist, and in the end science took with him the place of religion. Yet he had begun as an ardent Catholic and to the end was emphatic that a man and woman should keep themselves chaste in body and soul until marriage, so as to produce healthy children for the nation. Yet, again, he was haunted by the dark side of sex, and talked by the hour about depraved customs.

When he decided to rebuild Linz, he wanted to include a great observatory and planetarium, and spoke of them as "our way of giving men a religious spirit, of teaching them humility – but without the priests. Put a small telescope in a village, and you destroy a world of superstitions." Yet he baulked at a thoroughgoing atheism, insisting that a creative force existed, and that a sense of eternity was "at the bottom of every man". Strangely, his speeches were full of the mention of God, while equally full of vituperation, and lack of charity, especially against the Jews – a hatred which ended in the deaths of at least between four and four and a half million Jews, to say nothing of those driven from their homes to take refuge abroad, a crime unequalled in history.

Hitler's reaction to bereavement was decidedly extreme. Even the death of his hated father, who used to beat him unmercifully, caused him, as he claimed in his *Mein Kampf,* severe pain: "A stroke of apoplexy felled the old gentleman, who was otherwise so hale, thus painlessly ending his earthly pilgrimage, plunging us all into the depths of grief." Indeed, when Hitler saw the body of this hated father, who had dropped dead, he broke down and wept.

It was the death of his adoring mother, however, four years later, when he was eighteen, which caused him devastating pain. He suffered dreadfully as she lay dying of cancer of the breast, after the removal of a breast, abusing the doctors for their inability to cure her. He devoted himself entirely to her, sharing the household duties with their servant, Paula, and his Aunt Johanna; sleeping beside his mother's bed in the warm kitchen so that he could be in constant attendance; and often cooking for her. He lived only for her. Nothing could save her though, and she died quietly in the early hours of the morning. After daylight a doctor, Dr Bloch, was asked to come to the house to sign the death certificate. Adolf was still at his mother's side, and on a sketchbook was his drawing of his mother, Klara, her son's last tribute. Dr Bloch tried to comfort him by saying that in this case death had been a merciful release. But there was no solace for him. "In all my career," recalled Dr Bloch, who had stood by many a death-bed, "I never saw anyone so prostrate with grief as Adolf Hitler." And, interestingly, Hitler not only expressed his deep gratitude to Dr Bloch for all he had done for his mother, but, as the doctor said thirty-three years later, he was quite sure that he *was* grateful. "Favours were granted to me," he said, "which I feel were accorded to no other Jew in Germany or Austria." Hitler never ceased to mourn his mother, and, sixteen years later, wrote a poem about the bitterness of losing a mother. Hitler himself wrote: "It was a dreadful blow. I had honoured my father, but my mother I had loved."

Even his grief for his mother, however, was almost undoubtedly less than that for the girl he fell in love with, not least because there was an element of guilt in that mourning. In 1925 Hitler's widowed half-sister, Angela Rabaul, came, with her two daughters, to keep house for him on the Obersalzberg. The daughter, Geli, was seventeen, simple, attractive, with a pleasant voice which she wanted to have trained so that she could become a singer. During the next six years Geli became his constant companion, and when Hitler acquired a luxurious flat on the Prinz-Regentenstrasse she spent a great deal of time with him in Munich as well as at the Obersalzberg – a period Hitler later described as the happiest in his life. He idolised this girl, who was nineteen years younger than he, and took her with him wherever he could.

He was, in fact, deeply in love with Geli, but he dominated her unbearably, refusing to let her have any life of her own, or to let her go to Vienna to have her voice trained. He was beside himself with fury when he discovered that she had allowed Emil Maurice, his chauffeur, to make love to her, dismissed Maurice, and forbade her to have anything to do with any other man. From then on she was escorted even to her singing lessons. Geli deeply resented his possessiveness and domestic tyranny, and the extent of that resentment was to be shown in a macabre fashion.

On the morning of 17th September, 1931, Hitler left Munich with Hoffmann, his photographer and friend, after saying goodbye to Geli. That night he stayed in Nuremberg, and had set off for Hamburg next morning, when he and Hoffmann saw a taxi following them. There was, it transpired, an urgent call from Hess for Hitler, at the hotel. They turned back, and Hitler rushed to the telephone. Hoffmann heard him cry out, "Oh, God, how awful!" and then scream, "Hess, answer me – yes or no – is she still alive?" But Hess had been cut off or had hung up.

Geli had shot herself in his flat after his departure. The reason for her death remains a mystery. Hoffmann thought she was in love with someone else, and committed suicide because of her uncle's despotic treatment; but Hitler's house-keeper believed she was in love with Hitler, and that her suicide was caused by disappointment and frustration.

Whatever the reason for her death, it dealt Hitler a formidable blow, greater than any other event in his life. For days he was inconsolable, and friends feared that he too might commit suicide. The chauffeur even hid his gun, and when his friends took him to the empty country house of his printer, Adolf Müller, on the Tergensee, he paced all night and all day for three days, without food. According to some accounts, his refusal to eat meat dated from this period – "It is like eating a corpse!" he said, when offered a piece of ham.

For the rest of his life Hitler never spoke of Geli without tears coming into his eyes, and, according to his own statement to a number of witnesses, she was the only woman he had ever loved. Her room at the Berghof was kept exactly as she had left it, and remained untouched when the original Haus Wachenfeld was rebuilt. Her photograph hung in his rooms in Munich and in Berlin, and flowers were always placed before it on the anniversaries of her birth and her death. He risked arrest, since he was banned from Austria, and she was buried in Vienna, to visit her grave at dawn, and place flowers on it. The marble slab bore a touching inscription:

Here Sleeps Our Beloved Child
Geli
She was Our Ray of Sunshine
Born 4 June 1908 – died 18 September 1931
The Rabaul Family

It is interesting that in 1932, less than a year after Geli's death, Eva Braun, at twenty-one, also attempted to commit suicide. Her attempt was not successful, and Hitler was anxious to avoid more scandal – for the suicide of Geli Rabaul had got into the newspapers, and his name had been linked with hers – so she was able to inveigle herself into his life and become his devoted slave, eventually even ousting Geli's mother from her position as housekeeper at the Berghof, in 1936. (One remembers, too, that Unity Mitford also attempted suicide, when Hitler turned against her.)

Hitler's isolation and reserve were always outstanding. Already, by the age of twenty-four, notably awkward and moody, he was consumed by hatred and fanaticism. Hardly anyone dented the shell with which he enclosed himself. Wary and secretive, he distrusted everyone, never let down his guard, or spoke without having thought out beforehand what he had to say.

At school there was one mentor who succeeded in making a profound impression on the difficult youngster – his history professor, Leopold Pötsch, who lectured on the ancient Teutons. "Even today," Hitler wrote in *Mein Kampf*, "I think back with gentle emotion on this grey-haired man, who by the fire of his narratives sometimes made us forget the present; who, as if by enchantment, carried us into past times, and, out of the millennial veils of mist, moulded dry historical memories into living reality. On such occasions we sat there, often aflame with enthusiasm, and sometimes even moved to tears."

Hitler's recklessness was notable. Capable of great patience until the right moment had, in his view, come, he would then make moves which shook his followers. Typical of these were the reoccupation of the Rhineland in 1936, and the invasion of Norway and Denmark just before the major campaign in the west. He believed in surprise and was willing to take risks to achieve it, often resorting to treachery, unscrupulousness, lying and cunning. He never blenched at the use of terror.

There is a strong suspicion that Hitler was a homosexual. As early as 1920, when he lived with Frau Carola Hoffman, a sixty-one-year-old widow, there was a good deal of drinking and sexual activities of all kinds in her house. Then, during the early days of the Nazi Party, many of the inner circle were well-known homosexuals. Röhm was an open homosexual, Hess was generally known as "Fraulein Anna", and there were many others. It was generally supposed that Hitler too belonged in that category. (Many men are, of course, capable of sex with both men and women.)

Again, when he was twenty, the home in which he lived had the reputation of being a place where homosexual men frequently went to find companions; and Hitler was actually listed on police records as a sexual pervert. Then, too, Rauschning claimed that a high Nazi had once confided in him that he had seen Hitler's military record, and that it contained an item of a court-martial, which had found him guilty of sodomy with an officer, and that it was for this reason that he was never promoted further. Rauschning also claimed that, later on, in Munich, Hitler was again found guilty of sodomy.

Many believed that Hitler was completely impotent; others believed that he was an obsessive masturbator; others, in the majority, thought him a homosexual. It was probably true that he was impotent, but it is accepted that his main perversion, already referred to, was of an extreme form of masochism, in which the individual derives sexual gratification from the act of having a woman urinate or defecate on him – in his case, on his head. If he was a homosexual he appears to have been a passive one. Rauschning reported meeting two boys who claimed that they were Hitler's homosexual partners. He seems, indeed, to have been impotent as far as heterosexual relations went. He is also reported as having used the term "Bubi", one used by homosexuals in addressing their partners. That, of course, would not be adequate proof that he had actually indulged in such practices.

The egotism of this man was unbelievable. To Schushnigg he once said, "Do you realise that you are in the presence of the greatest German of all?"; to Rauschning, "I do not need your endorsement to convince me of my historical greatness"; and Oechsner gave it as his opinion that Hitler believed that no one in German history was equipped, as he was, to bring the Germans to a position of supremacy which all German statesmen have felt they deserved but were unable to achieve. He believed he was not only a great leader, but a great strategist. To Rauschning he said: "I do not play at war. I do not allow the generals to give me orders. The war is conducted by *me*. The precise moment of attack will be determined by *me*. There will be only one time that will be truly auspicious, and I will wait for it with inflexible determination. And I will not pass it by." He believed, besides, that he was the greatest of all architects, although he had failed to pass his examination for admission to Art School, and spent much time sketching buildings. Further, he believed himself to be an unquestioned authority on economics, education, foreign affairs, propaganda, movies, music, and women's dress. He was proud of his hardness and brutality. "I am one of the hardest men Germany has had for decades," he said, "perhaps for centuries, equipped with the greatest authority of any German leader . . . but above all I believe in my success. I believe in it unconditionally."

Inevitably, this boundless faith in his own genius led to a feeling of infallibility and invincibility, and soon he would not tolerate either criticism or contradiction, which he regarded as *lèse-majesté*, and opposition to his plans was sacrilege, leading to punishment. The astonishing thing is that the German people took him at his own valuation. Hermann Rauschning reported that the Nazi Party had adopted what could only be called a creed: "We all believe, on this earth, in Adolf Hitler, our Führer, and we acknowledge that National Socialism is the only faith that can bring salvation to our country." Indeed, a Rhenish group of so-called German Christians passed the resolution in April 1937: "Hitler's word is God's law; the decrees and laws which represent it possess divine authority." More, the Reichminster for Church Affairs, Hans Kerrl, actually said: "There has arisen a new authority as to what Christ and Christianity really are – that is Adolf Hitler. Adolf Hitler . . . is the true Holy Ghost."

So Hitler's propaganda machine presented him as a deity, no less.

The wonder is that this man, cheap, vulgar, and compacted of hatred and malice, persuaded the German nation that he was a man of superhuman quality and genius. Perhaps he was indeed a political genius, he who had begun as not even a citizen of the country he aspired to rule. But he had to dominate and destroy, and the instrument of anti-Semitism came readily to hand.

It is also of interest that Hitler probably had syphilis. Doctors have suggested that his later symptoms were those of a man suffering from tertiary syphilis – stooped, with a pale and puffy face, hunched in his chair, his hands trembling, his left arm subject to a violent twitching which he did his best to conceal, and one leg dragging behind him when he walked. Towards the end he seems to have deteriorated mentally, too, making long rambling speeches of self-justification. He suffered from continual headaches and stomach cramps, as well as a throat condition. During his last six months he seemed an old man, with an ashy complexion, a shuffling walk, and shaking hands and legs. By then, the whole left side of his body trembled, and he not only walked awkwardly, stooping noticeably, but his gestures were slow and jerky. When he wanted to sit down, a chair had to be pushed under him. Whether this was syphilis, or, as has also been suggested, Parkinson's Disease, he was in a terrible state. A few months before the end, an adjutant later recalled that there was an indescribable flickering stare in his eyes that was at the same time shocking and completely unnatural.

It is now known that Hitler had been taking huge quantities of "Doctor Koester's Anti-Gas Pills", which contained strychnine and atrophene; reducing pills to prevent him from becoming obese; at least a dozen different kinds of sleeping pills since he suffered, not surprisingly, from nightmares and insomnia; and, because he feared impotence, injections of pulverised bull's testicles in grape sugar; as well as massive doses of dexedrene, pervatin, caffeine, cocaine, prozymen and ultra-septyl, and huge amounts of vitamins. Perhaps it is surprising that he looked as well as he did. All his movements, Gerhard Boldt recalled, were those of a senile man. It seems, indeed, that in his last days in the bunker Hitler presented, at times, the picture of a man who was bordering on insanity.

When the Russians performed an autopsy on Hitler's body they found that he had only one testicle – was, in medical terms, monorchic. Men who are monorchic are supposed to suffer from impatience and hyperactivity; the sudden development of difficulties in learning and lack of concentration; distinct feelings of social inadequacy; chronic indecision; a tendency to exaggerate, to lie and to fantasise; the identification of the mother as the person responsible for the defect; concern about bowel training, and castration fantasies. Such people, say those best qualified to speak, are defensive when criticised; believe that they are "special people with an unusual mission to perform", and are given to fantasies of revenge and megalomaniac day-dreams. In all of this, again, we can readily recognise our Adolf Hitler.

Hitler, it is said, also had the disturbing experience, at the age of three, of watching his drunken father rape his mother. Whether this was true, or fantasy, it not only intensified his hatred of his father, but made him feel that his mother had been disloyal to him, and left him disgusted and impotent.

Here was a man who achieved a more complete measure of power than Napoleon or Stalin or Mussolini, largely because

35

he never permitted any institution which might check his power to flourish. Was there ever such a climb to unchecked domination? And was there ever such a fall since Phaeton drove the chariot of the sun? His country was in ruins, and he and his wife, as well as the faithful Goebbels and his wife and children, were dead. Hitler had once said that only Eva Braun, and his Alsatian bitch, Blondi, were faithful to him, and had quoted the remark of his hero, Frederick the Great, "Now I know men, I prefer dogs." Only those two gave him the unquestioning devotion he demanded, and both died for it. Eva Braun, now his wife, had proved her courage and determination by flying into Berlin to die with him. As the Soviet Army advanced on Berlin that April afternoon, Hitler sat on a sofa with Eva next to him. At three-thirty he swallowed cyanide. It worked efficiently, having been tried out in a cold-blooded experiment to test it on Blondi, the dog. Hitler thrashed about and kicked the coffee table. Eva put the muzzle of her 6.35 Walther to his left temple and pulled the trigger. She then poisoned herself. The shot brought aides, who wrapped the bodies in grey army blankets and carried them out to the courtyard of the Chancellery. There was to be no grand Wagnerian funeral, and no seven-hundred-foot-high memorial to him, as he had planned. First there was an unsuccessful attempt to burn the bodies, and then a bungled attempt to bury them. Four days later, a patrol of Soviet soldiers found the stinking corpses, and identified Hitler's body by an examination of his brown, rotting teeth.

Perhaps one of the most interesting points about Hitler, who killed millions of Jews, was that he may well have been part-Jewish himself. His father's mother, a cook named Maria Anna Schicklgruber, had worked for a Jewish household, that of the Frankenbergers, and had produced a bastard child, which was probably the offspring of the nineteen-year-old son of the house. The boy's father paid her a paternity allowance until her son was fourteen. Hitler knew this, but it did nothing to decrease his hatred of the Jews – indeed, it increased it, if anything. The Jews, too, had been good to Hitler. Dr Bloch had, as we know, earned his gratitude by his attentions to his dying mother; his landlady in Vienna had been extremely kind to him; Antonescu, the Rumanian dictator, had sent him his Jewish cook; Jewish art-dealers had paid him generously for his mediocre water-colours; and he would not have received the Iron Cross, First Class, and Second Class, as a Lance-Corporal in the war, without the persistent efforts of the regimental adjutant, Hugo Guttmann, a Jew. Yet none of this diminished his desire for some form of vengeance on the Jews.

So there we have the Phaeton characteristics – an ascetic; a believer in magic and the supernatural, one with a decidedly extreme reaction to bereavement; a man of extreme isolation and reserve, with a great interest in religion, very reckless on occasion, and devoted to his mentor, Leopold Pötsch, to the end of his life. He showed an obsessive need for love. His aggression is indisputable. He demonstrated, indeed, the Phaeton characteristics in extreme form, for which Europe paid a terrible price.

AUTHORS

Hans Christian Andersen, son of a shoemaker's widow. (Father went mad, mother became an alcoholic and died of drink.)

The Brontës: mother died when Maria was 8, Elizabeth 6, Charlotte 5, Branwell 4, Emily 3 and Anne 2.

Lewis Carroll (The Revd. Charles Dodgson), mother died when he was an infant.

Fyodor Dostoevsky, mother died when he was 15.

Nikolai Gogol, father died when he was 15.

Maxim Gorky, orphaned when he was 7.

The Brothers Grimm, father died when Jacob was 11, and Wilhelm 10.

Nathaniel Hawthorne, father died when he was 4.

Edgar Allan Poe, mother died when he was 3, and his father deserted him, and soon died.

George Sand, father died when she was 4, mother banished by paternal grandmother.

Mary Shelley, mother died just after her birth.

Jonathan Swift, father died before he was born.

Leo Tolstoy, mother died when he was 1, father died when he was 9.

Ivan Turgenev, father died when he was a child.

Mark Twain, father died when he was 10.

Voltaire (François Marie Arouet), mother died when he was 7, and he was probably a bastard.

CHAPTER 4

Mary Shelley (1797 – 1851)

Mary Shelley's mother died four days after her birth.

Mary was the daughter of William Godwin, radical author of *Political Justice*, and Mary Wollstonecraft Godwin, unsuccessful suicide, mother of a bastard child, Fanny Imlay, and famous for her treatise, *A Vindication of the Rights of Woman*. They had been living together, and Mary Wollstonecraft was four months pregnant when, despite their declared contempt for marriage, they decided to opt for it after all.

With Mary Godwin's death from puerperal fever, the two little girls were left in the care of a notably undomesticated Godwin, then forty-one, and a woman friend. With unusual sensitivity, Godwin kept the secret of Fanny's illegitimacy from her, and gave her his name. He seemed incapable of showing affection, however, and, after one of his visits to him, Coleridge said, "The cadaverous silence of Godwin's children is to me quite catacomb-ish; and thinking of Mary Wollstonecraft I was oppressed by it."

The fictional characters in the novels and short stories that Mary would later write were strongly drawn from life. In one of her stories, *The Elder Son*, she described her father in striking detail, and then had her heroine say: "He never caressed me; if ever he stroked my head or drew me on his knee I felt a mingled alarm and delight difficult to describe. Yet, strange to say, my father loved me almost to idolatry; and I knew this and repaid his affection with enthusiastic fondness, notwithstanding his reserve and my awe. He was something greater, wiser,

39

better, in my eyes, than any other human being."

When Mary was four Godwin remarried, and Mrs Mary Jane Clairmont, now the second Mrs Godwin, moved into the house with her own two children, Charles and Mary Jane, who were almost certainly both bastards – Mary Jane was, undoubtedly. Her obvious preference for her own children aggravated an already difficult situation, to which Mary reacted strongly. She became rebellious and demanding, yearning for love and affection, though remaining quite incapable of expressing her own warm feelings. All her life she would seem to others cool and detached. Her feelings of being ill-used were exacerbated by her stepmother's insistence that she should do housework, while her own daughter, Mary Jane, was excused so that she could take singing lessons.

Mary's escape was into the world of books, and very early in her life she decided to become a writer. "As a child I scribbled," she later wrote; "and my favourite pastime during the hours given me for recreation was to 'write stories'." Solitary, reserved, and very self-willed, one of her biographers has pointed out that all her novels were to deal in varying degrees with loneliness and isolation. (The one which would make her name famous to coming generations would deal with a pathetic, isolated creature, rejected even by his creator, shunned by society, and denied any form of love.) Her strength of will struck those who knew her as formidable. When she was still under fifteen her father described her as "singularly bold, somewhat imperious, and active of mind. Her desire of knowledge is great, and her perseverance in everything she undertakes almost invincible." She herself later said that when she wanted something she was prepared to "go through fire and water to get it".

Mary grew into an attractive girl, very fair, with a white skin – the "moon" of Shelley's delight.

The cold chaste Moon, the Queen of Heaven's bright isles,
Who makes all beautiful on which she smiles,
That wandering shrine of soft yet icy flame,
Which ever is transformed, yet still the same,
And warms not but illumines.

It was in 1812 that the twenty-one-year-old Percy Bysshe

Shelley, baronet's son, and expelled from Oxford, with his friend Jefferson Hogg, for publishing a pamphlet, *The Necessity of Atheism*, appeared in Godwin's home. He was already married, having eloped at nineteen with the sixteen-year-old Harriet Westbrook, and had declared himself as a believer in free love as well as atheism.

Mary and Shelley felt an immediate attraction for each other, and soon they were meeting by the tombstone on the grave of Mary's dead mother. There they exchanged confidences about their unhappy childhoods.

"Passive obedience was inculcated and enforced in my childhood," Shelley declared; "I was required to love because it was my *duty* to love . . . I was haunted with a passion for the wildest and most extravagant romances . . . my sentiments were unrestrained by anything within me; external impediments were numerous, and strongly applied – their effects were merely temporary." (*Letters*, vol. 1, letter no. 157.) Doubtless, too, he told her of the sense of betrayal he had felt at being sent to Eton, where he had been miserably unhappy.

For her part, Mary would tell him of her positive hatred of her stepmother, her lonely childhood, and her feeling of irreparable loss for her dead mother, whose grave she haunted. "I detest Mrs G.," she wrote once. "She plagues my father out of his life."

It was the sixteen-year-old Mary who, on 26th June, 1814, proposed to Shelley by her mother's grave, offering herself to him on any terms. Once again, Godwin refused to countenance the free love he advocated, when it appeared in his own family. So Mary and Percy eloped, with Mary Jane Clairmont. Soon Jefferson Hogg joined them, and Mary faced the duty of carrying Shelley's principles of free love into effect. She avoided a physical consummation with Hogg until after the birth, and death, of a premature baby, but then, it seems, gave way. Shelley was delighted to give Hogg, as he put it, "your share of our common treasure". Shelley and Mary Jane Clairmont were also, most probably, lovers.

By the year 1816 Mary and Shelley were living in Switzerland at the Maison Chappuis on Lake Geneva, and by then they had a baby son, William. It was at Byron's villa, the Villa Diodati, also on Lake Geneva, that Mary, Shelley, Byron, Mary Jane Clairmont and Byron's doctor and travelling secretary, Dr Polidori, held their famous conversation about writing ghost stories. Each undertook to write one. Byron's was to be about a vampire, Shelley's about some early ghostly experiences he claimed to have had, and Dr Polidori invented a story about a woman with a skull for a head who peered through keyholes. Only Mary and Mary Jane Clairmont – now known as Claire – could not think of anything to write about. Yet it was Mary who produced the chilling *Frankenstein*, the story of the manufacture of a human body, and its dreadful results.

"My imagination, unbidden," she wrote, "possessed and guided me, gifting the successive images that arose in my mind with a vividness far beyond the usual bounds of reveries. I saw – with shut eyes, but acute mental vision – I saw the pale student of unhallowed arts kneeling beside the thing he had put together. I saw the hideous phantasm of a man stretched out, and then, on the working of some powerful engine, show signs of life, and stir with an uneasy, half-vital motion. Frightful it must be; for supremely frightful would be the effect of any human endeavour to mock the stupendous mechanism of the Creator of the world. His success would terrify the artist; he would rush away from his odious handiwork, horror-stricken. He would hope that, left to itself, the slight spark of life which he had communicated would fade; that this thing which had received such imperfect animation would subside into dead matter, and he might sleep in the belief that the silence of the grave would quench forever the transient existence of the hideous corpse which he had looked upon as the cradle of life. He sleeps; but he is awakened; he opens his eyes; behold, the horrid thing stands at his bedside, opening his curtains and looking on him with yellow, watery, but speculative eyes . . .

"I recurred to my ghost story – my tiresome, unlucky ghost story! Oh! If I could only contrive one which would frighten my reader as I myself had been frightened that night!

"Swift as light and cheering was the idea that broke in upon me. 'I have found it! What terrified me will terrify others; and I need only describe the spectre which had haunted my midnight pillow.' "

So was born the story of *Frankenstein*, known to infinitely greater numbers of people than the poems of Percy Bysshe Shelley, whatever their comparative merits.

In 1816 came two suicides, which were to have a great effect on Mary. In October poor, plain Fanny committed suicide, most likely because she had discovered the fact of her illegitimate birth. Mary was overwhelmed with guilt and remorse, feeling that she had neglected her half-sister. Next, in December, came the suicide of Harriet Shelley, who, pregnant by some unknown man, had drowned herself in the Serpentine. With more reason than in the case of Fanny, Mary blamed herself for Harriet's misery, and suffered great remorse. But that same month she married Shelley.

By 1817 Shelley and Mary had again left England. With them they took William and a new baby, Clara, and Claire and her daughter, Allegra, born of a brief liaison with Byron. It was the child Allegra who was to prove the indirect cause of intolerable grief to Mary.

Determined that her child, even if illegitimate, should be brought up as the daughter of a peer, and hopeful that this would bind Byron to her in some way, Claire sent Allegra to her father in Venice from Bagni di Lucca, where they were all staying. Then, when the nursemaid, Elise, sent disquieting reports of Allegra's treatment, Claire panicked, and decided to go and see for herself. She could not go alone. Shelley had to go with her so that, unknown to Byron, a meeting with the child could be arranged. On 17th August they left for Venice.

On 28th August Mary received a letter from Shelley, ordering her to pack and set off for Padua – a five-day journey at the worst time of year – in order to back up Shelley's assurance to Byron that Claire was with Mary and the children at Padua. Claire could then be produced.

On her twenty-first birthday Mary packed. A disastrous journey followed, during which the baby, Clara, already weak from a summer illness, developed dysentery, and almost died. However, when Byron lent the Shelleys a house at the village of Este, between Padua and Ferrara, where Claire joined them, the baby began to recover gradually. Then Claire complained of not feeling well, and set off, with Shelley, to seek a doctor in Padua. They missed their appointment, and Claire returned to Mary with a letter from Shelley: "Am I not like a wild swan, to be gone so suddenly?" He had travelled on to Venice, after making a new appointment for Claire with the doctor for eight-thirty in the morning. "You must therefore arrange matters," Shelley wrote, "so that you should come to the Stella d'Oro [in Padua] a little before that hour – a thing only to be accomplished by setting out at half past three in the morning."

The result was the death of Mary's baby, Clara. She became ill at once. At Padua Shelley decided they must take her on to Venice; but the baby had a convulsive fit in the gondola in which they were travelling. Mary sat in the inn, and watched her baby die in her arms. No doctor could save her. In less than an hour she had died.

Mary's reaction was extreme. She walked like a zombie, and refused her husband any affection, and, apparently, any sexual intercourse.

This blow, which affected her so deeply, was only the precursor of another. In February 1819, Mary and Shelley, Claire, and Milly Shields, an English girl, arrived in Rome. There the Shelleys' adored only surviving child, William, aged three, had an attack of worms. Then dysentery developed, and convulsions. In her book, *The Last Man*, so largely auto-biographical, Mary described the agony of watching her child die.

"We watched at his bedside, and when the access of fever was on him, we neither spoke nor looked at each other, marking only his obstructed breath and the mortal glow that tinged his sunken cheek, the heavy death that weighed on his eyelids. It is a trite evasion to say that words could not express our long-drawn agony; yet how can words image sensations, whose tormenting keenness throw us back, as it were, on the deep roots and hidden foundations of our nature, which shake our being with earthquake throe."

Her beloved "Willmouse", as well as Clara, and her first, premature, baby, were all dead, and her grief was devastating. The blow destroyed her. Still only twenty-one, she had lived through devastating tragedy, which had marked her for life. Never again would she be able to give her heart to a child as warmly as she had given it to her William and Clara.

She could not share her grief with Shelley. She retired completely into herself. The result was bitter resentment and estrangement from Shelley. He wrote:

> My dearest Mary, wherefore hast thou gone,
> And left me in this dreary world alone?
> Thy form is here indeed – a lovely one –
> But thou art fled, gone down the dreary road

That leads to Sorrow's most obscure abode;
Thou sittest on the heart of pale despair, where
For thine own sake I cannot follow thee.

The world is dreary,
And I am weary
Of wandering on without thee, Mary;
A joy was erewhile
In thy voice and thy smile,
And 'tis gone, when I should be gone, too, Mary.

She had in fact had what is today called a nervous break-down. Nearly three months later she would write: "I ought to have died on the 7th of June last" – the day of William's death. In her novel *Mathilda*, written shortly after, she set down a record of her feelings, including her revulsion from any sexual drive. Ostensibly the story of the incestuous love of a father for his daughter, her portrait of the father, as her biographer points out, is in many ways recognisably one of Shelley, and the death by drowning of the father in *Mathilda* is an extra-ordinary coincidence, in view of Shelley's fate.

In November, however, Mary gave birth to another son, and life began for her again. That child, Percy Florence Shelley, would live to inherit his grandfather's baronetcy.

Tragedy in plenty was still in store for Mary Shelley. In 1822, pregnant again, she had a massive haemorrhage, which ended in the loss of her baby, and, almost, of her life. It was Shelley, always surprisingly capable in times of emergency, who saved her life by sitting her in a bath filled with ice. Years later Mary recalled how she had faced the thought of imminent death.

"My feeling . . . was, I go to no new creation. I enter under no new laws. The God that made this beautiful world (and I was then at Lerici, surrounded by the most beautiful manifest-ation of the visible creation) made that into which I go; as there is beauty and love here, such is there, and I felt as if my spirit would when it left my frame be received and sustained by a beneficent and gentle Power. I had no fear, rather, though I had no active wish, but a passive satisfaction in death."

Worse was to come. Shelley had arranged for Leigh Hunt and his family to come to Italy, and live in Byron's palazzo in Pisa, so that Hunt could publish a paper, *The Liberal*, backed by Byron's money. On hearing that the Hunts had sailed from Genoa, Shelley decided to set off to meet them at Leghorn. Mary, full of foreboding, tried to persuade him not to go, but he would not be dissuaded. On July 1st, 1822, he and Edward Williams, who was staying, with his wife, at Lerici, with the Shelleys, and Captain Roberts, who had built *Ariel*, their boat, set off to welcome the Hunts, and install them in Pisa. That done, on Monday, July 8th, Shelley and Williams, and their ship's boy, Charles Vivian, set sail on their journey home. Before long a violent squall struck the little vessel.

On July 12th an anxious note from Leigh Hunt addressed to Shelley arrived at Lerici: "Pray write to tell us how you got home, for they say you had bad weather after you sailed Monday, and we are anxious." Mary and Jane Williams opened it, and realised that something was very wrong. Mary was still weak from her miscarriage, but they set off at once for Pisa. At midnight they arrived at Byron's palazzo. There Mary, white and exhausted, asked Byron's mistress, the Countess Guiccioli, "*Sapete alcuna cosa di Shelley?* (Have you any news of Shelley?)" There was none. Not until July 19th did they learn that the three bodies had been washed ashore.

The rest of the story is well known, particularly the dramatic burning of the bodies of Williams and Shelley on the sands.

Mary's mourning lasted for the rest of her life. She blamed herself bitterly for her withdrawal from Shelley during his last days, and wrote:

> Now fierce remorse and unreplying death
> Waken a chord within my heart, whose breath,
> Thrilling and keen, in accents audible
> A tale of unrequited love doth tell . . .
> It speaks of cold neglect, averted eyes,
> That blindly crushed thy soul's fond sacrifice: –
> My heart was all thine own – but yet a shell
> Closed in its core, which seemed impenetrable,
> Till sharp-toothed misery tore the husk in twain,
> Which gaping lies, nor may unite again.

Now more than ever reserved and isolated, she turned in on herself. "All I ask is obscurity," she wrote once; and when a magazine asked for an interview with her she replied, "I do not see what the public have to do with me – I am a great enemy to the prevailing custom of dragging private life before the world, taking the matter generally – and with regard to myself there is no greater annoyance than in any way to be brought out of my proper sphere of private obscurity.''

Mary was, of course, very sensitive to the possibility of the irregularities of her earlier life being given publicity in the remorseless press of the day. She still sought fame, as well as money, by continuing to write her books. For the rest, like Victoria with her Albert, she devoted herself to Shelley's memory, editing his works, and cherishing anything that remained of his. She never remarried, though the American actor-manager, John Howard Payne, proposed to her. She died in 1851, at only fifty-three, her beauty ruined by small-pox.

There is no doubt that in Mary Shelley we can recognise the Phaeton's traits of abnormal sensitivity, of isolation, and of an icy reserve, of a marked austerity in her life, and, most remarkably, of extreme reaction to bereavement. She had an intense devotion to her own children; and recklessness was all too evident in her elopement with Shelley. She had a notable concern with religion, as she showed when facing possible death from haemorrhage, and she had a noticeable propensity to depression. Her books are full of descriptions of the emotional deprivation of the motherless or orphaned. To mention only one or two, Lionel Verney, in her novel, *The Last Man*, grew up solitary and unloved. Mathilda lost her loving and brilliant mother exactly as Mary had done hers, and Elizabeth Raby, in *Falkner*, was a lonely girl who paid daily visits to her mother's grave.

From her childhood Mary had been ambitious, writing her stories, and determined to succeed as an author – to drive the fiery chariot.

Mary Shelley also shared with other Phaetons a fascination with storms. One of her biographers goes so far as to call it a love of storms, and it seems to have been perhaps more than a mere fascination. She had been excited by the great tempests which broke over Lake Geneva. Then, after the terrible trauma of Clara's and William's deaths, when she and Shelley had left Rome for the Villa Valsovano, between Leghorn and Monte Nero, she seemed to derive some strange comfort from watching those which broke over the waters which the villa over-looked.

"Sometimes the dark and lurid clouds dipped towards the waves, and became waterspouts that churned up the waters beneath as they were chased onwards and scattered by the tempest," she wrote in her notes to her dead husband's poems, still unable to forget the storms on Lake Geneva.

Perhaps, too, it may not be going too far to suggest that the story of Frankenstein's monster had something of the magical about it.

POETS

Charles Baudelaire, father died when he was 6.
Robert Burns, mother died when he was 10.
George Gordon, sixth Lord Byron, father died when he was
   3½, and he had not seen him for six months.
Samuel Taylor Coleridge, father died when he was 9.
Stratis Haviaras, father killed by Nazis when he was 9.
A.E. Housman, mother died when he was 12.
John Keats, father died when he was 13.
John Masefield, mother died when he was 6.
Jean Racine, mother died when he was 3 months and his father
   when he was 4.

> "I had the choice of many inglorious years,
> Or a short life followed by a long renown,
> But since the grave stands open to us all,
> Never will I, encumbering the earth,
> Too sparing of a goddess mother's blood,
> Waiting at home till obscure age comes on,
> And shunning still the path that leads to fame,
> Nameless, go down to all-effacing death.
> Let us not forge these shameful obstacles."

William Wordsworth, mother died when he was 7, father
   when he was 14.

CHAPTER 5

George Gordon, Lord Byron
(1788 – 1824)

George Gordon, the sixth Lord Byron, lost his father when he was three and a half, and had not seen him for six months.

Lord Byron was not only a Phaeton of Phaetons, he also had an extraordinary insight into that condition, as is evidenced by the passage from *Don Juan*, Canto XVII, written shortly before his death, which appears at the front of this book.

> The world is full of orphans: firstly, those
> Who are so in the strict sense of the phrase;
> But many a lonely tree the loftier grows
> Than others crowded in the Forest's maze –
> The next are such as are not doomed to lose
> Their tender parents, in their budding days,
> But, merely, their parental tenderness,
> Which leaves them orphans of the heart no less.

Byron had an extreme reaction to bereavement. He had never got on at all well with his mother, a tactless woman, capable of taunting him about his lameness, though very good to him in other ways. Yet when, on his return to England after an extended tour abroad, he reached the Byron estate, Newstead Abbey, too late to see her alive, his reaction was extreme. The night after his arrival, his mother's maid found him sitting in the dark beside her corpse, and he burst into tears and exclaimed, "Oh, Mrs By, I had but one friend in the world, and she is gone!"

Then, before his mother was buried, another blow struck. Charles Skinner Matthews, the most brilliant of Byron's Cambridge friends, died horribly, trapped in a bed of weeds at the bottom of the Cam, in a pool where he was bathing alone. To Byron, this was unbearable. "Some curse hangs over me and mine," he wrote to another friend, Scrope Davies, "my mother lies a corpse in this house; one of my best friends is drowned in a ditch . . . Come to me, Scrope, I am almost desolate – left almost alone in the world."

On the morning of his mother's funeral, Byron could not bring himself to follow the remains to Hucknall Torkard Church, where they were buried in the family vault. He stood in the door of the Abbey, watching until the procession passed out of sight. Then he turned to his page, Robert Rushton, the only person besides himself left behind, and engaged in a violent sparring match. Then, suddenly, he flung away the gloves, and retired to his room.

Yet a third death, that of his Harrow school-friend, John Wingfield, came to afflict him at this time. To his friend, John Cam Hobhouse, he wrote: "I am really so much bewildered with the different shocks I have sustained, that I can hardly reduce myself to reason by the most frivolous occupations . . . There is to me something so incomprehensible in death that I can neither speak nor think on the subject. Indeed, when I looked on the mass of corruption which was the being from whence I sprung, I doubted within myself whether I *was*, or whether she *was not* . . . I have neither hopes nor fears beyond the grave, yet if there is within us 'a spark of that Celestial fire', M[atthews] has already 'mingled with the gods'."

More sorrow would come to him in the near future. The choir-boy, John Edleston, with whom he had had a very close friendship – probably innocent in the beginning, certainly homosexual later on – had died of tuberculosis while he had been away, and his sister, Ann Edleston, wrote to break the news to him. To his friend, Robert Dallas, he wrote: "I have been again shocked with a *death*, and have lost one very dear to me in happier times . . . an event which, five years ago, would have bowed down my head to the earth. It seems as though I were to experience in my youth the greatest misery of age. My friends fall around me, and I shall be left a lonely tree before I

51

am withered . . . I am indeed very wretched, and you will excuse my saying so, as you know I am not apt to cant or sensibility."

He poured out his feelings in a poem *To Thyrza*, and, by using a woman's name, was able to give full release to his sorrow for the loss of Edleston.

> The whispered thought of hearts allied,
> The pressure of the thrilling hand;
> The kiss, so guiltless and refined,
> That Love each warmer wish forbore;
> Those eyes proclaimed so pure a mind,
> Ev'n Passion blushed to plead for more –
> The tone, that taught me to rejoice,
> When prone, unlike thee, to repine;
> The song, celestial from thy voice,
> But sweet to me from none but thine;
> The pledge we wore – *I* wear it still,
> But where is thine? Ah! where art thou?

There is no doubt that Edleston was a homosexual; and indeed he had been in trouble for the crime of "indecency" while Byron had been abroad. It is equally certain that Thyrza and Edleston were one and the same. Byron even added a stanza to *Childe Harold*, beginning:

> There, Thou – whose Love and Life together fled
> Have left me here to love and live in vain.

To Hobhouse, his closest friend, he wrote: "At present I am rather low, and don't know how to tell you the reason – you remember *E*. at Cambridge – he is *dead* – last May – his sister sent me the account lately – now though I never should have seen him again (and it is very proper that I should not) I have been more affected than I should care to own elsewhere."

It was hard for him to forget Edleston. Before the year ended he wrote another poem to Thyrza, *Away, Away, Ye Notes of Woe*. It concluded:

> Sweet Thyrza! waking as in sleep,
> Thou art but now a lovely dream;
> A Star that trembled o'er the deep,
> Then turned from earth its tender beam.

But he who through Life's dreary way
Must pass, when Heaven is veiled in wrath,
Will long lament the vanished ray
That scattered gladness o'er his path.

In 1812 he was still yearning for Edleston, writing: "I believe the only human being that ever loved me in truth and entirely was of, or belonging to, Cambridge, and in that no change can now take place. I almost rejoice when one I love dies young, for I could never bear to see them old or altered."

Again he set his thoughts to verse:

The love when Death has set his seal,
No age can chill nor rival steal,
Nor falsehood disavow.
And, what were worse, thou canst not see
Or wrong, or change, or fault in me.

In all he wrote at least five poems inspired by the shock of Edleston's death, or later reflections on it; and it is possible that the poem:

There be none of Beauty's daughters
With a magic like thee

was really written to Edleston, and not to Claire Clairmont as is often supposed – a most unlikely supposition, as Byron never pretended, least of all to her, that he was in love with her.

Even for the death of Lady Noel, whom he had cordially disliked, Byron went into deep mourning.

However, the deepest grief Byron ever felt, largely, perhaps, because of an element of guilt in it, was that for the death of his little bastard daughter, Allegra, by his mistress Claire Clairmont. By then, exiled from England, and living in Pisa with a new mistress, the Contessa Teresa Guiccioli, Byron had insisted on leaving the little girl in a convent at Bagnacavallo, about twelve miles from Ravenna, on the road to Bologna. The child was only four when she went to the convent, and she died there at the age of five years and three months.

The news was brought to Pisa by special messenger, arriving on April 22nd, 1822, and Byron's mistress, the Contessa Guiccioli, broke it to him as carefully as she could. His reaction, however, was severe. In the Contessa's words: "After a short interval of suspense, with every caution which my own sorrow suggested, I deprived him of all hope of the child's recovery. 'I understand,' said he, 'it is enough, say no more.' A mortal pallour [sic] spread over his face, his strength failed him, and he sunk into a seat. His look was fixed, and the expression such that I began to fear for his reason; he did not shed a tear; and his countenance manifested so hopeless, so profound, so sublime a sorrow, that at the moment he appeared a being of a nature superior to humanity. He remained immovable in the same attitude for an hour, and no consolation which I endeavoured to afford him seemed to reach his ears, far less his heart . . . He desired to be left alone, and I was obliged to leave him."

The child's mother, Claire Clairmont, a bastard, also suffered excruciatingly from her death.

Four days after Allegra's death, Byron wrote to Shelley: "The blow was stunning and unexpected, for I thought the danger over, by the long interval between her stated recovery and the arrival of the express. But I have borne up against it as best I can, and so far successfully that I can go about the usual business of life with the same appearance of composure, and even greater . . . I do not know that I have anything to reproach in my conduct and certainly nothing in my feelings and intentions towards the dead. But it is a moment when we are apt to think that, if this or that had been done, such an event might have been prevented – though every day and hour shows that they are the most natural and inevitable. I suppose that Time will do his usual work – Death has done his."

Byron would never pronounce Allegra's name afterwards. His suffering was long-lasting. Three years later, he spoke of the misery of bereavement to Lady Blessington – exceptionally, mentioning the child's name – on the subject of the misery caused to men like himself whose imagination was warmer than, as he put it, their hearts. "This is our misfortune but not our fault," he said, "and dearly do we expiate it; by it we are rendered incapable of sympathy, and cannot lighten, by sharing, the pain we inflict . . . *But let the object of our affection be snatched away by death, and how is all the pain ever inflicted on them avenged!* The same imagination that led us to slight or overlook their suffering, now that they are for ever lost to us, magnifies

54

their estimable qualities and increases tenfold the affection we ever felt for them.

> Oh! what are thousand living loves
> To that which cannot quit the dead.

"How did I feel this when Allegra, my daughter, died! While she lived her existence never seemed necessary to my happiness; but no sooner did I lose her than it appeared to me as if I could not live without her. Even now the recollection is most bitter."

So overcome was Byron by his little daughter's death, indeed, that he was willing to brave the inevitable scandal by asking that his bastard child should be buried in Harrow Church, with her name on a plaque and an inscription composed by him.

> In memory of Allegra
> Daughter of George Gordon Lord Byron
> who died at Bagnacavallo
> in Italy, April 20th, 1822,
> aged five years and three months.
> I shall go to her, but she shall not
> return to me
> (2 Samuel XII 22)

It was not his fault that the plaque was not put up. First the Vicar objected on the ground that it would be an offence against taste and propriety, and then the churchwardens protested, objecting "on behalf of the parish to admit the tablet of Lord Byron's child inside the church". So Allegra was buried outside in the churchyard, under the trees, in unconsecrated ground, and no tablet or memorial stone marked her final resting-place. Her father, at least, had tried to do more for her in death than he had ever done in her lifetime – he had not even bothered to inspect the convent to which she had been sent – and make a sacrifice for her. (It is pleasant to think that now, at long last, there is a memorial to Allegra, in the church near Newstead Abbey, in the very words composed by her father.)

Byron became very nervous about his legitimate daughter, Ada, after Allegra's death. He always remembered her birthday, December 10th, even writing to his publisher, "This day, and this hour (one, on the clock) my daughter is six years old. I wonder whether I shall see her again, or if ever I shall see her at all. I have remarked a curious coincidence, which almost looks like a fatality. My *mother*, my *wife*, my *daughter*, my *half-sister*, my [half-] *sister's mother*, my natural daughter (at least as far as *I* am concerned) and myself, are all *only children*. I heard the other day that her [Ada's] temper is said to be extremely violent. Is it so? It is not unlikely, considering her parentage. My temper is what it is – as you may perhaps divine – and my Lady was a nice little sullen nucleus of concentrated savageness to mould my daughter upon – to say nothing of her two Grandmothers, both of whom, to my knowledge, were as pretty specimens of female spirit as you might wish to see on a summer day."

It was as well that he did not live to see the death of this beloved daughter, suffering from cancer, yet even on her death-bed betting heavily on Epsom race-meetings, and giving her diamond parure to her lover, so that he could get her more money for settling her racing debts, and for paying her blackmailing married lover.

Worthy of mention, too, on the score of Byron's reaction to bereavement, was his sorrow even at the death of his beloved Newfoundland dog, Boatswain. He wrote a poem to him, and erected a monument with a prose inscription, preceding the verses, which were inscribed on it. The prose inscription read:

Near this spot
Are deposited the Remains of one
Who possessed Beauty without Vanity,
Strength without Insolence,
Courage without Ferocity,
And all the Virtues of Man without his Vices.
This Praise, which would be unmeaning Flattery
If inscribed over human ashes,
Is but a just tribute to the Memory of
BOATSWAIN, a Dog,
Who was born at Newfoundland, May, 1803
And died at Newstead Abbey, Nov. 18, 1808.

He announced the death of this beloved animal to his friend Hodgson, "Boatswain is dead! he expired in a state of madness on the 18th, after suffering much, yet retaining all the gentleness of his nature to the last; never attempting to do the least injury to anyone near him. I have now lost everything except old Murray." In the will which Byron executed in 1811, he stipulated that he should be buried in the vault with his dog.

The poem he wrote in Boatswain's memory, which was inscribed on his monument, ran:

When some proud son of man returns to earth,
Unknown to glory, but upheld by birth,
The sculptor's art exhausts the pomp of woe
And storied urns record who rest below:
When all is done, upon the tomb is seen,
Not what he was, but what he should have been:
But the poor dog, in life the firmest friend,
The first to welcome, foremost to defend,
Whose honest heart is still his master's own,
Who labours, fights, lives, breathes for him alone,
Unhonour'd falls, unnotic'd all his worth –
Denied in heaven the soul he held on earth:
While Man, vain insect! hopes to be forgiven,
And claims himself a sole exclusive Heaven.
Oh Man! thou feeble tenant of an hour,
Debas'd by slavery, or corrupt by power,
Who knows thee well must quit thee with disgust,
Degraded mass of animated dust!
Thy love is lust, thy friendship all a cheat,
Thy smiles hypocrisy, thy words deceit!
By nature vile, ennobled but by name,
Each kindred brute might bid thee blush for shame.
Ye! who perchance behold this simple urn,
Pass on – it honours none you wish to mourn:
To mark a Friend's remains these stones arise;
I never knew but one – and here he lies.

Byron's interest in religion was life-long, and extreme. His mistress, Claire Clairmont, outlined in her diary, in November 1820, four pages of suggestions for caricatures of him. These were, she wrote, to be called "Lord Byron's Morning, Noon and Night. The first, he looking at the sky, a sun brightly shining – saying, 'Come, I feel quite bold and cheerful – there is no God.' The second towards evening, a grey tint spread over the face of Nature, the sun behind a cloud, a shower of rain falling – a dinner-table in the distance covered with a profusion of dishes, he says, 'What a change I feel in me after dinner; where we see design we suppose a designer; I'll be, I am, a Deist!' The third – evening – candles just lighted, all dark without the windows (a cup of green tea on the table) and trees agitated much by the wind beating against the panes, also thunder and lightning. He says, 'God bless me, suppose there should be a God – it is well to stand in his good graces. I'll say my prayers tonight, and write to Murray to put in a touch concerning the blowing of the last Trump.' "

Exaggerated? Of course; and intended to be so. But Byron was deeply concerned about religion all his life. Calvinism had been instilled in him from his earliest years in Scotland, and he never forgot it. When he was courting his future wife, Annabella Milbanke, in 1814, it was he who raised the subject of religion. "When I tell you," he wrote, "that I am so convinced of its importance in fixing the principles that I could never have had perfect confidence in any woman who was slightly impressed with its truth, you will hardly believe that I can exact more tolerance than I am willing to grant. I will not deny that my own impressions are by no means settled; but that they are perverted to the extent which has been imputed to them on the ground of a few passages in works of fiction, I cannot admit to those whose esteem I would secure – although from a secret aversion from explanations and vindications I have hitherto entered into none to those who would never have made the charge but from a wish to condemn rather than convert. To you, my conduct must be different as my feelings. In a word, I will read what books you please, hear what arguments you please, and in leaving the choice to your judgment let it be a proof that my confidence in your understanding and your virtues is equal. You shall be 'my Guide, Philosopher and Friend'; my whole heart is yours – and if possible let me make it not unworthy of her to whom it is bound, and from whom but one event can divide it."

Not the least convincing evidence of his interest in religion was Byron's attending the marathon religious meeting held by Dr Kennedy, a worthy Scottish Methodist, and staying there for four hours, taking an active part. One amusing exchange between him and the divine went, according to Dr Kennedy, as follows:

" 'I would have no Hell at all,' said Dr Kennedy, at one point of the subsequent discussion, 'but would pardon all, purify all . . .'

" 'I would save,' cried his Lordship, 'my sister and my daughter, and some of my friends, and a few others, and let the rest shift for themselves.'

" 'And your wife also?' I exclaimed.

" 'No,' he said.

" 'But your wife, surely you would save your wife?'

" 'Well,' he said, 'I would save her too, if you like.' "

He considered the Catholic religion to be, on the whole, the best, as well as the oldest; and he put his illegitimate daughter into a Catholic convent to be brought up as one. And when she died the inscription he wrote for her closed with the words, taken from the Book of Samuel, "I shall go to her, but she shall not return to me." When he composed that memorial, at least, he seemed to believe in a life after death. To Pietro Gamba, brother of his mistress, Teresa Guiccioli, he said, *"Vous confondez vos idées religieuses avec vos antipathies politiques. Je considère l'athéisme comme une folie."* He often argued with his wife during their unhappy marriage, acting the part of devil's advocate, but at the end of all his arguments he would exclaim violently, "The worst of it is, *I do believe*." Shelley, shocked, commented to his Mary, "I do believe, Mary, he is little better than a Christian."

Byron himself said, "I have often wished that I had been born a Catholic. That purgatory of theirs is a comfortable doctrine. I wonder that reformers gave it up, or did not substitute something as consolatory in its room. It is an improvement on the transmigration, Shelley, which all your wiseacre philosophers taught. You believe in Plato's three principles. Why not in the Trinity? One is not more mystical than the other. I don't know why I am considered an enemy of religion, and an unbeliever . . . I know, however, that I am considered an infidel. My wife and sister, when they joined parties, sent me prayer-books."

Byron was always superstitious, and was given to presentiments. On his honeymoon there was a terrible outburst when his bride, who was wearing the wedding-ring with which his own mother had been married, and which was much too large for her, appeared with a black ribbon holding it on her finger. He insisted on eating a goose on Michaelmas Day, claiming that otherwise the year would prove fatal. So he travelled with cackling geese swinging in a cage behind his carriage. In fact, in the end, he decided not to wring the necks of those particular geese, and they became pets. That did not stop him, however, eating others, and becoming extremely angry when his foreign servants gave him his Michaelmas goose on the wrong day.

He believed that it was unlucky to wear a black gown; he never started any enterprise on a Friday; and when he lay in his final illness in Greece he gave orders that a search should be made for "an old and ugly witch", who might be able to cure him. More, in that last, terrible illness, he said that a Scottish fortune-teller had warned him, "Beware your thirty-seventh year." The fortune-teller was proved right, for Byron died in his thirty-seventh year.

The amusing quirk by which Phaetons born after Sir Walter Scott seem particularly addicted to his works, appears once again in Byron. As early as his university days, at Trinity College, Cambridge, Byron was reading his poetry. He attacked him in his *English Bards and Scotch Reviewers,* accusing him of writing "stale romance" for money, but later regretted it, after a talk with the Prince Regent, a devotee of Scott's, and wrote to Sir Walter to apologise and atone for his fractious remarks. By 1815 he had met Scott himself at Murray's, his publisher's, and had talked to him for nearly two hours. The two got on well together, and Murray's son later recalled seeing "the two greatest poets of the day – both lame – stumping downstairs side by side". They continued to meet at Albemarle Street nearly every day, he said, and remained together for two or three hours at a time. They often met, too, in society. Scott agreed with Byron, except on religion and politics; and predicted that Byron would turn Catholic. They became such friends that Scott recited *Christabel* to Byron, and Byron dedicated his *Cain* to Scott. He treasured Scott's autograph, too, only parting with it when he was actually on his way to Greece. Of his works he wrote: "To me these novels have so much of 'Auld Lang Syne' (I was bred a canny Scot till I was ten years old) that I never move without them, and when I removed from Ravenna to Pisa the other day, and sent on my library before, they were the only books that I kept by me, although I already have them by heart."

Phaetons are much affected by storms. There, once again, we find Byron's having a noticeable interest in them. In February 1821 he wrote, "Came home *solus* – very high wind –

lightning – moonshine – solitary stragglers muffled in cloaks –
women in masks – clouds hurrying over the sky, like spilt milk
blown out of the pail – altogether very poetical. It is still
blowing hard – the tiles flying, and the house rocking – rain
splashing – lightning flashing – quite a fine Swiss Alpine
evening, and the sea roaring in the distance."

More remarkably, on December 9th, 1823, there was a
violent thunderstorm which Byron insisted on watching, with
Teresa Guiccioli beside him, at an open window. Leaning on
his arm, she said, she found the courage not to show herself
afraid. But then the lightning actually struck the lightning-
conductor immediately outside the window, half-blinding
and stunning them both. "Madame Guiccioli was frightened,
as you may suppose," Byron wrote to Murray, adding that,
doubtless, if they had been killed, "your bigots" would have
"saddled me with a judgment".

He also wrote a vivid poem called *Stanzas Composed During a
Thunderstorm.*

1

Chill and mirk is the nightly blast,
Where Pindus' mountains rise,
And angry clouds are pouring fast
The vengeance of the skies.

2

Our guides are gone, our hope is lost,
And lightnings, as they play,
But show where rocks our paths have crost,
Or gild the torrent's spray.

3

Is yon a cot I saw, though low?
When lightning broke the gloom –
How welcome were its shade! – ah, no!
'Tis but a Turkish tomb.

4

Through sounds of foaming waterfalls,
I hear a voice exclaim –
My way-worn countryman, who calls
On distant England's name.

A shot is fired – by foe or friend?
Another – 'tis to tell
The mountain-peasants to descend,
And lead us where they dwell.

And so on, for eighteen verses, expressing most vividly the anguish of being caught out in a storm of frightening force.

Having no father, Byron was very ready to have a mentor. The solicitor, Hanson, who had been on the scene before the boy was born, persuaded Frederick Howard, fifth Earl of Carlisle, to become his guardian during his minority. Things did not go well, however. Carlisle had already acted as guardian to Byron's half-sister, Augusta, and was probably bored at the thought of more responsibility for the offspring of their feckless father. Byron dined with him in January 1805, and actually dedicated his first book of poems, *Hours of Idleness*, to him. Carlisle, however, did not even offer to introduce him into the House of Lords. Angered, Byron retaliated, and over-reacted. He wrote:

Lord, rhymester, petit-maître, pamphleteer,
So dull in youth, so drivelling in his age,
His scenes alone had damned our sinking stage.

When he was abroad, he made matters even worse, writing:

No muse will cheer with renovating smile
The paralytic puling of Carlisle.

Later he regretted his behaviour, when he discovered that the Earl suffered from a nervous disorder, and said: "I thank Heaven I did not know it – I would not, could not, if I had, I must naturally be the last person to be pointed on defects or maladies." The mischief had been done, however, and his half-sister Augusta was greatly hurt by his attack on Lord Carlisle. Byron actually sent a note to Samuel Rogers, asking: "Is there any chance or possibility of making it up with Lord Carlisle, as I feel disposed to do anything reasonable or un-reasonable to effect it?" Lord Carlisle sent an empty carriage to Byron's funeral – as did most others, embarrassed by his history. It was a sad end to what might have been a fruitful relationship for one clearly seeking a father-substitute.

Hanson became his father-substitute instead. He was genuinely impressed by the boy, and did everything for him that he could. The creditors of Byron's predecessor had seized everything the law allowed, and it was a pathetic inheritance that the boy came into. Hanson threw himself into making life as comfortable for Byron as possible. He did not merely persuade Carlisle to become his guardian; he arranged for an examination of his club foot, in the hope that it was not too late to cure it; he helped Mrs Byron to obtain a pension; he chose Dr Glennie's school to prepare the boy for Harrow; and he actually took him to Harrow himself, when the time came for him to go there, went to speech-days, and secured a grant for his education there. Indeed, he became more like a stepfather than a solicitor to the boy.

With Byron, of course, no relationship was ever without its strains and stresses. Yet he was prepared to act a most reprehensible charade for Hanson, actually giving away his daughter, Mary Anne, in marriage to the imbecile Earl of Portsmouth, so that she could become Lady Portsmouth, the imbecile being over forty and the girl twenty-four. Shortly afterwards, the Earl's brother took out a commission of lunacy to try to annul the marriage, and Byron swore an affidavit to the effect that Lord Portsmouth seemed "perfectly calm and rational on the occasion", and that his preferring "a young woman to an old one, and . . . his own wishes to those of a younger brother seemed to me neither irrational nor extraordinary". Probably because of this statement, Lord Chancellor Eldon ruled that Lord Portsmouth was capable of entering into a marriage contract. Yet in the end a jury would return a unanimous verdict of lunacy since 1809 – and the marriage had been in 1814.

It was the first Lady Melbourne, however, his wife's aunt, whom he had known long before his marriage, who perhaps meant most to him. For once disinterested, this accomplished woman did all she could to discourage Byron from his suicidal love-affair with his half-sister, and was very helpful in encouraging his marriage to her niece. Byron was extremely devoted to her, and mourned her deeply when he learned of her death, in 1818, when he was abroad, calling her "the best, and kindest, and ablest female I ever knew – old or young".

Byron's search for love was never-ending. Even if one

dismisses his ordinary womanising, the score of positive love-affairs is considerable. To quote but a few: Mary Duff; Mary Chaworth; Margaret Parker; Elizabeth Pigot; Lady Jersey; Lady Falkland; Henrietta d'Ussières; Susan Boyce; and Lady Frances Webster. (This, too, ignoring his predilection for keeping girls in boy's clothes, making servant-girls pregnant, and supporting a series of Venetian mistresses.)

His sexuality was developed very early because, as his friend Hobhouse put it, "When [Byron was] nine years old at his mother's house a free Scotch girl used to come to bed to him and play tricks with his person – Hanson found it out and asked Lord B – who owned the fact – the girl was sent off – "

Claire Clairmont, mother of his bastard child, Allegra, was another of his female, transient, loves, and he once planned to elope with a Mrs Constance Spencer Smith, three years older than he, whom he met at Malta. That romance was forgotten as soon as he sailed from Malta, however, and he embarked on another with Teresa Macri, whose mother actually offered her to him. The only love which lasted his whole life, however, was that for his half-sister, Augusta, and she betrayed him, falling completely under the sway of his estranged wife.

His love-affairs with men were also numerous. Robert Rushton, a handsome boy, was probably the first. Byron actually had his portrait painted by Sanders, standing by Rushton on the seashore with a steep mountain in the background. He was extremely angry when he discovered that his man, Fletcher, had taken the boy to a prostitute. Hobhouse was well aware of Byron's homosexuality, and when Moore commented on Byron's desire to be alone in Greece, suggesting that even Hobhouse's society "grew at last to be a chain and a burthen on him", he wrote contemptuously in the margin, "On what grounds does Tom say this? He has not the remotest grasp of the real reason which induced Lord Byron to prefer having no Englishman immediately and constantly near him." (Sodomy, one should remember, was a hanging offence at the time. At the very least Byron would have been afraid of blackmail.)

Long, long before this, indeed, Hobhouse had been aware of Byron's homosexuality, and he wrote, again in his copy of Moore, opposite Moore's reference to "an intimacy having sprung up between Lord Grey and his noble tenant", "and a circumstance occurred during [this] intimacy which certainly had much effect on his future morals".

The fact is that Lord Grey, his mother's tenant, had made sexual advances to Byron, which disgusted him at the time, but apparently opened his eyes to a new form of sexuality, which he subsequently practised.

He kept Eustathios Georgiu in Vostitza; Nicolo Giroud in Athens; and his last passion was for Loukas Chalandritsanos. The greatest male love of his life was, however, John Edleston, as the greatest female love of his life was his half-sister Augusta. The Contessa Teresa Guiccioli was the most faithful to him, though, forgiving him all his faults, and even his cruelty to her at the end, and never forgetting him all her life, though she remarried on the death of her estranged husband.

Ambition? While he was a boy at Harrow he wrote to his mother: "The way to *riches*, to *greatness* lies before me. I can, I will cut myself a path through the world or perish in the attempt." Those ambitions went far beyond achieving fame as a poet. At first he dreamed of making his name in politics, taking his seat in the Lords at the earliest opportunity. He himself was very pleased with his début, but Lord Holland was scathing about it, saying categorically, "His fastidious and artificial taste, and his over-irritable temper, would, I think, have prevented him from ever excelling in Parliament."

He never gave up hope of achieving fame of the kind he desired, saying to Moore: "I don't mean in literature, for that is nothing; and it may seem odd enough to say it, I do not think it my vocation. But you will see that I shall do something or other – the times and fortune permitting." It was that ambition, to make a glorious name for himself before all men, which took him to Greece. He himself said, in 1823, "For after all, it is better playing at nations than gaming at Almack's or Newmarket." He was absolutely serious, and saw himself as, one day, possibly the King of Greece.

Byron had a great propensity to depression, which at times reached frightening depths – frightening not least to friends like Hobhouse, and to Annabella Milbanke, during their brief marriage.

Byron was capable of great austerity. He had a terror of getting fat, and when he showed any sign of it he reduced his diet to the point of absolute starvation. To some extent this was because when he added to his weight even standing was painful, so he made up his mind not to exceed eleven stone. According to Trelawny, the strange buccaneer-type who lived in Florence with the Byron-Shelley circle, he was exceedingly abstemious in eating and drinking. When alone, he drank no more than a glass or two of claret or hock, in days when men drank a great deal, and when exhausted at night a single glass of grog, which Trelawny watered down to what sailors call "water bewitched". Byron would exist on biscuits and soda-water for days together, and then to sate his hunger make up what Trelawny called "a horrid mess of cold potatoes, rice, fish, or greens, deluged in vinegar, and gobble it up like a famished dog".

In 1816, too, in Switzerland, he lived only on a thin slice of bread and tea for breakfast; a light dinner, consisting only of vegetables, a bottle or two of Seltzer water with a drop of Graves wine in it, and in the evening a cup of tea without milk or sugar. To appease the pangs of hunger he chewed tobacco and smoked cigars. He had grown heavy from much eating out with his friends before his departure from England, and this rigid abstinence was in order to lose weight.

One would expect a poet to be abnormally sensitive, and there is no question but that Byron was so. It was not strange that from childhood he could not bear any mention of his club-foot. On one notable occasion a nurse met his own nurse and her charge on one of her walks, and remarked, "What a pretty boy Byron is! What a pity he has such a leg!" The boy flared up immediately, and struck at her with his little whip, shouting, "Dinna speak of it!" He had a violent temper, like his mother, and reacted angrily all his life to any suggestion of criticism.

So there we have this Phaeton of Phaetons, showing all the signs we look for: austerity; abnormal sensitivity; extreme religious concern; isolation and reserve; the need for a mentor; a propensity to depression; extreme reaction to bereavement; aggression; an obsessive need for love and the achievement of total support; intense feeling for his own children; reckless-ness; superstitiousness; and, even, a fascination with storms, and with Sir Walter Scott.

HEROES AND HEROINES

Admiral Earl Beatty, bastard.
Julius Caesar, mother died at his birth.
Charlemagne, bastard.
Donaldson sons, father killed when young, and 26-year-old
mother brought up her sons herself. The sons won eleven
decorations for bravery.
Joan of Arc, bastard.
Lawrence of Arabia, bastard.
Charles Martel, bastard.
Horatio Nelson, mother died when he was 9.
Henry Morton Stanley, bastard.
Duke of Wellington, father died when he was 12.

CHAPTER 6

Horatio Nelson (1758 – 1805)

Horatio Nelson lost his mother at the age of nine.

He missed her so acutely that even when he was over forty and a national figure he wrote to an old Norfolk friend: "The thought of former days brings all my mother to my heart, which shows itself in my eyes." All his life he searched for a mother, and when, in Emma Hamilton, he discovered motherliness and sexuality combined, he behaved in a reckless way, to the horror of his family and his friends.

He had an extreme reaction to bereavement. The death of his brother, Maurice, whom he went home to see on his death-bed, upset him dreadfully, as did the death of his sister Anne, caused by a chill caught on leaving a ball-room. When his friend, Vice-Admiral Sir Hyde Parker, died of his wounds, he was extremely emotional and distraught. Nelson was also deeply upset by his father's death in 1802, a sorrow increased by the fact that he was so afraid of meeting his estranged wife at the funeral that he did not go to it. He was upset, too, by the death of his old friend, Sir William Hamilton. The old man was generous and forgiving, as well as being, in Nelson's eyes, "an upright and accomplished gentleman". He left him Madame le Bruin's picture of Emma, writing, "I give [it] to my dearest friend Lord Nelson . . . the most virtuous, loyal and truly great character I ever met. God bless him and shame fall on those who do not say Amen." Forgiveness could go no further, and Nelson at least had qualms about deserving it. To Perry, the editor of the *Morning Chronicle*, he wrote, "Our dear Sir William left this world at ten minutes past ten this morning in Lady Hamilton's and my arms. Her attentions to him to the last and altogether for nearly twelve years have been such as to call forth all our admiration for this excellent woman. As I should wish neither to have too much nor too little said in your paper on this occasion, I entreat that I may see you as soon as possible." He was clearly worried by the prospect of rekindled criticism of his illicit passion for Emma, putting his career and his reputation in jeopardy. Fortune was with him, however. Within a month he was given an appointment which took him away from Emma for all but one brief period two years later – not that either Nelson or Emma would have considered that fortunate.

This sickly man never grew taller than five foot five and a half inches. He was so skinny that to a German at Dresden he appeared "one of the most insignificant figures I ever saw in my life . . . His weight cannot be more than seventy pounds." Yet he set out determinedly on his path to fame. He was convinced to the end of his life that providence was guiding his destiny, and that that destiny would take him to glory.

The family, by the gentry's standards were poor, so that his elder sister, Susannah, had to be apprenticed to a milliner at Bath. His father had an influence on him, but it was his uncle, his dead mother's brother, who set his course – Captain Maurice Suckling. When his father asked Suckling's aid in getting his son sent to sea in the navy, Suckling wrote: "What has poor Horatio done, who is so weak, that he, above all the rest, should be sent to rough it out at sea? But let him come and the first time we go into action a cannon ball may knock off his head and provide for him at once."

Nelson decided early, and precisely, to be a hero. When cut down by fever in the East Indies, and sent home to recuperate, he was in deep depression. Then, in his own words, "After a long and gloomy reverie, in which I almost wished myself overboard, a sudden glow of patriotism was kindled within me, and presented my King and Country as my patron; my mind exulted in the idea. 'Well, then,' I exclaimed, 'I will be a hero, and confiding in providence I will brave every danger!' "

All his life Nelson searched for love, particularly maternal

69

love. He was twenty-two when he fell in love, at Quebec, with Mary Simpson, daughter of the provost-marshal of the garrison. She was only sixteen, and excited Nelson so much that when ordered to join Lord Hood's fleet at New York he was on the verge of resigning his commission in order to continue his courtship. Mary Simpson was, however, not interested in this unattractive lover, and, sadly, he departed.

His second passion was for a Miss Andrews, the daughter of an English clergyman at St Omer. There Nelson, who was in France to try to learn to speak French, was badly smitten. He had only a hundred and thirty pounds a year, however, and felt that he could hardly propose marriage on so miserable a sum. Without shame he begged help from his other maternal uncle, William Suckling, an official in the Navy Office. His uncle gave him a hundred pounds a year, as he had asked, but the clergyman's daughter did not want him either. Nelson returned to London to forget her, successfully. He had decided to stand as a candidate in the General Election to be held in March 1784, but failed to find a seat. The "greasy pole" has always appealed to Phaetons.

Once again, in command of the frigate *Boreas*, he lost his heart to Mrs Mountray, the wife of the Admiralty Commander at English Harbour, the naval base at Antigua. In 1785 he wrote, "I think I have found a woman who will make me happy" – not, one might note, a woman whom *he* would make happy.

But it was Frances Nisbet, the widow of a doctor, with a five-year-old son and a few months older than he, whom he was to marry. Motherly and feminine, elegant and graceful, she appealed to him at once. She came of good family, being the niece of John Herbert, the President of the Council of Nevis, and was accomplished in needlework, music and French. Nelson wooed her enthusiastically, writing, "Dearest Fanny, All my happiness is centred with thee . . . With my heart filled with the purest and most tender affection do I write this . . . I daily thank God, who ordained that I should be attached to you."

To William Suckling Nelson wrote, "I open a business which perhaps you will smile at, in the first instance, and say, 'This Horatio is for ever in love.' " To his brother he wrote, "The dear object you must like. Her sense, polite manners, and, to you I may say, beauty, you will much admire; and although we may not be a rich couple, yet I have not the least doubt that we shall be a happy pair." Prophetically, he added, "The fault must be mine if we are not." They were married at Nevis on March 11th, 1787, and two months later Nelson sailed for Portsmouth in the *Boreas*, his wife and stepson following in a more comfortable ship. He was not yet twenty-nine.

At home again, kept on board ship for a while, he wrote to her on August 19th: "Absent from you I feel no pleasure: it is you, my dearest Fanny, who are everything to me. Without you I care not for this world . . . This [sic] you are well convinced are my present sentiments. God Almighty grant they may never change. Nor do I think they will: indeed, there is, as far as human knowledge can judge, a moral certainty they will not: for it must be real affection that brings us together."

The next step in his endless search for love is all too well known. At Naples he found Sir William Hamilton, then in his thirtieth year as ambassador there, having abandoned all hope of promotion, and Lady Hamilton, who had lived with him for five years, the last two as his wife. This woman, a year or two past thirty (the date of her birth is uncertain and she may indeed have been a bastard), exuberant and bossy and mother-ly, had been born of working-class parents in North Wales. She had been brought by her mother to London, her father having died before she was a year old. It is said that she acted the part of the "Goddess of Health" in the famous exhibitions of James Graham. Long before that, however, she had been, probably, first a nursemaid in the family of Dr Richard Budd, and then a prostitute; and it is likely that she was actually taken off the streets to become the mistress, at Uppark, of the dissolute young baronet, Sir Harry Fetherstonhaugh. Legend has it that the giddy girl danced on the dining-table there. He tired of her, and dismissed her, it is said, when she was six months' pregnant.

Charles Greville had met her at Uppark in 1781, and took her up, and they lived together for four years in London, with her mother acting as cook-housekeeper. Romney, Hoppner and Lawrence all painted her during this period. Emma loved Greville, and was heart-broken when he gave her, almost literally, to his uncle, Sir William Hamilton, who wanted a lively young mistress. Taking her mother – now known as "Mrs Cadogan" – with her, she departed for Naples. There her

71

triumph was complete. She not only pleased her husband-to-be, but became the confidante of the formidable Queen Maria Carolina, and a political force. This was the woman with whom Nelson was to fall so passionately in love. There was always a streak of vulgarity in him, and this met its response in Emma.

She had, according to one Mrs St George, a well-shaped figure, but was "colossal", with "hideous" feet, and her "very attractive face" was seriously marred by a coarse complexion and a brown spot in a pair of blue eyes. Her voice was loud, "yet not disagreeable", and she had dark hair which was "never clean". Yet even this stringent critic admired the famous "attitudes", or poses, which were Emma's forte. Lord Fitzharris admired Nelson, but of Emma he would write that she was "without exception the most coarse, ill-mannered, disagreeable woman I ever met". At any rate, Emma took command of Nelson's life, nursing him like a mother, loving him like a mistress, giving enormous banquets and balls to celebrate his birthdays and his victories – for example, in 1798, a banquet for eight hundred to celebrate his victory at Aboukir Bay, and a ball for eighteen hundred after the banquet. From the moment that Emma and Nelson met, his marriage was doomed. His search for love was over, and the ailing Fanny, who found England forbidding and chilly, was a poor rival for the lively Emma. Nelson was a very lecherous man, too, and Emma satisfied his lust. In an amusing passage he wrote to her: "My longing for you, both person and conversation, you may readily imagine. What must be my sensations at the idea of sleeping with you! It sets me on fire, even the thought, much more would be the reality. I am sure my love and desires are all to you, and if any woman naked were to come to me, even as I am at this moment from thinking of you, I hope it might rot off if I were to touch her even with my hand." Again, "Would to God I had dined with you alone, what a dessert we would have had!" and, "With my present feelings I might be trusted with fifty virgins naked in a dark room." Fanny had never aroused him to that extent, it seems, and she had no hope of breaking his liaison with Emma Hamilton.

Nelson had two predominant mentors in his life – his uncle, Captain Maurice Suckling, and Captain William Locker, who was to be a lifelong friend and dominant influence. "Lay a Frenchman close and you will beat him," he used to say, and many years later Nelson wrote, "I have been your scholar; it is you who taught me to board a Frenchman . . . and my sole merit in my profession is being a good scholar."

Nelson could be reckless. When he was only fourteen he went on the Royal Society's polar expedition. His ship was locked in pack ice, and was, incidentally, in danger of being crushed. Nelson walked on the ice, and met a polar bear. He decided that he wanted its skin for a fine rug, but his musket misfired. With reckless courage he tried to club the seven-foot animal with its butt. Luckily the captain of the *Carcass* fired a signal gun, and the bear loped away. The crestfallen boy returned to protest, "Sir, I wished to kill the bear that I might carry the skin to my father."

Again, when, in 1794, Hardy was nearly drowned, he ordered his crew to "back the mizzen top-sail", and saved him. The enemy, taken by surprise, hesitated, and he rescued his friend simply because of his reckless boldness. Once more, at the Battle of St Vincent, in 1797, recklessness paid off. In direct defiance of orders, he hauled the *Captain* out of line, and, putting the helm hard over, sailed her into the gap between the enemy squadrons. This was a most serious crime, literal disobedience, but he was right, and, fortunately for him, Admiral Jervis saw the point, and backed him up. His ship was badly damaged, but he decided not only to board the nearest enemy ship but to board her himself. The famous story of his putting his telescope to his blind eye was yet another example of his disregarding clear orders, which paid off once again. His attack on Boulogne, however, was a bloody failure. He admitted this trait in his character, once writing to Fanny, "I wish to be Admiral and in command of the English fleet. I should very soon do much, or be ruined. My disposition cannot bear tame or slow measures. Sure I am, had I commanded our Fleet . . . that either the whole French fleet would have graced my triumph, or I should have been in a confounded scrape."

The very fact that he went to Naples, refusing to obey orders to go to Minorca, was another act of disobedience. Events proved him right, but if Admiral Keith's fears had been justified this disobedience would have been catastrophic.

Horatio Nelson was very religious. From the beginning of his career he used to write prayers in his journal. In 1793 he wrote: "When I lay me down to sleep I recommend myself to the care of Almighty God, when I awake I give myself up to

His direction, amidst all the evils that threaten me I will look to Him for help, and question not but that He will either avert them or turn them to my advantage; though I know neither the time nor the manner of my death, I am not at all solicitous about it because I am sure that He knows them both, and that He will not fail to support and comfort me."

After the loss of his right arm he sent a note to the vicar of St George's, Hanover Square, saying, "An Officer desires to return thanks to Almighty God for his perfect recovery from a severe Wound, and also for the many mercies bestowed upon him." Again, in 1798, after the devastation of the French fleet, when Bonaparte lost more than five thousand men, nearly six times as many as the British, Nelson's first reaction was to make "a solemn act of gratitude to Heaven", even before sending the news home.

He encouraged the King of Naples to join the coalition of Britain, Russia and Austria against the French, and to "advance, trusting to God for his blessings in a just cause . . . or remain quiet, and be kicked out of his dominions". At the end of January, 1801, when he heard that Emma had given birth to a daughter, the survivor of twins, he wrote – using the *nom de plume* for himself which they adopted – "I believe poor dear Mrs Thompson's friend will go mad with joy. He cries, *prays* and performs all tricks, yet dare not show any of his feelings . . . I cannot write, I am so agitated by this young man at my elbow. I believe he is foolish; he does nothing but rave about you and her." And when he spoke of living with Emma, part of his plan was to make squirearchical appearances at church, where "we will set an example of goodness to the under-parishioners".

When he left Emma for the last time, in 1805, he wrote: "Drove from dear, dear Merton, where I left all which I hold dear in this world, to go and serve my King and Country. May the great God whom I adore enable me to fulfil the expectation of my Country; and if it is His good pleasure that I should return, my thanks will never cease being offered up to the Throne of His Mercy. If it is His good Providence to cut short my days upon earth, I bow with the greatest submission, relying that He will protect those so dear to me, that I may leave behind. His Will be done. Amen, Amen, Amen."

Then, just before his death, he wrote in his journal his last prayer: "May the Great God whom I worship Grant to my

Country and for the benefit of Europe in General a great and glorious Victory, and may no misconduct in anyone tarnish it, and may humanity after Victory be the predominant feature of the British Fleet. For myself individually I commit myself to Him Who made me, and may his Blessing light upon my endeavour for serving my Country faithfully. To Him I resign myself and the just cause which is entrusted to me to Defend. Amen, Amen, Amen."

But as he died he was haunted by anxiety about his sinfulness. To the chaplain attending him he said, "I have not been a great sinner" – presumably a question, rather than an assertion.

The Phaeton shows intense devotion to his children. There was no doubt about Nelson's devotion to his daughter, Horatia – a devotion amounting to recklessness, in the circumstances. He wrote her touching letters. For example, in 1804, he wrote from *Victory*: "My dear Horatia, I send you a Watch which I give you permission to wear on Sundays, and on very particular days, when you are draped and have behaved exceedingly Well and obedient. I have kissed it and send it with the *Blessing* of *Your*

Nelson and Bronte
Victory. Jan.ʳʸ 20th, 1804"

Nelson was intoxicated at the thought of having a child of his own, for he and Fanny never produced one, and from the moment that Horatia was born, if there had ever been any hope for his marriage left, it was doomed.

There is no doubt of Nelson's great courage, demonstrated every time he was wounded, for instance at the amputation of an arm – when his stepson, Josiah Nisbet, saved his life by applying a tourniquet, and collected a crew to take him back to the flag-ship to have his arm amputated, without an anaesthetic, and very high, near to the shoulder. He was equally brave when he had been blinded in one eye. This slight, far from handsome, straightforward fellow overcame these major disadvantages, and created a picture of an active, animated personality, apposite and vehement in conversation, able to charm and convince.

Nelson was superstitious. Just before his death he had premonitions of doom. He took prolonged farewells of the five-year-old Horatia, and looked his last at Emma in the

75

setting they had created for themselves. Despite the brave front he put on, he went away afraid that he might never return. He was right.

Nelson was austere in his personal habits, eating little, and, according to at least one witness, sedate in his behaviour. "A man of more temperate habits," he said, "could not . . . have been found. He always looked what he was, a gentleman. He was, it is true, a sailor, and one of a warm and generous disposition, [but] he was not 'a rude and boisterous captain of the sea'."

There is no need to recount the details of Nelson's death, known to every Englishman and Englishwoman. It took more than a month to bring back his body. It did not reach Spithead until 23rd December, 1805, when it was placed in a coffin which had been made from the mainmast of *Orient*, and which Nelson, with the Phaeton's preoccupation with death, had kept in his cabin for this very eventuality, saying that he would be buried in it. His hair had been cut off, the body stripped of all clothes except for the shirt, and put into a cask of the largest size on shipboard, which had then been filled with brandy. At Gibraltar the brandy had been replaced with spirit of wine. The body lay in state in the Painted Hall at Greenwich Hospital, and Frances, Lady Nelson, was informed of his death by the First Lord of the Admiralty. The Controller of the Navy Board wrote to Emma, at Merton. She took to her bed, and remained there from the sixth of November, when the news reached her, until at least, by her own account, the twenty-ninth.

To Nelson went a posthumous earldom, an estate, and a hereditary pension of five thousand pounds a year, bestowed on his elder brother; nineteen thousand pounds went to each of his sisters; and for Lady Nelson there was an annuity of two thousand pounds. But for Emma Hamilton there was nothing, then or later, except his last letter and the codicil to his will, leaving her "a legacy to my King and Country, that they will give her ample provision to maintain her rank in life". She had been left well enough provided for, with eight hundred pounds a year from Sir William Hamilton, and a like sum from Nelson, as well as Merton Place. But she was recklessly extravagant, and gambled so heavily that in 1813 she was gaoled for debt. A year later, after a second term in prison, she fled to France, taking Horatia with her, to live at number 111

Rue Française, Calais. There she became an alcoholic, and, in the year of Waterloo, contracted jaundice, and died.

Horatia was adopted by Nelson's sister, Catherine Matcham, and her husband, and in 1822 married an eminently respectable clergyman, the Reverend Philip Ward. She acknowledged Nelson as her father, to the extent of adopting the married name of Nelson-Ward, but, to the end of her life, at the age of eighty-one, never admitted that Emma had been more than a guardian, who, "with all [her faults] – and she had many – had many fine qualities, which, had [she] been placed in better hands, would have made her a very superior woman. It is but justice . . . to say that through all her difficulties, she invariably till the last few months expended on my education etc. the whole of the interest of the sum left to me by Lord Nelson, and which was entirely at her control." Nelson had left two hundred pounds a year for Horatia. Later, in September 1854, Lord Aberdeen would be faced with the problem of Nelson's "adopted daughter", Horatia, by Lady Hamilton, recommended by him to the care of the country before Trafalgar. Aberdeen would add her three daughters to the Pensions List, to avoid the "much scandal and disagreeable debate" in Parliament, which a special vote would entail.* Aberdeen himself had walked and talked with Sir William Hamilton and his wife at his father-in-law's house, Bentley Priory, and he was a man who never failed to be discreet.

On 8th January, 1806, Nelson was carried up the Thames from Greenwich to Whitehall, to lie in the Captains Room in the Admiralty. Next day he received a State funeral, and burial in St Paul's Cathedral. Thirty-one admirals and a hundred captains followed the body. The Prince of Wales and the Duke of Clarence attended it. Lady Hamilton did not. Even the beggars left their stands, forgetting to beg. The Garter King of Arms, after formally reciting Nelson's many honours, was moved to add, in breach of all precedent, "The Hero who in the moment of Victory fell covered with immortal glory". In St Paul's Nelson was accorded the rare honour of being buried in the crypt, beneath a great marble sarcophagus, inscribed only with his name and the dates of his birth and death.

So the sickly, undersized, bereaved child, who had been determined to become "a hero", had achieved his ambition. In

* Royal Archives. A3 23/145 September 1, 1854.

Norfolk to this day inns are simply called "The Hero"; and when, on the anniversary of Trafalgar, officers drink the toast, "The immortal memory", there is no need to explain to whose memory they are referring.

ARTISTS

Guillaume Apollinaire (Wilhelm-Apollinaire de Kostrowit-sky), bastard, champion of Cubist painting, also a poet.

Antonio Caracci, bastard son of Agostino Caracci.

Francesco Caracci, bastard brother of Agostino and Annibali Caracci.

Edgar Degas, mother died when he was 13.

Marcus Gheeraerts the younger, lost his mother in childhood.

Augustus John, mother died when he was 6, and hated his father.

Toulouse Lautrec, mother died at his birth.

Bernard Leach, potter, mother died at his birth.

Fra Filippo Lippi, orphan, and put into the Carmine to get him out of the way – not fitted temperamentally to be a monk.

Edvard Munch, mother died when he was 4.

Sir Henry Raeburn, orphaned young and apprenticed to a jeweller.

Raphael, father died when he was 11.

Dante Gabriel Rosetti, father died before he was 15.

James McNeill Whistler, father died when he was 15.

Leonardo da Vinci, bastard, who never knew his mother.

CHAPTER 7

Augustus John (1878 – 1961)

Augustus John's mother died when he was six and a half.

His mother, Augusta, was the wife of a young solicitor, Edwin John. She was a delicate woman, suffering from chronic rheumatism, perhaps aggravated by the damp climate of Haverfordwest, in Wales, where they lived. Augustus was terrified of his father, who kicked him violently upstairs when he was only four. He only really felt at home in the kitchen with the servants, for the family was uncommunicative. His mother's health deteriorated rapidly, and she was less and less at home. In the second week of August 1884, the day came when the servants were lined up in the hall, and Edwin John informed them that his wife had died. The servants stood in line, some crying but, in a macabre way, the children ran from room to room, chanting with senseless excitement, "Mama's dead! Mama's dead!"

That was the first of several tragedies for Augustus John during the course of his long life, and to all of them he reacted with extreme emotion. The death of his wife, Ida, in Paris, much later, after giving birth to her fifth child, a boy, was a terrible blow, and his behaviour at that time illustrated the abnormally intense reaction to a tragedy which, admittedly, would shake even the most phlegmatic of husbands.

Complications set in immediately after the birth. Luckily Ida's mother was in Paris, as Augustus was paralysed with fear. She selected a specialist, paid him sixty pounds, and organised Ida's move to a *Maison de Santé* for an operation. She paid for the sixteen-shillings-a-day cost of her room there as well, since Augustus remained in a state of terror and stupor. Ida was suffering, not, as they thought, from a little abscess, but from puerperal fever and peritonitis. Yet she was euphoric, laughing, smiling and joking, and insisting that Augustus drink a toast in Vichy water, "Here's to love!" At last unconscious, she died, in comparative peace.

Augustus's reaction was extreme and unexpected. He was seized with an uncontrollable, hysterical elation. "Strange," he wrote, "after leaving her poor body dead and beaten I had nothing but a kind of bank holiday feeling, and had to hold myself in." He was dead drunk for three days – as his biographer, Michael Holroyd, has written, it was "a desperate bid for the sort of optimism he needed to keep him from the descent into paralysing melancholia". He could not forget, either, that Ida's death had been caused by childbirth, and that her children were deprived of a mother, as he had been.

Ida was cremated on the Saturday following her death at the crematorium of Père Lachaise. Determined not to give way to depression, Augustus John could not bring himself to go; and he did not care if he outraged everyone. He even refused the offers of friends in England, who wanted to come over. Nor did Ida's mother attend the cremation. Only Ambrose McEvoy, defying Augustus, and Henry Lamb, who lived in Paris and had taken Ida to a music-hall the night before she had entered hospital, attended the cremation. When the coffin and the body had been consumed, and the skeleton was drawn out on a slab through the open door of the furnace, Lamb and McEvoy were still able to recognise the strong bone-structure of the girl they had known. An attendant tapped the slab with a crowbar, and the skeleton crumbled into ashes. The ashes were put in a box and taken back to Augustus, and later a memorial service was held in Lamb's rooms. Gwen John, Augustus's sister, and something of a manic-depressive herself, under-stood Augustus's feelings, and for a short time came to look after him in his new studio.

The third major tragedy in Augustus John's life came with the death of Pyramus, his son by his mistress Dorelia. By the end of February 1912, Dorelia was expecting a baby at any moment, and Pyramus was ill with meningitis. In March Dorelia gave birth to what she called "a big nice girl"; and Pyramus died. To Lady Ottoline Morrell John had written on

March 10th, 1912, "Pyra is still breathing feebly, but happily has been unconscious for the last two or three days. I do not think he will outlive today. He was indeed a celestial child, and that is why the gods take him . . . The mind refuses to contemplate such an awful fact." Then, on May 9th, 1912, he wrote to his friend Quinn, "It was a terrible event. I must say the missus behaved throughout as I think few women would – with amazing good sense, and a splendid determination not to give way to the *luxury* of the expression of grief."

The death of Henry, the son Ida had died giving birth to, was to be the cause of another severe reaction to bereavement. In love with Olivia Plunket-Greene, who refused to sleep with him, and expressed a preference for Paul Robeson, Henry drove down to Cornwall. Olivia did not join him. On 22nd June, 1935, Henry bicycled to a desolate stretch of the cliffs, unbroken for miles by any house. He was seen walking along, swinging a towel, his aunt's Irish terrier at his heels. Then he vanished. The dog returned home, but Henry did not.

Police searched the cliffs, scouts explored the caves, aeroplanes circled above, and motor-boats manned by coastguards with binoculars patrolled the seas. John rushed down to join the hunt, and was persecuted by the press. He stayed in Cornwall for a week, tormented by the thought that the son Ida had died giving birth to should so recklessly have lost his own life, but resolved to banish the thought from his mind. Thirteen days after the disappearance, Henry's body was washed up on a beach at Perranporth, dressed only in a pair of shorts. The birds and crabs had eaten his face, but John was able to identify the body. Father D'Arcy of Jesuit House, at Roehampton – where Henry had hoped to be groomed for the priesthood, and had entered as a novice, but had failed to get a good enough class, and had had to abandon his ambition – was certain that there was no question of suicide, and that it had been an accident. John, however, suspected otherwise, and, in 1943, on a train travelling from London to Salisbury, he suddenly became very talkative, and spoke to the young man sharing his compartment of the suicide of his son.

His attempt to control his feelings reached a certain depth of bad taste. To many people who wrote to him, he replied that it was a tragedy that, having climbed out of the Society of Jesus, Henry should have fallen into the sea. (His mistress, Dorelia, was callous. "It's perfectly all right," she said. "Henry wasn't mine.")

82

Even for his mother-in-law, Mrs Nettleship, with whom he had never been on good terms, Augustus John mourned. And when John Sampson, the gipsy scholar, died, he wept openly after the scattering of the ashes, while he chanted a poem in Romany. "I myself saw the tears rolling down Augustus John's cheeks as he tramped in silence back to Llangwin," Dora Yates remembered.

Equally for those not in his family, Augustus could feel grief when they died. In 1935 Horace de Vere Cole, the practical joker, died in exile, at Ascaigne, but was buried near London. Augustus went to the funeral. "As the coffin was lowered into the ground," he wrote, "in dreadful tension I awaited the moment for the lid to be lifted, thrust aside, and a well-known figure to leap out with an ear-splitting yell. But my old friend disappointed me this time. Sobered, I left the churchyard, with his widow on my arm."

Only for Edwin, his hated father, did he show no grief when he died, on the afternoon of 7th April, 1938, after calling out, politely, to his housekeeper, "Goodbye, Miss Davis, goodbye." The inscription above his grave could not have been bleaker.

Edwin William John
1847 – 1938
WITH LONG LIFE WILL I SATISFY
HIM AND SHOW HIM MY SALVATION

John and his son Caspar attended the funeral. Thornton and Winifred, two of Edwin John's other children, were too far off to come, and Gwen John, another daughter, did not attend.

Then Gwen herself collapsed and died, in September 1939, only a year after her father, in Dieppe. Augustus mourned her deeply, calling her "the greatest woman artist of her age, or, as I think, of any other".

There can be no doubt whatever about Augustus John's obsessive need for love, and his desire to achieve total support. All his life he pursued women, seeking it. When he believed that Ida had failed him he turned to Dorelia, and to any other woman who crossed his path, beseeching her to sleep with him and to love him. To name but a few, he pursued Euphemia Lamb; Lady Ottoline Morrell; Frieda Stringberg (who took poison when he appeared to be ignoring her, tried to shoot him, and eventually committed suicide); Joe Hone's wife, Vera

Hone; Lady Tredegar; Iris Tree; Sybil Hart Davis; Mavis Wright; Caitlin Thomas, wife of Dylan Thomas; and Chiquita. He expressed his selfish philosophy frankly and crudely: "Lock antlers with the men; copulate with the women; scatter your image through the land. There will be wounds given and received, but there will be no deception or the sour sediment of regrets and frustrations taken to the grave. The wounds will be honourable, and will heal, not fester."

He was frank with his women, too, telling Lady Ottoline Morrell when she confessed her love for him, "Since my wife's death there have been few opportunities of excitement or intoxication that I have let pass." Even without counting his adventures with whores – for example, in his own phrase, the "inveterate whores of Marseilles" – his extra-marital copulations must have run into hundreds, if not thousands. When he eventually offered to marry Dorelia she did not bother to reply.

Augustus John had an intense devotion to his own children, giving as his prime motive for considering the possibility of marrying Dorelia, after Ida's death, that she would be able to look after them. "It is precisely because she is the only possible mother to Ida's children, now Ida has gone," he wrote to Ida's mother, "since I love her, knowing her to be such. And for no less reason would she consent to marry me, or I her . . . she is . . . in a word, the one woman with whom I can live, work, and still be a father to all my children. Without her I would have to say goodbye to the children, for I cannot recognise them or myself in a house and atmosphere which will ever be strange and antipathetic to me, as it was to their mother." Ida's mother did her best to hang on to her daughter's children, even threatening to take proceedings against Augustus, and to have him committed to prison. It was only after a hectic chase round the zoo, where she had gone with his three eldest boys, ending with Augustus's running them to earth behind the pelicans' enclosure, seizing two children, and bearing them off in a cab, to leave them in a remote village in charge of an elderly but devoted woman, that he recovered his children. From then on, Augustus and Dorelia brought up Ida's four eldest sons. Only Henry remained with the Nettleships, to die, as we have seen, in tragic circumstances.

Augustus John had a decided propensity to depression – one that at times could be frightening. Suddenly, for instance, in

December 1909, in the midst of decorating Sir Hugh Lane's Lindsay House, in Cheyne Walk, he was seized by the most appalling melancholia, became lethargic, and lost all interest in his commission. In a desperate effort to combat the depression, he even brought a band of gipsies to make merry in every room of Lane's house, frightening the unfortunate owner almost out of his wits.

Unlikely as it may seem, Augustus John also had an extreme religious concern. In Nice, in 1929, when staying with Frank Harris, he objected most violently to his host's habit of dragging the name of Jesus Christ into any conversation, especially as "coming from a man of Harris's moral standards" – a case of the pot calling the kettle black.

Austerity might also seem foreign to Augustus John's nature. Yet one story perfectly illustrates a strange asceticism in his life. When he was hard up he would bargain, obtain his price, and then light his pipe with the cheque. Again, when John was grumbling that he had no money, his friend Hugo Pitman searched the house and turned up with notes and cheques worth almost twelve thousand pounds.

John's recklessness, already mentioned, was proverbial. Once he jumped into the bucket at the top of a deep well, and went crashing down to the bottom, from which he had to be hauled back. On another occasion he stabbed himself in the leg so as to mingle his blood with a friend's, and was laid up with incipient blood-poisoning.

Nor was Augustus John without a certain superstitiousness and a belief in magic. His "fragments of autobiography", written under the title *Chiaroscuro,* which took him thirty years to write, is full of references to occultism, and the fascination which the gipsies held for him was to some extent due to their "magic" rituals.

In ending this chapter, I can do no better than to quote from Michael Holroyd's excellent biography of him.

"He had been aged six when his mother died, and though he nowhere laments her death, his obsessive theme as a painter – a mother with her children in an ideal landscape – illustrates the deep effect this loss had produced. If his father, whom he so disliked, represented the actual world, the deprivation of his mother became the source of that fantasy world, happy and beautiful, he created in its place. It was an example of how art can transmute deprivation into an asset."

So there we are once again with the distinctive Phaeton characteristics: an extreme reaction to bereavement; an obsessive need for love and the need to achieve total support; an intense devotion to his own children; a decided propensity to depression; a marked religious concern; a notable austerity; recklessness and superstitiousness; to say nothing of the driving ambition which impelled him all his life.

This very extraordinary Phaeton, in fact, showed all the Phaeton characteristics in extreme form.

THE STAGE AND SCREEN; RADIO AND TELEVISION ACTORS, ACTRESSES AND DRAMATISTS AND BROADCASTERS

Fatty Arbuckle, mother died when very young.

Lauren Bacall, orphaned young.

Ingrid Bergman, mother died when she was 2, father when she was 12.

Reginald Bosanquet, father died when he was 4, mother when he was 7.

Mel Brooks, father died when he was 3.

Christopher Fry, father died when he was 3.

Jean Harlow, father died when she was 9.

Al Jolson, mother died when he was 9.

Charles Laughton, father died when he was very young.

Jayne Mansfield, father died when she was an infant.

Millicent Martin, mother died when she was 12.

Warren Mitchell (Alf Garnett), mother died when he was 13.

Marilyn Monroe, bastard.

Pola Negri, father died when she was 6.

David Niven, father killed at Gallipoli, when he was 12.

Merle Oberon, father died when she was 3 months.

Sir Laurence Olivier, father died when he was 13.

Dennis Potter, dramatist, mother died before he was 8.

Mickey Rooney, mother and father died when he was 11.

Robert Shaw, father died when he was 12.

Tom Stoppard, father died when he was 5.

Barbra Streisand, father died when she was 15 months.

CHAPTER 8

Marilyn Monroe (1926 – 1962)

Marilyn Monroe was a bastard.

In fact, it was in an article written about her, shortly after her death, in a French magazine, that I first learned of the "Phaeton", as Maryse Choisy called the type of personality she had noted as peculiar to bastard children in a Paris orphanage.

The child who was to make herself so famous as Marilyn Monroe, and whom it will be convenient to refer to as Marilyn, was born in Los Angeles General Hospital, on June 1st 1926, to a widow called Gladys Mortenson. The infant was named Norma Jean, and registered for the sake of respectability under the surname of Mortenson.

Mortenson was, indeed, the name of Gladys's second husband. She had been divorced from her first, by whom she had two children, Jack and Berneice. She then married a man called Edward Mortenson, who soon left her, and was later killed in a motor-cycle accident, long before Marilyn's birth.

Marilyn's father, at this stage in the story a barely discernible figure, was one C. Stanley Gifford, a Lothario, divorced and remarried, and a fellow-employee of Gladys's at Consolidated Film Industries, where she was known as Gladys Baker. Gladys Mortenson had been hoping that when her illegitimate baby was born they would both be able to stay in the home of her mother, a Mrs Grainger. When, however, she arrived at her mother's to explain her pregnant state and her need for somewhere to stay, she found that her mother had just let the house and was about to depart for India, to seek her second husband, Mr Grainger. Mrs Grainger had long since obtained a divorce from her first husband, whose name was Monroe, and who was Gladys's father. Monroe had eventually been committed to a state asylum. It was the name of this maternal grandfather which Norma Jean Mortenson was later to adopt, together with the made-up Marilyn, on her climb towards the driving seat of the fiery chariot. Other classic Phaetons, Hitler among them, have assumed a public name better calculated in their eyes to enhance their public personalities.

With no prospect of a family home, her mother farmed out her newly-born infant to a woman named Ida Bolender, who had for some years been caring for small children. Marilyn's grandmother, having failed to run her second husband to earth in India, returned to America. There she attempted to smother the infant, Marilyn. Sent for trial, she was then committed, like her first husband, Marilyn's grandfather, to a state asylum, where she died. She had a son, who also gradually retreated from reality. In the end, too, Marilyn's mother was to be committed to a state asylum. It was a thoroughly bad heredity. But what Marilyn remembered as the most devastating experience of her childhood was the death of the one upon whom she bestowed love, and who gave her unquestioning devotion – her dog, Tippy, shot by a neighbour for rolling on his garden.

Marilyn Monroe had an extreme reaction to bereavement. She had had an affair with one Johnny Hyde, who played a considerable part in creating her fame, and the Monroe legend. It was he who had started her on her upward path, after insisting that she take a part, though not an important one, in *All About Eve*. He had been warned against Marilyn, but it was she who refused to marry him. He went for frequent weekends to Palm Springs with her, and they toured Hollywood clubs together. Soon his weight began to drop alarmingly, and his heart specialist warned him not to climb stairs. His chauffeur had to carry him up to the master bedroom every night. In his last weeks he arranged minor plastic surgery to remove a small lump from the tip of Marilyn's nose, for she was living in his house. Then he complained of difficulty in his breathing, and was sent to the Cedars of Lebanon Hospital, where it was discovered that he had suffered a mild coronary occlusion. Marilyn made an effort to leave his house, but he persuaded her to stay. Divorced, he had every right, as his friends maintained, to his own life; and he was not even sleeping with Marilyn.

Johnny Hyde's final heart attack occurred in the late afternoon of Saturday, December 17th, 1950. He had specified that Marilyn was to be treated as one of the family; but it was not to be. On Sunday he died. His last words were ignored by his brother and other members of his family. Marilyn was told to get herself and her belongings out of the North Palm Drive house immediately.

Word was sent to Marilyn that she was not to appear at the funeral. Johnny Hyde's sons, it was said, would not understand, and if she had really cared for Johnny she would make the sacrifice. Marilyn, however, went, encouraged by Hyde's closest friends and associates.

Nearly twenty years later, Hyde's second son, Jimmy, declared of his father's funeral at Forest Lawn: "All I can recall clearly is Marilyn screaming my father's name over and over again. It shook everyone." It was an extreme reaction to bereavement – a bereavement she never forgot. Later, perhaps remembering that outburst, and distrusting herself, she did not go to Clark Gable's funeral.

Marilyn Monroe had an extreme religious concern. The Bolenders, with whom she spent her early years, were religious, and went to the Christian Science church in their district, and kept a coloured print of Christ on their living-room wall. There Marilyn learned to sing, "Jesus Loves me, this I know"; but when she went, at long last, to live with her mother, she found the adults playing rummy and poker, and very uncomfortable when she sang her hymn. Years later, she took up her interest in Christian Science once more, going to the Christian Science church, and responding to the creed's ethic – "God as love, and the underlying principle of the universe". For eight years, in that later period, she remained a faithful member of the Christian Science church.

When Marilyn married her first husband, Jim Dougherty, she took him to the Sherman Oaks Christian Science Church every Sunday morning. She took her mother to services too, when she was out of the mental hospital.

Later on, Marilyn, in distress, was persuaded to visit a Catholic church, St Victor's, where she sat silently for two and a half hours, but never went back. Much later, too, she would visit on her walks the statue of the Reverend Henry Ward Beecher in the churchyard of what had been his famed Plymouth Church.

Strangest of all, perhaps, was her determination, on her marriage to the playwright, Arthur Miller, to become, not a mere Gentile married to a Jew – a *shiksa* – but a *mishpacha,* or proper Jewess. She shrugged off all Christian beliefs, apparently without difficulty, as well as Christian Science, and insisted on being married as a Jewess. If in the end there was only a civil wedding in the White Plains court-house, and not a marriage by a rabbi with an exchange of two rings, it was no fault of hers. (Early the following week Miller bought a gold wedding ring for Marilyn, inscribed "A to M, June 1956. Now is Forever". Forever was four and a half years.) Before the ceremony Marilyn was given instruction in the Jewish faith for over two hours by Rabbi Robert Goldberg, a friend of Miller's for several years. He explained his view that there was no after-life. After those two hours Marilyn believed that she was a Jewess. Even Miller was never quite sure how Jewish Marilyn really became, but she certainly did all she could to become what she believed was a real Jewess.

Marilyn Monroe's search for love was displayed in its most poignant form by her desire to be united with her father. In 1951 she suddenly decided to try to meet him. She located Gifford on a farm, the Red Rock Dairy, outside a rural village near Palm Springs, and set out to drive to see him. C. Stanley Gifford, now remarried, had established a successful dairy, having had some luck with investments. His new wife, however, died of cancer within a few months, and he himself began having heart trouble. Despite two attacks in a period of a few months, he remarried once again, and his new wife, a few years younger than he, ran the dairy after his second attack. Ignorant of all this, Marilyn was on her way to the longed-for meeting, driving steadily, when she suddenly decided to telephone her father. At a highway telephone booth she pulled over, and rang through. The following conversation then took place.

"Hello, is Mr Gifford there?"

"Who's calling him?" a woman enquired sternly.

"This is Marilyn. I'm his child . . . I mean, the little girl, years ago. Gladys Baker's daughter. He's sure to know who I am."

"I don't know who you are, but I'll tell him you're on the 'phone."

Finally the woman returned, Marilyn having waited, leaning back, eyes closed, fighting, it seemed, an impulse to hang up.

"He doesn't want to see you," the woman said when she returned. "He suggests you see his lawyer in Los Angeles if you have some complaint. Do you have a pencil?"

"No," Marilyn replied, "I don't have a pencil. Goodbye." She walked back to the car and slumped over the wheel.

Years later, by then famous and recently ill, Marilyn received an expensive greetings card made of embossed silk, reading, "Best wishes for your early recovery". It was signed "From the man you tried to see nearly ten years ago. God forgive me."

"What does it mean?" Marilyn asked. "It's all too late."

That was not the end. In 1962, the year of her own death, Gifford again tried to contact his daughter. A nurse in a Palm Springs Hospital rang, asking to speak to Marilyn, and said that she was calling for "your father". She said it seemed unlikely that her patient, Mr Gifford, would survive his heart attack. His condition was grave, and one of his strongest desires was to see her. "He keeps talking about it all the time," the nurse told Marilyn.

Marilyn seemed uncertain only for a moment. Then she spoke clearly into the telephone: "Tell the gentleman I have never met him. But if he has anything specific to tell me, he can contact my solicitor. Would you like his number?" The nurse declined to take his number, and rang off. However, the call must have upset Marilyn, and she later took the trouble to ascertain that Gifford had recovered from the heart attack.

Marilyn's first marriage, to Jim Dougherty, took place when she was only sixteen. Less than four years later, at the end of the Second World War, Dougherty went ashore in Shanghai and bought his wife a present of a carved camphor-wood chest. On his return to his ship, he found a letter from an attorney, telling him that Marilyn wanted a divorce. Rather poignantly, he became a policeman after the war, and part of his duties at one time was keeping Marilyn's fans under control.

Her second husband, whom she married when she was already famous, was Joe Di Maggio. The marriage was unhappy, and lasted only ten months – months of quarrels, scuffling and banging, that woke their neighbours in the hotel where they were staying. It ended with Di Maggio announcing to a crowd of newspapermen and sightseers that he was going back to San Francisco – "That's my home" – and with Marilyn heavily sedated and unreachable. Yet it was to be Di Maggio who, with another friend, Inez Melson, eventually buried her when all other friends had abandoned her. Her third marriage was to Arthur Miller, the famous writer and playwright. She was determined to marry him, and pursued him. His first marriage, to Mary Slattery, was dead, and had been dying, he claimed, for at least two years before their divorce in 1956.

It was not long before Miller realised, on a visit to England in that year, how vulnerable and exposed he would be as Marilyn's husband. Things grew worse, and rapidly. It was not long, either, before Marilyn discovered an entry in Arthur Miller's notebook, about how disappointed he was in her; how he had believed her to be "some sort of angel", but had found he was wrong; that his first wife had let him down but that she had done something worse; that Laurence Olivier had begun to think her a troublesome bitch; and that he, Arthur Miller, no longer had an answer to that. Later Marilyn changed and exaggerated what she had read – as she invented and exaggerated the horrors of her childhood. It had been, indeed, an emotional desert, but it had not really been peopled by dirty old men with rape on their minds, or brutal disciplinarians armed with straps. By the winter of 1959–1960 the marriage was over. Miller, it seemed, represented a long series of betrayals to Marilyn – but so did every other lover in her life. He tried to be compliant and stoical, but the strain told on him. Yet he stayed with her, at least counting the pills on which she was becoming more and more dependent, and sleeping with her. But Marilyn was growing more and more erratic. By this time, too, she had had two miscarriages – one tubular, one not, at almost three months – and the marriage was under severe strain. In the end it was Marilyn who ordered Miller out of her life. She was thirty-four.

Marilyn's life was one long effort to find a mentor. Hardly had she embarked on her Hollywood aspirations, in 1948, than she had thrown herself at the feet of Natasha Lytess. Soon Chekhov's son, Michael, joined her, persuading Marilyn to try to become a "straight" actress. But Natasha Lytess had such a hold on her that when Natasha had suspected cancer Marilyn sold her mink coat to pay for the operation – thus deferring her death until 1964. By 1952 three older men had played a part in her life – Joe Schenck; Arthur Miller's father, Isidore; and George Solitaire, a Broadway ticket-broker. Paula Strasberg would follow Natasha Lytess, and Milton and Amy Greene, husband and wife, would play a dominant role in her life. Then her, which lasted until her death and burial. So close was she with the Strasbergs that Lee Strasberg gave her away at her marriage to Miller. Towards the end, too, Ralph Roberts, her masseur, became a confidant. Yet perhaps her most poignant choice of mentor was Yves Montand. Never having known a father, and deeply mistrustful of men, she usually sought to have a man who could fulfil several functions – to reassure her, to satisfy her sexual needs, and to take the place of her missing father. She felt that she had been set adrift by Arthur Miller, and that only a close emotional attachment could keep her from foundering. She told Clark Gable, too, that he represented the kind of father she wished she had had.

There is no doubt about the risk-taking in Marilyn's life. She always ran up large bills, and once even sold her engagement ring to meet them. The episode of selling her mink coat – in a film star's life a mink coat was almost an essential sign of success – was characteristic. Her posing for nude pictures, which had such devastating results later, when she was famous, is all too well known. She drank far too much; and she became addicted to drugs, increasingly so as time went on, and she grew more and more isolated. She took to analysts, notably Dr Ralph Greenson. She discarded Natasha Lytess after seven years, and the Strasbergs after a similar period. By 1962 she was pregnant again, by a married man. Once again the pregnancy was tubular, and terminated.

It was not very long before her death that Marilyn had a new will drawn up. She made her half-sister, Berneice, in Florida, the main beneficiary. She left a legacy to May Reis, her secretary, and, to some extent, substitute mother. The residue went to Lee Strasberg, who came nearest to personifying the father figure she sought and who sincerely believed that she had a rare talent.

As Marilyn deteriorated, she was taken to a section of the Payne-Whitney Clinic, which was concerned mainly with mental and nervous disorders. She was not told this, and was frightened by the security arrangements that confronted her.

Under an assumed name, Faye Miller, she was hospitalised in a bare and comfortless room. Desperately, after three days, on being permitted one telephone call, she called Di Maggio for help, and he rescued her, and had her transferred to a private room in the Neurological Institute of the Columbia-Presbyterian Hospital.

By her thirty-sixth birthday Marilyn was in a state serious enough to cause concern to her lawyer and her two doctors. By the second Friday in June she had been fired from the picture she was making, and had gone into seclusion. She was shocked, crying, and emotionally drained, but was able to send rude messages about her studio bosses to the press reporters constantly calling her number – especially about Peter Levathis, who had actually dismissed her.

Desperately lonely and frightened, Marilyn began to telephone her friends for comfort. She started to talk about going on the stage, and joined a small group of actors in one of Strasberg's classes. Now, her pregnancy by the married man terminated, and attempting to regain her strength in her Brentwood house, she was miserable and alone.

One night Marilyn telephoned her masseur, Ralph Roberts, at two o'clock in the morning, the pills prescribed by her doctor having failed to work. Paula Strasberg came to see her, filled her empty refrigerator, and went back to her husband.

On Friday, August 3rd, 1962, Marilyn got up late, pulled a dressing-gown round her, and prepared her own simple breakfast of coffee and grapefruit. Later she persuaded a doctor to give her a prescription for twenty-five tablets of Nembutal. By next day she had had a poor night, the normal doses of Nembutal pills not having sent her to sleep. At breakfast she continued to take pills to calm her nerves. Her friend, Patricia Newcombe, who was staying with her, saw nothing unusual in her behaviour.

That night Marilyn went to bed, and turned on a stack of Sinatra records on her portable record-player. Between ten and eleven that night panic must have aroused her from the stupor that always preceded an overdose coma. If she tried to get through to Patricia Newcombe or one of her doctors she did not reach them. She did get through to the two men who had invited her out for the evening, and told one of them that she had just taken the last of her Nembutal pills and was about to slip over the edge into unconsciousness. One of the two then tried to telephone Mickey Rudin, her Hollywood attorney, but he was out for the evening. No one telephoned the police, probably from fear of taking a decision which might have resulted in bad publicity for Marilyn.

In a last desperate attempt Marilyn dialled the number of Ralph Roberts, her masseur. His answering service told him later that he had received a call from a woman with a drawling, troubled voice, who had left neither name nor number. That was her last attempt to contact a human being.

When Marilyn's body was found in the dark, early hours of Sunday morning, the telephone was still in her hand.

When Dr Greenson came home he rang to find out whether Marilyn was all right. He still had no knowledge of her purchase of a new supply of pills. The housekeeper walked a few steps to Marilyn's room, and saw a light under her closed door. She did not knock for fear of waking her, and reassured Dr Greenson that she was safe in her room. Next morning, however, a little before 3 a.m. she called Dr Greenson again. He arrived within minutes, and broke a window-pane to get into the bedroom. He saw at once that she was dead, but telephoned Dr Hyman Engelbert to confirm it. Dr Engelbert reached the house at about 3.30 a.m., confirmed Marilyn's death, and, shortly after four o'clock, the police were called in.

The coroner's verdict was "probable suicide". Certainly, as Miller knew, she had had overdoses of sleeping pills before, and was aware of the danger. And certainly she had contemplated suicide before – for example when she had read in a newspaper that Clark Gable's wife believed that Marilyn had caused her husband's death by prolonging the picture in which they were both acting, and so bringing on his fatal heart attack. She had leaned out of a high window, contemplating throwing herself down, and had refrained, she claimed, only because she thought she recognised someone walking on the pavement whom she believed she knew.

"There is too much pain in living," she had said on another occasion. "When they brought me back to life after my suicide attempt, I was very angry. People have no right to make you live when you don't want to."

Yet her end seemed more like accident than suicide, on the whole.

Coroner's Case No. 81128 lay unclaimed at the Los Angeles County Morgue. Her body was stretched on a slab in a chilled storage vault where unidentified bodies await burial. No one came to identify her. Her life had ended as it had begun – unwanted and unwelcome.

Eventually Marilyn's half-sister, Berneice Miracle, from Gainesville, Florida, and Inez Melson, surfaced. Di Maggio agreed to handle the funeral arrangements until they could fly out.

Marilyn had left word, over a year before, that no one but "Whitey" Snyder, her make-up man, was to touch her body. She had given him, years before, a gold-plated money-clip. It read simply, "To Whitey. While I'm still warm. Marilyn." Costumier Margie Plecher was asked to dress her body, and Agnes Flanagan was to do her hair. "Whitey" Snyder stopped at a liquor store and bought some gin, unable to face his task sober.

Joe Di Maggio broke down at the funeral. Arthur Miller did not attend it. He had remarried the year of the divorce. Some say that his first play after her death, *After the Fall*, was an attempt to exorcise her ghost. Certainly there are many factual biographical details, which awaken echoes, such as the mother of the girl having attempted to smother her with a pillow; Quentin's recognition that she wanted to die; Quentin's telling the audience that Maggie had been "chewed and spat out by a long line of grinning men! Her name floating in the stench of locker-rooms and parlour-car cigar-smoke!", while at the same time suggesting that she slept with men only out of a sense of charity. The play made more money for Miller than anything he had written since *Death of a Salesman*, but he was pilloried in the press for "bad taste and lack of respect for the dead".

The bastard child, who was religious, superstitious, reckless, and always seeking a mentor, died miserably, and alone. Her search for love was never successful. She had died, as she had lived, alone, and still seeking.

THE WORLD OF MUSIC

Innumerable celebrated performers – singers from Caruso to Piaf, dancers such as Diaghilev, and so on – could, like Paderewski, claim admittance to "The World of Music". However, it seemed to me that there was one more or less finite group at which it would be worth looking to see what proportion qualified, merely by the crude criterion of being orphans or illegitimate, as Phaetons. This group I defined as the indisputably great composers, of whom the list I made totalled thirty-three. Any such list is arbitrary, and susceptible to argument here and there, but I doubt whether anyone else's list would be significantly different. Of my thirty-three I found that twelve – some 36% of the total – qualified, as follows:

Johann Sebastian Bach, mother died when he was 9, father died when he was 10.
Béla Bartók, father died when he was 7.
Alexander Porfirevich Borodin, father died when he was 1.
Anton Bruckner, father died when he was 13.
Claude Debussy, father died when he was 1.
Charles Gounod, father died when he was 3.
Joseph Handel, father died when he was 12.
Giacomo Puccini, father died when he was 5.
Jean Sibelius, father died when he was 2.
Pyotr Tchaikowsky, mother died when he was 14.
Ralph Vaughan Williams, father died when he was 3.
Richard Wagner, father died when he was 6 months, and stepfather when he was 8.

CHAPTER 9

Ignace Jan Paderewski (1860 – 1941)

Ignace Jan Paderewski's mother died when he was three months old.

I quote Paderewski's own words as he wrote of the death of his mother, in his own, authorised, autobiography, *The Paderewski Memoirs*.

"My father was everything to us, father and mother both; he was all we had as my mother died soon after my birth. I was born [on] November 6, 1860, and a few months later the mother whom I was never to know, died. I grew up without a mother. My mother's name was quite unusual – Polixena, and her family name was Nowicki."

It was clear that that loss haunted him all his life, and he added, "There was no woman in our house when we were small except my aunt, who came only from time to time to visit us, before my father was sent to prison." He proceeded to an eulogy of his mother as an artistic, well-educated woman, very musical, very gentle, and beautiful, the niece of a member of the government of Poland, and the daughter of a university professor.

Soon he was deprived of his father, too. Again, let me quote his own words as he described the removal of his father to prison.

"It was this revolution of '63 and '64 which ruined many thousands of people in Poland. Many were executed or sent to Siberia; their properties were confiscated and given away to Russian functionaries, to those, for instance, who had

99

discovered that they had been guilty of some intrigue or some participation in the propaganda against the Russian Government. My father supported all that. Whatever he could do he did, except that he could not take an active part in the fighting, for that was against his nature.

"I still remember very well what happened the day they came to take him away. Suddenly the house was surrounded by Cossacks, and nobody was permitted to leave before a thorough search was accomplished. There was a large company of Cossacks, perhaps 150 on horseback. They seemed very big and terrifying to a small boy. They completely encircled our house, and proceeded with the search. I was frightened, of course, and could not realise then what was going on, and I wanted to know, to understand; so I approached a Cossack very timidly and asked him about my father, because he was the most important thing in our lives. I was rather badly received, with the knout!

"The incident was of great importance in my young life – my first contact with the Russian authorities. They were searching our house to find forbidden things – papers and propaganda and so on. Of course I had no idea who they were – I was only interested in the fate of my father. He was very dear to us – there was a tremendous bond.

"When the Cossacks first surrounded the house I felt that something terrible was going to happen, but when they entered the house, then I knew that it was for my father they had come. I realised the danger. So I ran again to the tallest of the Cossacks, frightened as I was, and cried, 'What is happening to my father?' But he never answered, or even looked at me. But I insisted, and kept on asking, as a child will, what had happened – why they were taking my father away, and if he would soon be back again. And then, the tall Cossack laughed, threw back his head, and again gave me several very heavy strokes with the knout.

"This first contact with the Russian authorities affected me very deeply – it will always affect me. First of all, it was very painful, it cut my flesh, but I also considered it a supreme insult – in the pride of boyhood, not quite four years old! It wounded my spirit."

It might have seemed impossible for an aspiring musician, however talented, whose hand was too small to span an octave, to become a world-famous pianist. It might have seemed, to anyone with an appreciation of European history and the realities of the time, even more impossible to succeed in persuading the President of a neutral United States of America to espouse the cause of Polish nationalism and, eventually, to commit his nation to the creation of an independent united Poland as one of the objectives of entering the First World War. More impossible still would it have seemed to be able to persuade representatives of the victorious allies at the Versailles Conference, including the highly sceptical and contemptuous Lloyd George, to effect the fulfilment of such a commitment.

Paderewski was born in the old manor house of Kurylowka in Podolia, one of the ancient palatinates of the old kingdom of Poland, by then under Russia's sway. Three years after his birth, the rising of 1863 was crushed by the Czar, and it was then that Jan Paderewski, Ignace's father, was arrested and imprisoned for keeping arms and uniforms for the Polish regiments secretly organising in his house. Kurylowka village, too, was burned to the ground, and its defenceless inhabitants whipped in herds by the brutal Cossack cat-o'-nine-tails, while scores of them were put to the sword and slaughtered in cold blood.

Paderewski's mother, Polixena Nowicka, had indeed been the daughter of a university professor, and came of a good family from Nowicki. His father was a gentleman of the landed classes, poor but educated, employed as administrator of the estates of the wealthy family, Iwanowski. His mother's father had been banished from Poland to Siberia, where he had died. His mother had, indeed, been born in exile, in the Siberian town of Kursk, a favourite deportation station of the Czar's. It can be claimed that with his mother's milk there came to Ignace Paderewski a sense of Poland's afflictions. Now, with his father being sent to prison, the boy was doubly deprived.

The memory of his mother was kept warm by the family – the sadness of the fate of one who had seen her own father die in exile, and had herself come out of it only to leave her own son an orphan, was never forgotten. No doubt the child, Ignace, heard many stories from his father and others in the family of the sufferings of his mother, as well as of those of his grandfather and grandmother in their banishment.

His mother had, indeed, been an accomplished musician.

101

Though she did not live long enough to instruct him herself, he inherited her talent. By the age of three he was keenly interested in the pianoforte, and by the age of six he was being instructed in it. His first teacher was a violinist, but he taught him how to work, for Ignace liked to improvise, and was inclined to be a little lazy. His tutor insisted on periodical performances by Ignace Jan and his sister Antonina before the family and guests in the drawing-room. When Ignace was seven, the violinist teacher was succeeded by the more accomplished Pierre Sowinski, this time a virtuoso performer on the pianoforte. For four years he taught Ignace, and the boy learned to love Chopin from him. Later, Paderewski would say: "It is a strange fact that the greatest music is in the minor mode . . . Music expresses first of all sadness rather than joy."

After being released from prison his father remarried. Ignace lavished his own affection on animals, especially on dogs. Sowinski convinced his father that the boy had exceptional talent, but his father could not afford to send him to the Conservatory at Warsaw. It would be nearly two years before his father was able to do so. Eventually, at twelve, he left home, to arrive in Warsaw in 1872.

There he had to face the great handicap that his hands were not those of a pianist. They were small, with short thumbs, and the third and fourth fingers were of almost equal length; it was only with difficulty that he could span an octave when he began his studies. However, he refused to study anything but the piano. To him it was "the greatest of instruments". All his life he was to practise, sometimes for seventeen hours a day. At this stage – and he was only a boy of twelve, of course – he ran wild sometimes, and played pranks on his teachers and fellow-students. But he was good-hearted and gay and generous. Soon, at thirteen, he won the first prize in composition and piano-playing. By the time he was sixteen he was anxious to join with Cielewicz, a violinist, to begin a public career. They planned to make a joint concert tour in the holidays, since pupils were forbidden to appear in public. The tour took place, and was all but disastrous – so badly arranged that in one hall there was a stage and an audience, but no piano, and when one finally arrived the keys stuck and the hammers would not move. They had to hire a boy to stand and whip the hammers back when they did not respond. It was a close thing, but the director, although aware of their escapade, took them back as students.

By the age of eighteen Paderewski was a fine-looking young man, with blue eyes, fair lashes and hair, a fine nose, a noble brow, and a good chin – masculine, but delicate, good looks. He fell in love with a fellow pupil, Antonina Korsak. Still only nineteen, and just graduated from the Conservatory, he decided to marry. At the same time he tried to support himself by giving piano lessons for a pittance. The marriage was short-lived, though happy. His wife, in giving birth to their son, died. The shock to Ignace Paderewski was tremendous. His dying wife gave him the money given her by her parents as a dowry, telling him to use it to go on with his studies. "You have great genius," she insisted, "you must have the best teachers in the world. When you have won your success you will repay our son many times over." Before she died she exacted the promise. So the idyll ended, and his life of toil and pain began. Stunned by his bereavement, at twenty, with an infant child to care for, he put his baby son in his father's care, and left the Conservatory for a year's leave of absence in Berlin.

In his own words, he said that he had married "a young girl who was a student at the Warsaw Conservatory. I had a little home of my own at last and I was happy – but it was a short happiness. A year later my wife died, leaving me alone with our child, a son. I had lived through a brief – a beautiful – experience. Even at twenty, one can plumb the heights and depths and feel the pain and mystery of life. I now faced another change – I must go forward alone. My wife had had some little money of her own, and before she died she asked me to use part of it to continue my musical studies, in which she had the deepest faith. We had in Poland an institution for which I think there is no equivalent in other countries, a very special kind of Trusteeship for orphans, controlled by a number of prominent people, the details of which are of no interest at this moment except that it was in that institution I deposited the money that was to go to my child. It proved to be a tragic choice, for every penny of it was stolen a few years later by certain of these very respectable Trustees, and nothing remained. The little safety that I had then hoped for proved a dream, like so many others."

Paderewski continued to compose, and wrote an elegy –

Opus 4 – in which the tragic bereavement he had suffered in the death of his wife echoes his mourning.

Then Modjeska, the famous Polish actress who was to become a lifelong friend, entered his life, to give him once again the self-confidence he had lost with that death. She rallied and helped him, insisting that Poland needed him. "Poland needs you," she said. "Every man and woman of Polish blood must fall in line. This one as a soldier; that one as a nurse; the other as a writer; you as a musician." Her faith roused him to a new determination. In 1905, in New York, he would organise a public testimonial to her, saying, "The first encouraging words I heard as a pianist came from her lips; the first successful concert I had in my life was due to her assistance, good, kind and generous."

Finally, she persuaded him, and helped to raise the funds for him. But before that, in Warsaw, for the first time he appeared in a programme consisting entirely of his own works – at only twenty-four.

So Paderewski went to Vienna, the Mecca of all musicians. There he submitted himself to the discipline of Leschetizky, the greatest of pianists; and was drilled like a schoolboy, practising sometimes up to twelve hours a day. Then he was offered a professorship at the Conservatory of Strasbourg, and gladly accepted – but only in order to return, a year later, to Leschetizky, with some money saved, and more experienced. His appetite for improvement and his determination to reach the top were insatiable.

By the age of twenty-six he was the soloist in the same programme as Pauline Lucca, the celebrated Italian soprano, and created a sensation. Next morning he awoke to find himself a musical celebrity. To him the best result would be what he could now do for his little invalid son, now six, but never to be strong and well.

The climb to the top was rapid. In March 1888 he went to Paris, there to join the evening gatherings of the exiled Poles in the Rue Jacob – for a century Paris had been the traditional refuge of Polish *émigrés,* particularly after the uprising of 1831. The Parisian audiences applauded him warmly, and his press notices were enthusiastic. He had conquered Paris, a consummate achievement. Soon he was being offered engagements by the most distinguished of French impresarios – Lamoureux and Colonne. Soon, too, he brought his little son to the home of friends, the Gorskis, to be mothered, for the remainder of his life, by Madame Gorska. From then on he was in great demand for his unforgettable interpretations of Beethoven, Schumann, Bach, Liszt, Mendelssohn, Schubert, Wagner, and more modern composers.

In 1890 he travelled to England – to initial failure. Only George Bernard Shaw praised him, in *The World*, finding him "alert, humorous, delightful, dignified, intelligent". (Needless to say, when London critics veered to uniform praise, Shaw could see Paderewski only as "sensational, empty, vulgar, violent".) By the third performance, however, the public was warming to him, and the fourth performance was sold out in advance. Receipts had soared from ten pounds to two hundred and eighty pounds.

But Paderewski wanted to conquer London as indisputably and totally as he had conquered Vienna and Paris. So he decided to tour the provinces, in preparation. By 1891, when he went back to London, London reversed its initial verdict. He returned to unanimous and extravagant acclaim. A few years later, Robert Newman would pay one thousand pounds for one Paderewski recital in the Queen's Hall. The strain of such adulation was, however, heavy. He had a crisis of nerves when his agent, Mayer, came to tell him of the sell-out for the Chopin recital. Bending over the keyboard he said, in a trembling voice, "Oh, I can't play at all! It's wrong. I can't take their money. I can't play at all!"

In England his fame was now assured. He had played in twenty-two cities, and in nearly every case the entire seating for his concerts had been sold out two months in advance. He was even received by Queen Victoria.

In her diary the Queen wrote: "2 July, Windsor Castle. Went to the green drawing-room and heard Monsieur Paderewski play on the piano. He does it quite marvellously, such power and such tender feeling. He is young, about twenty-eight, very pale, with a sort of aureole of red hair standing out."

After that recital she sent him a tie-pin; her daughter, the Princess Louise, painted his portrait; and Alma-Tadema and Burne-Jones made portraits of him. At only thirty, all doors were open to him, largely because of the Queen's favours.

Next time he played for Queen Victoria she received him like an old acquaintance, and made him play many encores.

This time three of her daughters, and the Princess of Wales, and Prince Battenberg, as well as other relations, and most of the ladies and gentlemen of the royal household were also there. This time, too, she sent him a signed photograph of herself, and, according to Paderewski, a ring. On the first occasion she had come in leaning heavily on a stick. On the second occasion she was wheeled into the drawing-room in a bath-chair. A few months later she was dead – another Phaeton, and one not sorry to join her beloved, long-lost Albert. That had been in 1901.

Next, Paderewski journeyed to America, a few days after his thirty-first birthday, in 1891 – and before his second visit to the Queen, of course. There he appeared in the Carnegie Hall. His success was again phenomenal, and when he transferred to the Madison Square concert hall, it could not contain the crowds wanting to hear him, and he had to move back to the Carnegie Hall, which seated three thousand. Before he left America he had performed at more than fifteen hundred concerts, appearing in every one of the forty-eight states of the Union, and playing in over two hundred cities, travelling three hundred and sixty thousand miles and playing to more than five million people. He was to make a great fortune from the piano on which, as a boy in Warsaw, he had been told that he was "wasting his time".

The nervous strain, however, was enormous, what with the demands of travelling, entailing living in railway-coaches and railway-yards, yet being fresh and ready day after day – *and* having to practise on the train. Fortunately he was a good sleeper, and used to strict self-discipline. With the Phaeton's austerity, he would take nothing but a cup of coffee or tea if playing at an afternoon concert. If playing in the evening, he would eat nothing beforehand except one soft-boiled egg. During the intermission he would drink a lemonade without sugar, and, sometimes, after the concert, before dining, a glass of sweet champagne. He smoked, but once gave it up for a whole year, to prove that he could do so. All his life his daily routine was rigorous and spartan.

Nothing made a stronger appeal to him during these years than a gifted child, and when he discovered one he always referred to the child's mother, saying that to a child of pronounced musical talent, a musical mother was a God-given aid, and stressing the great and invaluable role such mothers have played in the lives of master musicians – a form of mourning, perhaps, for what he had missed. He declared, with Joseph Conrad, that imagination, not invention, was the supreme master of art; and he insisted that the chief qualification of a great pianist was, apart from technical excellence, simply, genius. Yet he was, it seems, himself entirely free from vanity, the most modest musician whom De Pachmann, at any rate, had ever met.

Eventually Paderewski decided to settle in America, and bought a ranch at Paso Robles, the Rancho San Ignacio, bought in 1913, and bearing one hundred and twenty thousand almond trees. Originally Paderewski had come seeking rest and the waters of the Paso Robles for his neuritis. Modjeska, too, lived there. But he toured London and Paris annually, sometimes extending his visits to Italy, Belgium, Russia, Holland and Germany, as well as England and France, and even going to Australia, South Africa and South America, drawing larger and larger crowds with each visit. His generosity to his father, his sister, his half-brothers and his half-sisters grew greater as he prospered. When Paderewski was thirty-nine, he married Helena Garska, the Baroness de Rosen, as his second wife.

Paderewski's father had died, to his great distress, in 1894. Far worse was the death of his son – a tragedy from which he never recovered. The child had suffered from infantile paralysis at the age of four. When he was six, Paderewski heard of one Monsieur Pomerol, a healer, in Paris, who offered a permanent cure for his halting walk. The first effect of his cure was that the child ceased to walk at all. Pomerol declared that this was only an indication of response to manipulation. Then Pomerol died, and Alfred never walked again. Yet the child was very bright, keen, and happy, a clever chess player, and an ardent champion of his father's achievements.

At nineteen the boy was still helpless in a wheelchair, but well educated, and showing a promising literary gift. Then he heard of a specialist at Augsberg, in Germany, whom he believed could help him. Paderewski sent him there, but the boy caught cold and died of pneumonia. Paderewski reached him, from Bilbao, too late – Alfred was already dead.

Paderewski's grief was deep and lasting. He was lost without his son, always remembering how he had helped to entertain his guests with original little comedies written by himself.

His earliest romance, ended by death, had, nineteen years later, produced another death.

In Paderewski's own words, as he wrote in his memoirs: "He was away from home undergoing a certain treatment of which we both had high hopes at that time. The sudden ending of his brief, mutilated span of life came with shocking force to me. I had still hoped there was help for him somewhere. Death put an end to that hope. I took his body to the Cemetery of Montmorency, near Paris, a cemetery sacred to my countrymen, where eminent Poles were buried in the days of the emigration. Chopin lies there, and Mickiewicz, our national poet. There I buried my son Alfred – not yet twenty-one. It was a blessing for me that I had work to do then, that I was forced to work, and could plunge into the final details of my opera, which was soon to be produced."

Paderewski kept his son's room locked for a long time. Then he took all the tributes and souvenirs which had been showered on him, including a wreath given him by the Boston Symphony Orchestra, and, as he put it, laid them at the feet of his son. He had the room filled with fresh flowers every day, and kept his son's wheel-chair, his table, and all the things the boy had used, exactly as he had left them. It was a grief from which he never recovered, to the end of his own life.

That was not the last blow death was to strike at him. When his godson, Edziu, son of Dr Fronczak, a fine, strapping six-footer of splendid character and manly bearing, who had last visited him at the age of eighteen, died, at twenty-four, Paderewski was deeply upset. A few months later the boy's parents visited him. Paderewski talked long and affectionately with the bereaved father about his son. But to spare the boy's mother he ordered every member of his household not to mention him in her hearing.

In 1898 Paderewski returned to Warsaw, and gave three large benefit concerts. There, too, came his début as an orator. The Russians forbade publication of his speeches, but manuscript copies were circulated throughout Poland. Then, in 1903, he was invited to Russia, by the Imperial Society of Music at St Petersburg. There the Czar remarked that he was pleased that the world's most eminent musician was a Russian. "Your Majesty is mistaken," Paderewski replied, "I am a Pole." To that the Czar responded, "There is no such country as Poland. There is only Russia." "Pardon my hasty remark,"

Paderewski rejoined. "Your Majesty speaks the truth." Then he played Chopin's funeral march. All his life Paderewski declared, *"La patrie avant tout; l'art ensuite"* – and his life bore it out that his patriotism was, indeed, more important than his art, to which he had dedicated all his energies, and which had already brought him great fame. Events proved his claim to be absolutely true. Internationally famous, and domiciled in neutral Switzerland, there was no compulsion whatever for him to allow the war of 1914 to 1918 to affect his way of life. He did not even have, in any but a romantic historical sense, as we know, any *patrie*, since there was no such thing as an independent Polish nation – only an amorphous, dismembered agglomeration of mid-European provinces, different parts of which were governed by Germany, by Austria, and by Russia. The idea of any possible resuscitation of the ancient kingdom of Poland, in some form or other, was kept alive only by desperate, and often conflicting, bodies of nationalist revolutionaries.

However, for those like Paderewski, to whom the idea was a passion at the heart of their being, the war between Germany and the Allies was primarily an opportunity for the "Poland" of their dreams to emerge into reality. And Paderewski, who had at no time involved himself deeply in the activities of any of the political nationalists, regarded this opportunity as more important than his musical career. With one enemy of "Poland" in the shape of Tsarist Russia at war with another enemy of "Poland" in the shape of the Kaiser, in alliance with a third enemy, in the shape of Austria, and with Poles fighting in the armies of all three, and with all three enemies offering beguiling promises of independence to a new, united "Poland", the situation of the Polish patriot was somewhat confused, to say the least. But Paderewski's patriotism was not subject to that sort of confusion, even though it was devoted to a country that did not exist.

Paderewski abandoned his musical life, and went to the neutral United States of America, as the representative of one of the exiled Polish Nationalist factions, with the purpose of promoting Poland's interests. The bleakness of the outlook can best be assessed by considering the war, and Poland's place in it, from the point of view of the President of the United States. Millions of loyal, voting Americans were, emotionally, Germans, and championing "Poland" against the Kaiser, who ruled a third of it, was likely to antagonise them – and without appealing to any deep, instinctive loyalties in most of the rest of the electorate. There was, certainly, a substantial, if less numerous, element of persecuted refugees from the Polish provinces of Russia to be considered. But currying favour with them meant antagonising Russia, which ruled another third of Poland, and that was undesirable since Russia was in alliance with Britain, and American sympathies were broadly, even at the beginning of the war, pro-British.

Paderewski's self-imposed mission would have seemed, to any impartial and realistic observer, at best mere fishing in troubled waters, and, at worst, both futile and hopeless. Yet the fact is – without going into the details of all the grinding, agonising, wearying months, running into years, of fund-raising and charity-promoting, and agitation and importunity – that President Wilson's Thirteenth Point was, at one remove, Paderewski's work:-

An independent Polish state should be erected which should include the territories inhabited by indisputably Polish populations, which should be ensured a free and secure access to the sea, and whose political and economic independence and territorial integrity should be guaranteed by international covenants.

That Point Thirteen was achieved by a pianist and composer with no experience or understanding of international politics and diplomacy – only with the passion and faith to move mountains. It was one of the six territorial points delivered by President Woodrow Wilson in his address, "Ideas of Essential Nature of Post-War Settlement, to the Joint Session of the United States Congress on the report of Colonel Edward House's Committee of Enquiry". Colonel House was the man on whom Paderewski had, at last, successfully imposed his will, and his vision of a united, independent Poland.

In the consequential political turmoil in Poland, Paderewski was briefly, at the outset, Prime Minister. Not having any background of previous political activity, and lacking any organised party support, it is hardly surprising that he did not become permanently involved in a life of politics. In fact he was not elected, as he probably hoped, President of Poland; but that does not detract from the magnitude of his achievement, in becoming not only a world-famous musician but Prime Minister of Poland, however briefly. The drives which impelled this Phaeton to two such heights were formidable.

Paderewski was religious. After the death of his son he was comforted by St Augustine's text: "Thou madest us for Thyself, and our heart is restless unless it repose in Thee." To him that text explained, too, the whole impulse behind music and art, what the German critic Walzel called "the intense longing of man as a reasonable thinking being for the Endless and the Eternal".

He was a Catholic, and was attacked by the radicals in Poland – his government, too, was attacked, both from inside and outside, on the pretext that it was anti-Jewish. "I am not a modest man," he once said. "Frankly, I am not modest before men. But I bow to God and to Art." And again, "I am a firm believer in God and destiny."

Paderewski was superstitious. He declared that he foresaw the death of his grandfather before he reached the house in which it had taken place. In his own words: "We arrived late in the afternoon and the first thing I saw were candles alight in the big room. This did not surprise me because I already knew that something was going to happen in my father's house. I felt this the day before I left Kieff. I said to myself, 'Something happens now in our home. There will be a great change when we return.' I could not sleep that night. I have always had a certain sensitiveness or intuition which made me foresee and expect things, especially death. So when I saw the candles burning, I knew that what I felt had happened. For there in the big room lay the body of my grandfather. He had died the day before.

"I have had several such experiences. I often had them as a child. Now I use more logic. Perhaps I am not so wise as I used to be, because now I apply logic to my intuition, and logic and intuition do not go hand in hand."

From his earliest youth, too, Paderewski showed signs of recklessness. As a boy he was twice expelled from school for reckless behaviour.

Perhaps one of Paderewski's most amazing achievements was that he became a gifted orator. This man, who had Polish as his native tongue, and who had a slight lisp, as well as a Polish accent, to overcome, did brilliantly. In Colonel House's words, describing one performance: "I have heard nearly all the great speakers of our time except Gladstone. I have heard none that seemed to have the power that Paderewski exhibited that day. He made me think of the great Greeks, and everybody felt as I did. For forty minutes, without a halt, his fine voice rolled on through the hall and filled it. One could have heard a pin drop until he concluded, and then the auditorium rose in unrestrained homage."

So there we have the Phaeton pattern once again – a man superstitious, isolated, reckless, sensitive, austere, with an extreme reaction to bereavement, an obsessive need for love, an intense devotion to his child, a great interest in religion, a notable aggression, and a dependence on mentors. His achievement, in becoming not only a world-famous musician but the Prime Minister of his own country, was remarkable – in fact, unique.

A MIXED BAG

Arthur Ashe, mother died in childhood.
William Beckford of Fonthill, father died when he was 9.
Jesse Boot (founder of Boots the Chemists), father died when he was 10.
Coco Chanel, bastard.
Marie Curie, father accidentally killed when she was 8.
Mamie Eisenhower, mother died when she was 4, father when she was 11.
Guy Fawkes, father died when he was 9.
Henry Ford, mother died when he was 12.
Milton Friedman, Nobel Prizewinner, father died when he was a child.
Emma Hamilton, Nelson's mistress, father died before she was 1, and she was probably a bastard.
Violette Leduc, bastard.
Archbishop Makarios, mother died when he was 11.
Edwina Mountbatten, mother died when she was 10.
Aristotle Onassis, mother died when he was 6.
Tsar Paul II of Russia, bastard, Grand Duke Peter impotent ("I don't know how it is that my wife becomes pregnant") and father died when he was 7.
Anna Pavlova, probably a bastard.
Eleanor Roosevelt, both mother and father dead before she was 11.
James Smithson, of the Smithsonian Institute, bastard son of the Duke of Northumberland and Elizabeth Keate Macie, a direct descendant of King Henry VII.
Saint Theresa, mother died when she was 6.

Dr Fred Young, Indian laser scientist at Los Alamos, father died when he was a child.

The Duchess of Windsor, father died when she was 5 months old.

CHAPTER 10

Aristotle Onassis (1906 – 1975)

Aristotle Socrates Onassis was born on January 20th, 1906, to a Greek exile, Socrates Onassis, and his wife Penelope. His mother died when he was six, to the boy's great grief, after a kidney operation and subsequent infection. His father married again in 1915, and produced half-sisters, Merope and Callirrhoe, for "Aristo" and his own sister, Artemis.

Onassis had an extreme reaction to bereavement. Although he was in Buenos Aires when his father fell ill, he made a point of travelling to his side, in Greece. There were tears of pride and affection as father and son said goodbye to each other. They never saw each other again; for the old man died soon after. Onassis had named his first ship after his father. The old man had never been able to fulfil his dream of sending his son to Oxford, but he had taught him enough to ensure that, at under thirty, his son possessed a fleet of ships, and had become a millionaire. They had parted in anger when Aristotle was sixteen, but all was forgotten as they said goodbye to each other.

That grief was, however, nothing to the blow which Aristotle Onassis received when his only son, Alexander Onassis, was killed, at the age of twenty-four, in an air-crash on the 22nd January, 1973. Onassis had, like all Phaetons, an extreme devotion to his children, and doted on this son, to whom he had planned to turn over his shipping empire. The light aircraft in which the young man was a passenger got into difficulties as it was taking off from Athens airport, causing the plane to cartwheel for four hundred and sixty feet, and then crash. The young man could only be recognised by the monogram on his bloodstained handkerchief. His brain was irreparably damaged – the right temple reduced to pulp. Although the relationship had not been by any means a wholly happy one, this son was the most important person in Onassis's life, his future, as he saw it. He was kept alive on a life-support machine in an oxygen tent, but there was no hope for him, and eventually Onassis decided to let him die. His grief was terrible. First he refused to have his son buried. Then, giving way to spells of excruciating pain and outbursts of rage and blasphemy, he wanted him deep-frozen. Then he wanted him buried inside the chapel on the island of Skorpios – a privilege reserved for saints. Finally, he agreed to have him buried by the side of the chapel, and to have the grave covered by an annex later. The death of this, his only son, indeed, seemed to unhinge him. He became convinced that the crash had not been caused by an accident, and that the plane had been sabotaged, and offered a reward of 500,000 dollars to anyone who could prove that his son had been murdered, and another million dollars to a charity of his choice, but no one with any proof came forward. So crushed was he that he could not bring himself to attend his son's funeral; and in his anguish he decided to sell Olympic Airways, and began negotiations to dispose of it to the Greek government. He could not agree on a price, and his negotiations were very unlike his usual style – loose, vague and imprecise. He seemed to have lost all control of himself, and was obsessed with violence, murder, death and vengeance. He himself would be dead in a little over two years, and his daughter Christina would inherit most of his fortune.

Even for the death of Sir Winston Churchill, for whom Onassis had a great admiration, he would shed tears, though his grief was, of course, infinitesimal as compared with that for his beloved son.

That Onassis was intensely devoted to his own children has already been suggested, in the extremity of his grief for his dead son. His love for his daughter, too, was warm, and lifelong.

The driving force which could take a young man who was almost penniless to becoming one of the richest ship-owners in the world was formidable. Born in Turkey, though he was a

Greek and not a Turk, and despised the Turks, in a world where Greeks had to worry about a knock on the door in the middle of the night, which might be followed by beating and blackmail, Onassis, like all Greeks, learned to be cunning in order merely to stay alive. From this miserable beginning he became a dollar millionaire at the age of twenty-three, and never looked back.

Aristotle Onassis was religious. As a child he sang in the Church choir, learned his catechism, and was drilled in theology at his local church for two hours a week. As a man he never broke away from the church.

He was far from outstanding in school, yet he tried to shine at everything he undertook, whether it was swimming, or water-polo, or sailing, or making a fortune. Disaster came to him and his family in 1922, when the Turks ran the Greeks out of Turkey, chased them into the sea, and slaughtered them. Thousands of Greek refugees poured into Smyrna ahead of the Turkish army, with dreadful tales of savagery and horror that echoed the bloody history of the Turkish massacres of centuries before. The Turks were taking a horrible revenge for the Greek atrocities of 1919 on the Turkish population. The old and beautiful city was burned on September 13th, 1922. The horror was unbelievable, with a pall of black smoke rising from the ruins, the dreadful smell of burning flesh, and hundreds of men, women and children crowding into every available craft, even small rowing boats, in order to escape. Not least in horror was the cruelty with which the escaping Greeks broke the legs of the mules in order to keep them from being useful to the Turks. When the Greeks had been in power they had burned the most prosperous towns in the west of Turkey. Now the innocent Greek population of Smyrna were paying with their blood.

Aristotle Onassis's father was thrown into a Turkish prison, and his new wife and three daughters were sent to an evacuation centre, to await transportation from Smyrna to Greece. Only the sixteen-year-old Aristotle and his grandmother were left at home – but not for long. Soon the Turkish general requisitioned the house and the old lady and the boy had to get out. The boy had to grow up overnight – somehow to rescue what was left of the family; somehow to save what was left of the family fortune; somehow to survive against dreadful odds; somehow to get them all out of Turkish Smyrna; and somehow to start again. Almost incredibly, he succeeded in all these aims. He made up to the Turks, and to the Americans, supplying the Turks with information, the Americans with liquor – for he hid bottles of *raki, ouzo* and even French brandy, and supplied them to the Americans. His commission would be a single bottle, and he would give that to his friend, the Turkish general. From the Americans he obtained an identification pass to take him in and out of the United States Marine zone; and from the Turks a Turkish army pass to enter and leave the still smouldering city. Now he could operate; but first he must find his family. His grandmother had disappeared, and his father was in a Turkish prison, for summary trial as a political offender – his death by hanging a certainty if all went as usual. His Aunt Maria and her husband, Chrysostomos Konialides, were already dead. His father's brothers were also arrested, and one of them, Alexander, had been hanged in the public square. Five hundred Greeks had been burned alive in a church.

Miraculously, Aristotle managed to rescue his relatives. Through the American Vice-Consul's intercession he obtained the release of his half-sisters and his stepmother from their camp, and they were put on an American ship and despatched to Lesbos. For his father he needed a great deal of money. His father had run a one-man banking business, and at his offices, on Grand Vizier Han Street, there were valuables belonging to Turkish friends in an old-fashioned black safe. Going with a Turkish friend of his father's to retrieve a parcel of papers and valuables left with his father for safe-keeping, Aristotle opened the safe, secured the parcel for his friend, and emptied the safe of his father's fortune in Turkish pounds. Next he organised a march of fifty leading Turkish businessmen, waving a banner, shouting against the arrest of Socrates Onassis, and demanding his release. This almost certainly saved his father's life.

Aristotle himself, however, about to leave Smyrna, was arrested on his last visit to his father, and put under guard. In a very difficult situation – for he was carrying secret messages from the prisoners, and the inevitable search would result in imprisonment, or worse, for him – and by sheer effrontery, he managed to escape, and once outside the gate ran to the safety of the United States Marine compound. In minutes he was with his friend the Vice-Consul; and, outfitted in an American uniform, was steaming within the hour for Lesbos and freedom. He would always believe that he owed his life to Vice-

Consul Parker and the United States Marines, and from then on he had a sincere love for America.

That was not the end. With great courage and cunning, Aristotle Onassis managed to save his father from incarceration in Smyrna: a delicate and expensive undertaking. With astounding ingratitude, all his relatives, and his father himself, thought he had spent too much. Resentful and angry – and who could blame him? – his son decided to leave home and make his way on his own. He refused to take more than fifty Turkish pounds. With fifteen of his Turkish pounds he got himself a special temporary travel document, then went to visit his grandmother's grave in Piraeus – for she was dead, killed in a struggle with Greek thieves when disembarking in Piraeus. That was a remarkable example of affection for the old lady, to spend so much out of so little, simply to pay his respects at her grave – and another example of extreme reaction to bereavement. Then he set off for Buenos Aires, half the world away.

In six years Aristotle Onassis would return, a dollar millionaire. The tale of his rescue of his father would grow in the telling, and Aristotle would claim in years to come that he had been in prison with his father, the shadow of the noose hanging over both of them; that he got out of gaol about a month before his father, who was released under a general Turkish amnesty; that three of his uncles were hanged by the Turks; and that he actually watched them hang. All this was denied by the Turks, who claimed that Greeks were prone to lying. At least it seems that his uncle Alexander *was* hanged, and that Vice-Consul Parker *did* get Aristotle out of Smyrna.

After a nightmare voyage in what has been described as a floating garbage-can, in which he could not afford a cabin, and slept on top of coiled stern lines, he reached Buenos Aires, on September 21st, 1923, a date he never forgot. Starting at the very bottom, rowing stevedores from one end of the docks to the other for a few cents a trip, he then got a temporary job as a construction worker, then became a dishwasher in a bar on the corner of Corrientes and Talcahuano. His climb began when he was employed by the telephone company – the British United River Plate Telephone Company – at a salary of twenty-five cents an hour, by lying about his age and his birthplace. According to him, he had been born in 1900, six years before he had been, at Salonika, in Greece. All he had to

119

do was to gather bunches of wires and fasten them together, and soon he was earning over a hundred dollars a month, with overtime. By 1925 he was working at nights, and sleeping only three hours a night. In his free time he sold cigarettes in the streets of Buenos Aires – cigarettes made by a company in which he would be a major stockholder in the future. Soon he was selling cigarettes manufactured and rolled by two workers in a back room, and finished by hand. Some, intended to appeal to women daring enough to smoke, and to prostitutes, had their tips made of rose leaves. He cheated, calling his cigarettes Bis, a famous Argentine brand, and sold them cheaper. He was sued by the owner of the Bis factory, Xoudis, and had to settle out of court for several thousand pesos, and stop using the Bis name. It was only the first of a chain of lawsuits which were to be brought against him – and the cheapest.

Hardly a year after his arrival in Buenos Aires he had become a fully-fledged citizen of two countries. He was not only an Argentine citizen – a citizenship obtained with false information – but also a Greek citizen, with two million other Greek wanderers. He always claimed to have made his first million by the time he was twenty-three. Whether he was referring to pesos or dollars, it was still a lot of money. He was decidedly on his way to great riches; and now he began to frequent night-clubs and to entertain beautiful women; and to deal in everything from salt to whale-oil. He raised a steamship sunk off Montevideo, spent a few thousand pesos on her, and sold her for an enormous profit. He took time for piano and language lessons, learning French, Spanish, English, Turkish, Italian and German. He threw himself into gaining knowledge of the arts, too; and Anna Pavlova's prima ballerina fell in love with him, and refused to leave Buenos Aires without him. Adamant, she hung on for a year before she left – possibly bought off by Onassis.

The climb became speedier – soon he was envoy-extraordinary of the Greek government in Argentina. Six years after arriving as a stateless immigrant with a few dollars and no prospects, he had two nationalities, a million dollars, a diplomatic passport, and was being entrusted with a delicate assignment which would affect international relations. By December of that year he had been appointed Greek Consul in Buenos Aires. He exploited his position as Consul to make contacts and utilise them, until 1935, when he gave up the consulate. He was on the way up, and, soon, he was the owner of a fleet of ships which had been laid up in the St Lawrence River, and which were owned by the Canadian National Steamship Company – ten ships which had been bought for about 30,000 dollars apiece; but he bought six for 20,000 dollars apiece. Starting in a tiny shipping office in the Calle Santa Maria in Buenos Aires, with his cousin, Nicholas Konialides, as his manager, he was launched on the business which would make him a millionaire.

His search for love was endless, and, interestingly, he had a great penchant for older women – clearly a search for a mother. His first real love was Ingeborg, or Ingse, Dedichen, unhappy, blonde, lovely, Nordic, whose father owned one of Norway's biggest whaling fleets. She was almost ten years older than he, but the short, dynamic Greek and the tall, emotional Norwegian soon fell in love. He behaved like a man in love for ten years, but he never married her. He took her to Buenos Aires, America, and England, and she played hostess for him, and dressed expensively in clothes bought at Schiaparelli and Worth. With her, Onassis began to appreciate the value of fine furniture and paintings, and the luxury of chauffeur-driven cars. It is almost certain, too, that she contributed money to his purchase of three tankers at the Göteborg shipyards.

So the climb continued, through the 1930s, with Adolf Hitler a threatening spectre; through the Spanish Civil War, lasting its three years, with Hitler and Mussolini supporting Franco and using Spain as a testing-ground for Germany's modern military equipment and new war tactics, including the mass air bombardment of civilians. Onassis carried cargoes of arms, oil and supplies to both sides.

By 1938 he had built the *Ariston*, flying the Swedish flag, and was getting really rich, taking oil to Japan. Onassis was able to stay at the best hotels everywhere – at the St Moritz Hotel on Central Park South in New York; in London at the Savoy; in San Francisco at the Mark Hopkins Hotel. In Buenos Aires he kept a permanent suite at the Plaza, and built a new house in Montevideo. In Hollywood he stayed at the Beverley Hills Hotel. Nothing held him back, not even the immobilisation of his ships in neutral Scandinavia; and not even the requisitioning of his ship, the *Aristophanes*, by the Norwegians. He managed to get a passage from Europe to the United States, crossing the Atlantic while the Germans were over-running France, and beating Stavros Niarchos, his partner in many ventures, to New York by a few weeks. He still had six ships sailing under the Panamanian flag; still had his interests in Argentina; and still believed that there was money to be made during the war. Pearl Harbour was more than a year away. When America entered the war, in 1941, Onassis' passport, most strangely, gave his age as forty-one, not thirty-four. So he did not serve in it. Now, based in New York, he became friendly with Simone Signoret, Veronica Lake, and Paulette Goddard.

Then he met Costas Gratsos, and went into the whaling business, for whale oil. Somehow the two turned an old tugboat, three sailors, and an abandoned whaling station in Northern California, bought for a mere 15,000 dollars, into a blue-chip investment. They never caught more than forty whales, but found that there was a fortune to be made selling whale-meat to the local mink farmers, and disposing of the enormous whale livers, to supply the chemically processed and desperately needed Vitamin A.

So the climb went on, ever upward, until May 1945, when Germany was defeated and the Führer had committed suicide in a blazing Berlin; and when Mussolini had been shot by the Italian partisans, and his body strung up by the heels in a square in Milan. Then, by September 1945, when the once invincible forces of the Japanese Emperor had humbly surrendered to General Douglas MacArthur on the deck of the U.S.S. *Missouri* in Tokyo Harbour, it was all over, and Onassis was free to pursue his rise to the top. Out of four hundred and fifty Greek ships, three hundred and sixty had been lost. Of the major Greek ship-owners, Onassis alone had not lost a single sailor or a single ship – though the two he had sold to the Japanese before Pearl Harbour had been sunk by the Americans. At the end of the war he was able to count his blessings – his immediate family was safe in Greece; his fleet was intact; he had made influential friends in the United States and Argentina; he had enjoyed his life in New York and in Hollywood; he had become something of a connoisseur; and he had a fortune of thirty million dollars, and big plans for the future.

At once he sent for his two stepsisters and other relations, and they arrived on the first Onassis ship from Piraeus to New York.

Now he meant to marry, but not the older Ingeborg, for he wanted to raise a family: he wanted a Greek girl of good family and good character, rich, preferably from a Greek shipping family, young, and very beautiful. On Saturday, April 17th, 1943, at seven o'clock in the evening, he had met the two Livanos daughters, sixteen and fourteen years old respectively, Eugenia and Athena – Eugenia dark, Athena blonde. He proposed to the fourteen-year-old Eugenia, but she refused him. Her sixteen-year-old sister had decided, however, that if Eugenia did not want Aristotle Onassis, she did.

So they married, and had a two-month honeymoon. It was a marriage very much motivated by expediency for Ari, but apparently Tina – as she was known – was happy, and very much in love with the man who was forty, but looked only thirty. Now the flight upwards was even steeper and swifter, with Onassis really beginning to build his oil-shipping fortune, finally even persuading the head of the National City Bank to lend him half the money with which to buy sixteen Liberty ships. Presently he was building brand-new, enormous tankers, with other people's money, and was on the way to one of the largest fortunes in the world. The days of hiring ships were soon over. Within a few months he had five supertankers under construction in the United States, which would sail under the Panamanian flag. At one stroke he had more than doubled his money. At once he gave Eva Peron ten thousand dollars for one of her charities.

Soon America's wartime romance with Russia was over; soon there was a post-war shipping boom; soon Onassis's fortune was made even greater. Careful to stay out of the anti-Communist struggle, he and Stavros Niarchos forged on, making more and more money. Ten Canadian frigates at scrap value for the whaling business; seventeen Canadian corvettes at bargain prices, manned by fifteen hundred veteran German sailors and Quisling gunners, and a flagship, the *Olympic Challenger,* sailing under the Panamanian flag – nothing went wrong and at the end of the first year Onassis had twenty thousand tons of oil, worth well over ten million dollars – all this at the expense of the whales. (On a later occasion, in 1952, Onassis took a group of New York friends and oil executives by chartered plane to a whale-killing party. On a single day the fleet killed over one hundred and fifty whales and the sea was red with blood as the whales bled to death.)

Onassis now began moving in more exalted circles, patronising the ballet, and becoming friendly with Dame Margot Fonteyn and her husband Roberto Arias.

His son had been born, and he and his wife lived more in Europe: a Paris apartment; the Côte d'Azur; Aristotle even bought the château where the Duke of Windsor, who could not afford it any longer, had lived. But they moved back to New York for the birth of his daughter, Christina, in December 1950.

By the age of forty-four Onassis had created the largest and most efficient whaling fleet in history; had engaged in a private war with Peru, and won; had built the most modern tanker fleet ever to sail the seven seas; had, in effect, bought, and greatly revived Monte Carlo; had feuded with her Prince and Princess and made world headlines. Had a deal with the ruler of Saudi Arabia gone through, he would have had an oil transport monopoly. He had, however, lost much reputation in the process. Still, phlegmatically, he had survived a boycott by the oil companies; had seen the Argentine dictator fall; had begun negotiations to buy a national airline; had bought many homes around the world; had built the largest and most luxurious yacht in the world, in which kings, presidents and prime ministers would accept his hospitality – and had made hundreds of millions of dollars. He had never been slow to bribe, and that had, apparently, paid dividends.

The climb was complete. He had reached the top of the tree, not only in wealth, but also in status. He owned most of Monaco, including the Casino, the hotels, the golf course, and the only theatre. Soon he got together with Prince Rainier – though later he called the friendship "the worst mistake of my life". The guests on his yacht would include ex-King Peter of Yugoslavia and Queen Alexandria; ex-King Farouk; Gianni Agnelli, the millionaire Italian industrialist; Norah, Lady Docker; Greta Garbo and her friend Dr Gayelord Hauser, and, later, George Schlee; the Begum Aga Khan; Argentine millionaire Arturo Lopez-Wilshaw; the Maharanee of Baroda; the Earl of Warwick; Darryl Zanuck and Juliette Greco; Jack Warner; Sir Laurence Olivier and Joan Plowright; Porfirio Rubirosa and his wife Odile; Anita Ekberg and, in due course, Sir Winston Churchill, with his wife and entourage.

But the ascent was not without its problems. In 1955 he was accused of taking half his catch illegally, and out of season –

eight and a half million dollars' worth – and much of it from blue-fin whales, which were protected by international law. The Norwegians accused him of falsifying his records and bribing Panamanian inspectors to sign them for him. They obtained a judgment of 665,000 dollars against him for his illegal hunting, and tied up the *Olympic Challenger* in port. He decided to sell out, and filed a counter-suit for three million dollars. Costas Gratsos sold his fleet to the Japanese for eight and a half million dollars. Onassis was out of the whaling business for good, with a profit of several millions, but with the loss of his reputation.

An indictment for fraud by the United States Government was also brought against him in the mid-1950s. The prosecutors were even using deals previously approved as a basis for legal action against him. His ships were taken over, and twelve of them immobilised so as to prevent him trading with Communist China, North Korea, and the Soviet ports, and the Attorney-General was preparing cases of criminal fraud against both Onassis and Niarchos. Onassis was actually placed under arrest by a United States Marshal – and the Attorney-General, Herbert Brownlow Junior, a member of the firm of Law, Day and Lord, one of those which had allegedly advised Onassis that his proceedings were legal. Formally committed to gaol for fifteen months, photographed and finger-printed for the criminal records, Onassis pleaded not guilty, was released on ten thousand dollars' bail and was allowed to leave the country. In the end, by the summer of 1955, the case was settled out of court – Onassis paying seven million dollars of the twenty million dollars claimed by the United States Government, and agreeing to build 198,000 tons of tankers in the United States, to be operated under the United States flag, and to be owned by Alexander and Christina Onassis, his children, and two *bona fide* citizens of America and Britain. In return he could sail fifteen of the seventy-two tankers under whatever flag he wished. The United States dropped the criminal charges against him as part of the package deal. If he had done as much for the British, Onassis claimed, he would have been knighted – "In America I was indicted." But he had been cleared.

It was not the end of trouble though. A string of lawsuits would dog Onassis – he was even accused of signing contracts with disappearing ink.

Suez saved him. On the brink of ruin when the canal shut down, by the time it was open again, in April, 1957, he was without question one of the richest men in the world.

His wife saw little of him – when she broke a leg skiing in St Moritz he was immersed in the Saudi-Arabian crisis; when she was seriously injured in an automobile accident he was not there, though he did arrive within twenty-four hours from New York. Her serious facial injuries later required plastic surgery, luckily successful.

The time was ripe for Maria Callas to come on the scene. Soon after Onassis and Niarchos combined to form their Olympic Airways, in 1957, with Onassis fifty-one, he and his wife Tina met the only Greek who had made a great success in opera. The association would lead to the end of both his and Maria Callas's marriages, and continue until he decided to marry again.

Onassis first met Maria Callas and her husband, Giovanni Battista Meneghini, in Venice, at a party given by the famous Elsa Maxwell. He pursued her, giving her three huge bunches of red roses the next day. Next he met her in London, and gave a party for her at the Dorchester, toasting her again and again. Soon they were cruising together aboard the *Christina*, with Sir Winston and Lady Churchill, his daughter Diana, his secretary, Anthony Montague Browne, and even Churchill's doctor, Lord Moran, and his canary, Toby. Soon Onassis was confiding everything to her, including details – as we may note, specially – of the death of his mother, who had died of a kidney operation when he was six; of his father's remarriage to her sister; of his adored grandmother, Gethsemane; of his time as a choir-boy, dressed in a gold-braided cassock and surplice, boasting that he still had a fine singing voice; of the time when he had pinched the attractive English teacher's bottom and been suspended; of the Turkish attack on Smyrna and the horror in which tens of thousands of Greeks had perished; of his father's arrest and the horror which had followed; of his decision to emigrate to Argentina, the crossing and his arrival in Buenos Aires. He opened his heart to her as he had done to no one else. They had both followed difficult careers, and had become what the popular press described as the world's two most celebrated Greeks. Each responded to the fighting qualities of the other. Poor Meneghini had also gone on the cruise, despite desperate efforts to get out of it, and had spent it being dreadfully seasick. By the time the ship returned to Monte Carlo, both Maria Callas's and Onassis's marriages were at an end. He flew to Milan, and Callas announced that she had separated from her husband, joined him on a private plane, and flew to the south of France. "She was a fat, clumsily dressed woman," Meneghini later said, with a strange turn of phrase. "She had not any prospect of a career, and I had to rent her a hotel room and put up seven hundred dollars so she could remain in Italy. I created Callas, and she repaid my love by stabbing me in the back."

It all ended in two divorces. The love-deprived Onassis had fallen, as so often happens, for another love-deprived person – for Callas's mother and father had refused even to look at her when she was born, since they had hoped for a boy, having lost their only son in a typhoid epidemic. Onassis did not want a divorce, and he did all he could to dissuade his wife from bringing an action against him, ringing her repeatedly, begging her to give up the idea, and crying like a baby. In June 1960, however, the adamant Tina was granted an uncontested divorce, with custody of the two Onassis children, after her lawyers had worked out a settlement. Just before the divorce, when Tina had broken her right leg, skiing in Switzerland, and been flown to a hospital in Oxford, Onassis visited her there. So did the Marquess of Blandford, known as Sonny Blandford. A year later Tina and Blandford were married, in October 1961.

Now Aristotle Onassis and Maria Callas lived together, openly, on land and sea. Both self-made, both considered foreigners by the other Greeks, they had much in common. Just before Onassis had gone to seek his fortune in Argentina, in 1922, Maria's father, George Kalogeropoulos, had left Greece to seek *his* fortune in America. He had been a small-town pharmacist in Meligala, and was glad to go. His wife Evangelia, one of eleven children, however, was the daughter of a Greek army officer, and had a will of iron. They had settled in Astoria, New York, with the six-year-old "Jackie". Four months later, on September 2nd, 1923, their second daughter, Maria, was born at the Old Flower Hospital. Maria was not even christened for three years – and then she was christened Cecilia Sophia Anna Maria Callas, her father having changed his name to Callas by then. Soon her father had lost his business, during the Depression, and had become a travelling salesman. Brought up in an unhappy home, full of bickering, with a father who was a womaniser, moving from cheap apartment to cheaper apartment, Maria and her sister were used by their mother as a form of compensation for the frustrations and disappointments of her own life. The shy, sensitive Maria was soon being pulled in and out of agents' offices, and pushed into auditions at radio stations. She won one talent contest on the Mutual Radio Network – a Bulova watch – but it was her mother's drive, not her own, which was pushing her onwards.

In 1937 her mother finally decided to go to Greece and take her children with her. There, forcing Maria to lie about her age and claim that she was sixteen when she was only fourteen, she got her into the Ethnikon Odeon, or National Conservatory. Her voice was good, but she was poor in appearance – awkward, with a bad skin, wearing glasses, weighing nearly thirteen stone, and chewing her fingernails to the quick, though aggressively determined to succeed. By April 1939 she had sung the leading role in *Cavalleria Rusticana*, and by December had been admitted to the Athens Conservatory, an improvement on the National Conservatory. But in 1940 the Italians invaded Greece, and, by April 1941, the Germans had occupied a defeated Athens. A terrible time had ensued for Maria Callas and her mother – virtual starvation. At least they were neither old nor weak, and could walk miles into the country for a handful of vegetables. So Maria Callas survived. More, Hitler loved opera, so the Germans tried to keep the opera going, for entertainment and propaganda. Many leading artists refused to perform for the invaders. Maria became a permanent member of Athens Opera during the Occupation, and her acquaintance with some of the Italian officers was very useful, especially as she would entertain them with selections from Italian opera, and they would repay her with food for her family. In 1942 she sang her first leading role, as Tosca, in occupied Greece – sang it well, but she was so fat she had to wear a waistless dress – and was paid a salary of only 3000 drachmas a month. She could, however, buy food, and no more money was coming from her father, with America now at war. So it all went on, until 1944, when Maria was singing the leading role in Beethoven's *Fidelio*, when Athens was liberated by the Greek resistance troops, and when civil war broke out. Maria's anti-Communist sympathies were known, her apartment was machine-gunned, and her pro-Communist janitor wrote, "We will kill Maria, first knocking out her brains with a sledgehammer." In the event, only her canaries were killed. The British occupied Athens, and the war was over – but only to bring new problems for Maria. The liberated Athens opera company refused to renew her contract, and she had to return to America at once to retain her citizenship. Her father sent her money, but she had to borrow more from the United States Embassy in order to pay her fare.

So she had gone back to her father's little drug-store, to make the rounds of managers and agents, while keeping house for him. Then her mother returned from Greece, and the quarrels began all over again. For two years Maria stayed in America, and got nowhere, until Edward Johnson, head of the Metropolitan Opera Company, heard her and engaged her to sing Puccini's *Madame Butterfly* – on condition she reduced her weight, by then nearer fourteen than thirteen stone, before the performance, a year away. She asked to be allowed to sing *Tosca* instead, but was refused.

In 1947, in desperation, she went to Italy, where she met her first husband, Meneghini, an older, moderately wealthy, Milanese business man, with strong operatic connections, and a deep passion for her. They were married in 1949, and two days later Maria, left, alone, for Buenos Aires, to sing at the Teatro Colon – a theatre which had much impressed the youthful Onassis. Thanks to Meneghini and his entire devotion to her – for he even turned over his business to his brother – her career took off. Now she grew slim, and sang in Rome, Naples, Mexico, Covent Garden, the Metropolitan, and La Scala. When she sang *Tosca* in Paris she emptied the ski-resorts. Temperamental, tyrannous, excessively unreasonable, she clashed with everyone. Her mother, who at one stage attempted suicide, even threatened to sue her for support, and a hostile press published a letter in which Maria told her mother she was not concerned about what became of her – a strong revenge on an unloving mother. Her singing in Athens was, however, a triumph, until her voice began to become uneven, possibly because of extreme dieting, possibly simply because she was tired.

The love-affair between the Phaeton who had been bereaved and the Phaeton who had been rejected at birth lasted until Jacqueline Kennedy, widow of the assassinated American

President, appeared on the scene. Onassis had been one of the first to call at the White House to offer his condolences after the death of her husband; and after Bobby Kennedy's death he had taken her on a cruise. Soon she had decided to accept his proposal of marriage.

The marriage was not all that either had hoped. When she married Onassis, in 1968, Jacqueline Kennedy probably hoped for security for the rest of her life. The public's reaction was one of shock. For Jacqueline Onassis the shock would come after Onassis's death, on March 15th, 1975, of *myasthenia gravis*, at the age of sixty-nine, when his wife was in New York with her children. She had stayed with him for weeks, but had finally departed, at odds with his family; and she was again, inevitably, subjected to criticism for leaving him. She issued a statement, which should have saved her from much of it, but it did not: "Aristotle Onassis rescued me at a moment when my life was engulfed with shadows. He meant a lot to me. He brought me into a world where one could find both happiness and love. We lived through many beautiful experiences together which cannot be forgotten, and for which I will be eternally grateful."

The shock of Onassis's will was still to come. Jacqueline Onassis would find that Onassis had taken a cruel revenge for what he considered her disappointing behaviour. He had somehow managed to achieve what might have seemed the impossible, getting the government to pass a new law, which benefitted him, and protected his fortune, but only after his death. He had waited for that death, knowing that he would have deprived his wife of a share of his fortune.

So Onassis died, fighting to the last, but broken by the death of his son, from which he never recovered. He had fallen in love with another Phaeton, Maria Callas, rejected at birth by her parents. His marriage, too, had been destroyed, both his children were at one time estranged from him, and his wife insulted to the point of divorce, subsequently embarking on two marriages, in a desperate effort to achieve the happiness she had lost. At the end she had been found dead, a year before Onassis, in the Hotel de Chanaleilles, in Paris, from an oedema of the lung, and Onassis had been so shaken that he could not, as with his son, attend the funeral.

With all his ambitions fulfilled, it seemed that this man had managed to make a complete failure of his life as far as happiness went.

Perhaps the cruellest thing that Onassis did to Maria Callas was to prevent her having the child she had always longed for. She was forty-three when she became pregnant, and he insisted on her having an abortion, saying that he would never see her again if she did not. Perhaps he deprived himself of a son who might have taken the place of the one he had lost.

A remarkable example of the Phaeton drive, Aristotle Socrates Onassis: religious; reckless enough to cheat on the sale of his cigarettes and be penalised, to risk prison by killing the blue-fin whales protected by international law, to falsify his records, to be indicted for fraud (it was only luck which saved him from actual imprisonment), penalised to the tune of 665,000 dollars and to suffer the loss of his reputation; capable of extreme austerity when he considered it necessary, even to the extent of sleeping only three hours a night on the way up; with an obsessive need for love and the achievement of total support, from the days of his early ten-year-long love-affair with the ten-years-older Ingeborg Dedichen, to his finding it with the devoted, ill-treated Maria Callas; aggressive enough to have made a fortune by the time he was twenty-three; given to bouts of depression; with an intense devotion to his own children; and with an extreme reaction to bereavement. Not at all a nice man, but a Phaeton of Phaetons.

He was buried, by his own wish, on Skorpios, next to his son.

CHAPTER 11

Charles Manson (1935 –   )

Murderers and criminals do not, of course, want to be discovered, put in prison, hanged, electrocuted, or subjected to any of the other penalties of the law. They are, none the less, frequently driven to commit crimes in order to achieve the power they long for; and a surprising number of those murderers and criminals were either bereaved in childhood or were bastards.

Ian Ball, the would-be assassin of Princess Anne, lost his father when he was five. Donald Nielson, the Black Panther, lost his father when he was eleven. Ronald Biggs, the "great" train robber, lost his mother when he was thirteen.

Even Lizzie Borden, of the well-known rhyme, was a Phaeton.

> Lizzie Borden took an axe,
> And gave her father forty whacks,
> When she saw what she had done
> She gave her mother forty-one.

In fact, it was not her mother, but her stepmother, whom she murdered. Her mother had died when she was two.

If Lord Lucan should ever be proved guilty of murder, he too would join our ranks, for his father died when he was thirteen.

James Hanratty also, known as "the A6 killer", the supposed murderer of Michael Gregsten, who inflicted severe injuries on his mistress Valerie Storie, as well as raping her, on Deadman's Hill, and who was executed for the crime, claimed that when he was a child he was locked in the cellar for days on end, and only had bread and water to drink. From the age of eight he had been sent to remand homes and Borstals, had done Corrective Training and was in line for Preventive Detention. He was devoted to his mother, who had no use for him – rejected him, in fact. He showed a penchant for older women, such as Mrs Louise Anderson, a middle-aged antique dealer, old enough to be his mother, clearly because he had been so deprived of love by his own mother.

The one I deal with here, however, is Charles Manson, who has been called the most dangerous man alive, and who founded a community called "The Family", and ordered his subjugated creatures to kill, simply for the sake of killing.

Manson was the bastard son of a sixteen-year-old girl named Kathleen Maddox, who later married a certain William Manson, who gave the boy his surname. Manson stated on numerous occasions that he never met his father, though his mother filed a bastardy suit in Boyd County, against one Colonel Scott, resident of Ashland, Kentucky. On the 19th April, 1937, she was awarded five dollars a month for the support of Charles Milles Manson. The colonel apparently did not honour his undertaking, and as late as 1940 Manson's mother was trying to file an attachment on his salary. It is believed that Colonel Scott died in 1954.

Not only was Manson a bastard, but his mother showed great indifference towards him. She would leave him with obliging neighbours, ostensibly for an hour, then disappear for days, or even weeks. In 1939 she went to gaol for armed robbery. While she was in prison, Manson lived with an aunt and uncle in McMechen, West Virginia. The aunt was very strict, and thought all pleasures sinful, but she gave him love. Torn between her and the mother who let him do anything he wanted as long as he did not bother her, Manson was caught in a tug-of-war between the two.

Let Manson speak for himself, in the words he used at his trial for mass murder.

"I never went to school, so I never growed up to read and write too good, so I have stayed in gaol, and I have stayed stupid, and I have stayed a child while I have watched your

133

world grow up, and then I look at the things you do, and I don't understand . . . You eat meat and you kill things that are better than you, and then you say how bad, and even killers, your children are. *You* made your children what they are. *These children that come at you with knives, they are your children. You taught them. I didn't teach them. I just tried to help them stand up.* Most of the people at the ranch that you call The Family were just people that you did not want, people that were alongside the road, that their parents had kicked out, that did not want to go to Juvenile Hall. So I did the best I could, and I took them upon my garbage dump and I told them this: that in love there is no wrong . . . I told them that anything they do for their brothers and sisters is good if they do it with a good thought . . . I was working at cleaning up my house, something that Nixon should have been doing. He should have been on the side of the road, picking up his children, but he wasn't. He was in the White House, sending them off to war . . . I don't understand you, but I don't try. I don't try to judge nobody. I know that the only person I can judge is me . . . But I know this: that in your own hearts and your own souls you are as much responsible for the Vietnam war as I am for killing these people . . . I can't judge any of you. I have no malice against you, and no ribbons for you. But I think that it is high time that you all start looking at yourselves, and judging the lie that you live in. I can't dislike you, but I will say this to you: you haven't got long before you are all going to kill yourselves because you are all crazy. And you can project it back at me . . . but I am only what lives inside each and every one of you. My father is the jailhouse. My father is your system . . . I am only what you made me. I am only a reflection of you. I have ate out of your garbage-cans to stay out of gaol. I have wore your second-hand clothes . . . I have done my best to get along in your world, and now you want to kill me, and I look at you, and then I say to myself, you want to kill *me*? Ha! I'm already dead, have been all my life.

"I've spent twenty-three years in tombs that you built. Sometimes I think about giving it back to you; sometimes I think about just jumping at you and letting you shoot me . . . If I could, I would jerk this microphone off and beat your brains out with it, because that is what you deserve. If I could get angry at you, I would try to kill every one of you.

If that's guilt, I accept it.

"These children, everything they done, they done for the love of their brother. If I showed them that I would do anything for my brother – including giving my life for my brother on the battlefield – and then they pick up their banner, and they go off and do what they do, that is not my responsibility.

"These children were finding themselves. What they did, if they did whatever they did, is up to them. They will have to explain that to you.

"It's all your fear. You look for something to project it on, and you pick out a little old scroungy nobody that eats out of a garbage-can, and that nobody wants, and that has been kicked out of the penitentiary, that has been dragged through every hell-hole that you can think of, and you drag him and put him in a court-room.

"You expect to break me? Impossible. You broke me years ago. You killed me years ago."

That was the excuse for programming teenaged girls through sex, sleeping with them, and telling the plain ones that they were beautiful; or, if one of them had a father-fixation, letting her imagine that he was her father. This was the man who used drugs to put them at his mercy; and who sent them out to kill.

It was the murder of Sharon Tate and her unborn child and four others which made world headlines; and which, after months of frustration, would be traced to Manson and what he called The Family. He called himself Jesus Christ, and his "family" seemed to accept him, and worship him, unbelievably, as a kind of Christ-like figure. Yet he even encouraged one girl to the point where she was prepared to kill her parents.

When Charles was eight, in 1942, his mother, paroled from gaol, reclaimed him, and he lived with her in run-down hotel rooms, always finding newly-introduced, heavy-drinking "uncles". His mother also drank heavily. When he was twelve, nearly thirteen, in 1947, his mother tried to get him into a foster-home, but failed. The court, however, sent him to the Gibault School for Boys in Terre Haute, Indiana. After ten months he ran away, and went to his mother. She didn't want him. He ran away again. He broke into a grocer's, and stole money to rent a room with. Soon he was breaking into other stores, and stealing whatever he could, including, among other

135

things, a bicycle. He was sent back to the juvenile centre in Indianapolis, escaped next day, was apprehended, and sent, under the misapprehension that he was a Catholic, to Father Flanagan's Boys Town.

Four days after his arrival he and another boy, Blackie Nielson, stole a car and fled to the home of the boy's uncle in Peoria, Illinois. On the way they committed two armed robberies, one in a grocery store, the other in a gambling casino. At the age of only thirteen, Manson had committed his first armed robberies. Soon, encouraged by Blackie's uncle, they were committing other robberies – once stealing fifteen hundred dollars from a grocery store and receiving a hundred and fifty dollars from Blackie's uncle as a reward.

They were caught two weeks later, trying to repeat a burglary, and implicated the uncle. Still only thirteen, Charles Manson was sent to the Indiana School for Boys at Plainfield. In the three years he was there, he ran away eighteen times. At last, in February 1951, he and two other sixteen-year-olds escaped and headed for California, stealing cars for transportation, committing burglaries in gas stations to get money – fifteen or twenty, according to Manson – before a road-block set up for a robbery suspect ended in their re-arrest; and, on March 9th, 1951, he was once more confined, this time in the National Training School for Boys, in Washington, DC, to remain until he reached twenty-one.

He was given many aptitude and intelligence tests. He had, they said, an IQ of 109; was illiterate; had an average intelligence, some mechanical aptitude and manual dexterity, and his favourite subject was said to be music. The case-worker reported of this boy: "Charles is a sixteen-year-old boy who has had an unfavourable family life, if it can be called family life at all," and, he pointed out, he was "aggressively anti-social". The psychiatrist, Dr Block, who examined him on June 29th, 1951, noted "the marked degree of rejection, instability, and psychic trauma" in his background. He noted, too, his sense of inferiority in relation to his mother, so pronounced, Dr Block commented, that Manson constantly felt it necessary "to suppress any thoughts about her". Because, he said, of his diminutive size, his illegitimacy, and the lack of parental love, "he is constantly striving for status with the other boys".

About to be released to live with his aunt, Manson ruined his chances. Shortly after his seventeenth birthday, in November, he held a razor-blade against another boy's throat while he committed sodomy with him. He lost ninety-seven days of remission, and, on January 18th, 1952, was transferred to the Federal Reformatory at Petersburg, Virginia. There he was considered dangerous, and by August he had committed eight serious disciplinary offences, three of them involving homosexual acts – his report stating, "Manson definitely has homosexual and assaultive tendencies". Classified as safe only under supervision, he was transferred to a more secure institution, the Federal Reformatory at Chillicothe, Ohio, and was sent there on September 22nd, 1952.

Suddenly, then, Manson changed, began to behave much better, and in January, 1954, he was actually given a Meritorious Service Award, because of his educational advancement, and his good record in repairing and maintaining vehicles. Far more important to him, he was granted parole on May 8th, 1954. He was then nineteen. He lived with his uncle and aunt for a time – a condition of his parole – then moved to live with his mother.

Manson married a seventeen-year-old McMechen girl, Rosalie Jean Willis, a waitress in the local hospital, in January 1955. Working as a bus-boy, service station attendant, or parking lot attendant, he scraped a poor living – and stole and sold cars. He himself admitted to stealing six. He drove at least two across state lines. His wife was by then pregnant, and he made much of that when he was arrested and detained, calling her "the best wife a guy could want". "I didn't realise how good she was until I got in her," he said. "I beat her at times. She writes to me all the time. She is going to have a baby."

He told the doctor examining him for a psychiatric report, Dr Edwin McNiel, that he had spent so much time in institutions that he had never really learned much of what "real life on the outside was all about". Now that he had a wife, he said, and was about to become a father, it had become important to him to try to be on the outside and be with his wife, and that she was the only person he had ever cared about in his life.

The doctor commented: "It is evident that he has an unstable personality, and that his environmental influences throughout most of his life have not been good. . . In my opinion, this boy is a poor risk for probation; on the other hand, he has spent nine years in institutions with apparently little benefit except to take him out of circulation. With the incentive of a wife and probable fatherhood, it is possible that he might be able to straighten himself out. I would, therefore, respectfully suggest to the court that probation be considered in this case under careful supervision."

So the court gave Manson five years' probation, on November 7th, 1955. But soon he had spoiled it all – he had taken a car across the border and abandoned it in Fort Lauderdale, Florida. The hearing of the charge was due, still with excellent chances of his getting probation, when, foolishly, he ran away; a warrant was issued for his arrest; he was picked up in Indianapolis, on March 14th, 1956, and was returned to Los Angeles; his probation was revoked; and he was sentenced to three years' imprisonment in San Pedro, California. By the time Charles Manson Junior was born, his father was back in gaol – and another Phaeton had come into the world.

At first his wife moved in with his mother in Los Angeles, and visited him every week – more often than his mother. But by March 1957 her visits had ceased, and she had gone to live with another man. He tried to escape, was caught and indicted, pleaded guilty, and got another five years' probation added to his sentence. Soon his wife filed papers for divorce, and it was made final in 1958. She had custody of Charles Manson Junior, remarried, and, wisely, had no further contact with Manson or his mother.

He was released on September 30th, 1958, on five years' parole. Soon he had a new occupation – pimping for one Frank Peters, a Malibu bartender and known procurer, with whom he was living. From pimping he went on to attempting to cash a forged United States Treasury cheque for thirty-seven dollars and fifty cents in a Los Angeles supermarket, to pleading guilty to avoid another charge for theft from a mail-box, conviction and a ten-year sentence – then to suspension of the sentence so that he could marry one Leona, a known prostitute, otherwise known as Candy Stevens, who lied about being pregnant by him, and convinced the judge of their intention to marry. By December he had been arrested twice, for "grand theft" of an automobile, and for the use of stolen credit cards, but both charges were dismissed for lack of evidence, and by November he was taking Leona, alias Candy, and a girl named Elizabeth to Lordsburg, New Mexico, to be prostitutes. Re-arrested on two charges, Manson, probably in order to prevent Leona from testifying against him, married her. Then the

138

nineteen-year-old daughter of one Ralph Samuels from Detroit, who had come to California in response to an advertisement for an airline stewardess school, only to learn, after paying for a course, that it was a fraud, had the misfortune to meet Manson. Not only did he drug and rape her room-mate, and con her into investing her savings in his non-existent company – he was masquerading as the President of "Three-Star Enterprises, Nile Club, Radio and Television Productions" – but he also got Jo Anne pregnant. More, it was an ectopic pregnancy, the foetus growing in one of the Fallopian tubes, and the nineteen-year-old nearly died.

He disappeared; a warrant was issued; and on April 28th a federal grand jury indicted him. Arrested in June in Laredo, Texas, after police had picked up one of his girls on a prostitution charge, he was brought back to Los Angeles. On June 23rd, 1960, the court ruled that he had violated his probation, and ordered him back to prison, to serve out his ten-year sentence. The judge, who had granted him probation the previous September, observed, "If there ever was a man who demonstrated himself completely unfit for probation, he is it." Ungrammatical, but correct.

Manson remained for a year in the Los Angeles County Jail, and appealed; the appeal failed; and in June 1961 he was sent to the United States Penitentiary at McNeil Island, Washington. He was twenty-six.

Manson claimed as his "religion" that he was a Scientologist. By the time he was twenty-eight, the prison report on him ran: "Charles Manson has a tremendous drive to call attention to himself. Generally he is unable to succeed in positive acts, therefore he often resorts to negative behaviour to satisfy this drive. In his effort to 'find' himself, Manson peruses different religious philosophies, e.g. Scientology and Buddhism; however, he never remains long enough with any given teachings to reap meaningful benefits. Even these attempts and his cries for help represent a desire for attention, with only superficial meaning. Manson has had more than the usual amount of staff attention, yet there is little indication of change in his demeanor. In view of his deep-seated personality problems . . . continuation of institutional treatment is recommended." On October 1st, 1963, prison officials were informed, "according to court papers received in this institution, that Manson was married to a Leona Mason in 1959 in the State of

California, and that the marriage had been terminated by divorce on April 10th, 1963, in Denver, Colorado, on grounds of mental cruelty and conviction of a felony. One child, Charles Luther Manson, is alleged to have been of this union" – the only mention, in any of Manson's records, of his second marriage and second child.

So on it went, with adverse reports on his progress, and constant references to his instability, his need to call attention to himself, his emotional insecurity, and his tendency to involve himself "in various fanatical interests". These "fanatical interests" ranged, the report repeated, from Scientology to an addiction to guitar-playing, and to an obsession with the Beatles, the four Liverpool young men who were taking America by storm. He believed that, given the chance, he would be "much bigger than the Beatles", said one report, and, in fact, he believed he would be an enormous success playing the guitar and the drums, and began writing songs – eighty or ninety of them in one year, which he hoped to sell when released. "He shall," the report ended, "need a great deal of help in the transition from institution to the free world."

At last, in 1966, he was released; and his final report read: "Manson is about to complete his ten-year term. He has a pattern of criminal behavior and confinement that dates from his teen [sic] years. This pattern is of instability whether in free society or a structured institutional community. Little can be expected in the way of change in his attitude, behavior, or mode of conduct." Now, it added, he was no longer an advocate of Scientology; but "has come to worship his guitar and music". He had no plans for the future, as he said he had nowhere to go.

The morning Charles Manson was to be freed, he begged the authorities to let him remain in prison. Prison, he said, had become his home. He did not think he could adjust to the world outside. Not unnaturally, his request was refused, and he was released during the morning of March 21st, 1967, and given transportation to Los Angeles, where he asked permission, and received it, to go to San Francisco. There, that spring, "The Family" was born. Charles Manson was thirty-two years old, and had spent seventeen of them in institutions. Burglar, car-thief, forger, and pimp, he was not yet a massmurderer. That was to come.

Living from hand to mouth, playing his guitar in the streets, soon he had met and moved in with an unattractive librarian, Mary Brunner, aged twenty-three. Then he brought in one girl after another to live with them, until there were eighteen in all. "The Family" had been created. And, somehow, Manson developed a control over his followers so all-encompassing that he could ask them to violate the most terrible of all taboos – he could order them to kill, and they would do it. Some believed that drugs lay behind his power. But the psychiatrist, Dr David Smith, believed that sex, not drugs, was the reason for his control over his followers. At any rate, Manson used both to bring his so-called Family into an extraordinary sub-jugation to him, so that they would do anything he asked of them. "Eliminating middle-class morality", as one follower of his called it, or making them dependent on drugs – it was all grist to his mill.

Before long Mary Brunner had a child by Manson, Michael Manson, with the whole Family watching the birth, and Manson biting through the umbilical cord himself. Mary Brunner would always be fanatically devoted to Manson.

During the court hearing, when Manson was being tried for the murder of Sharon Tate and her unborn child and four others, it became clear that The Family regarded Manson as a Christ-like person. Susan Atkins (alias Sadie Mae Glutz) her-self said: "He represented a Jesus-Christ-like person to me." Sometimes Manson called himself the Devil, sometimes Satan, sometimes Soul, and there is no doubt that his followers regarded him as a Satan or a Christ, and that they would do anything he wished them to do, without remorse. Soon they had killed thirteen people: Center Parker; Gary Hinman; John Philip Haught, a young boy; Charles Denton (or Tex, for Texas) Watson; Steven Grogan; Donald Jerome (Shorty) Shea; "Bruce" and Bobby Beausoleil, plus the five murdered at the ranch. The murder of Shorty, or Donald Jerome Shea, was particularly brutal. He had annoyed Manson extremely because he had married a black topless dancer, and Manson was preju-diced against inter-racial marriages. They demanded money from this thirty-six-year-old cowboy. When he gave trouble they killed him, cut his head off, and then cut his arms off, leaving him, as one of the Manson gang put it – "in nine pieces, and his head and his arms were off".

In all, the Family seemed to have committed between thirty-five and forty murders – and all horrifying. If it was horrible to kill the eight-months-pregnant Sharon Tate, stabbing her six-teen times, it was also appalling to stab the woman who tried to escape across the lawn – stabbing *her*, in fact, fifty-two times.

After a trial lasting two and a half months and costing a quarter of a million dollars, Manson was convicted.

"We, the jury . . . having found the defendant Charles Manson guilty of murder in the first degree as charged in Count 1 of the Indictment, do now fix the penalty as death."

Three girls, too, were found guilty, and condemned to death. Poignantly, Sharon Tate's father, Colonel Paul Tate, said, regarding the death sentence, "That's what we wanted. That's what we expected. But there's no jubilation in something like this, no sense of satisfaction. It's more a feeling that justice has been done. Naturally I wanted the death penalty. They took my daughter and my grandchild."

The Manson girls, waiting outside the court, had threatened to burn themselves to death by pouring gasoline over themselves and igniting it if he was found guilty. In the end they merely shaved their heads, being a good deal kinder to themselves than they, and Manson, had been to others.

At one point The Family robbed a store selling guns and ammunition. It was believed that their objective was to release Manson from gaol by staging a commando-type raid on the court-house on the day Manson appeared in court. In fact, they had, according to one member of The Family, intended to hijack an aeroplane and kill one passenger every hour until Manson and all the other imprisoned Family members were released.

Manson, it has been pointed out, had a great admiration for Hitler, calling him "a tuned-in guy who levelled the karma of the Jews". Both were small men; both suffered deep wounds to their egos in youth; both were conscious of the stigma of illegitimacy, Manson because he was a bastard, Hitler because his father was, until his grandmother later married his grand-father. Both were vagrants for years; both were frustrated, and rejected, artists; both liked animals more than people; both also believed that the blood of the people they despised ran in their veins – Hitler was seriously, and probably correctly, worried that he had a Jewish ancestor, Manson that he might have had a black father. Both surrounded themselves with unctuous flatterers; both used the weaknesses of others to their own needs; both programmed their followers through endless repetition; both realised and exploited the psychological impact of fear; both had a favourite epithet for those they hated, *"Schweinehund"* for Hitler, "pigs" for Manson; both had eyes which their followers described as "hypnotic"; both had charisma and an incredible ability to influence others. Generals, as Vincent Bugliosi, the prosecutor in the Tate-La Bianca trials, has pointed out, went to Hitler to dissuade him from what they considered insane military plans, and left him as victims of his persuasion. Dean Moorehouse went to Spahn Ranch to kill Manson for stealing his daughter, Ruth Anne, and ended up worshipping. (It is hard to believe, looking at pictures of Manson, this short, unimpressive, dirty little murderer, that this could be so, but, it seems, it was.) Like Hitler, Manson believed that women are inferior to men; that the white race is superior to all other races; and that it is not necessarily wrong to kill. Kill they both did, believing that mass murder was permissible, and right, even desirable, if it furthered their wishes, or the attainment of some grand plan. Hitler's was the Third Reich; Manson's was Helter-Skelter – a vast difference in kind. If Manson, however, had had the opportunity, he believed, he would have become another Hitler – certainly no qualms about murdering huge masses of people would have deterred him.

Manson, it is said, bragged that he had committed thirty-five murders. It is true that when, on October 13th, 1968, two women, Clida Delaney and Nancy Warren, were found dead, beaten and strangled with leather thongs a few miles south of Ukiah, California, there were several members of the Manson Family in the area at the time, and two days later Manson moved the whole Family from Spahn to Barker Ranch. There was probably a link. But it was never proved.

Then, at about 3.30 in the morning of December 30th, 1968, seventeen-year-old Marina Hake, daughter of writer Hans Hake, was abducted outside her mother's West Hollywood home as she was returning from a date with a boy-friend. Her body was found on New Year's Day, off Mulholland, near Bowmont Drive, and the cause of death was multiple stab-wounds in the neck and chest. It was rumoured that Marina had been acquainted with one or more members of the Family; and Manson was in Los Angeles on that December 30th, returning to Barker next day. Once again there seemed to be a connection, and once again the murder remains unsolved.

On the night of 27th May, 1969, Darwin Orell Scott was hacked to death in his Ashland, Kentucky, apartment. The killing was so savage that the victim, who was stabbed nineteen times, was pinned to the floor with a butcher's knife. This sixty-four-year-old Darwin Scott was the brother of Colonel Scott, the man alleged to be Charles Manson's father. Manson, it seems, was in California on the day of Scott's murder – and had appeared in the area with several female followers, calling himself "Preacher", and dispensing free drugs to the local teenagers. Manson claimed to have moved from Death Valley to Spahn Ranch, probably a deliberate alibi. The person to whom he wrote did not receive his letter until seven days after it had, supposedly, been written. That murder, too, remains unsolved. Was it a deliberate attempt to revenge himself on the Scott family? His father had, it is believed, died, in 1954; but Manson might have decided to kill his brother, as second best.

Early on the morning of 17th July, 1969, sixteen-year-old Mark Walts left his parents' home in Chatsworth and hitchhiked to the Santa Monica Pier to go fishing. His fishing pole was later found on the pier. His body was found at about 4 a.m. on 18th July, off Topanga Canyon Boulevard, a short distance from Mulholland. His face and head were badly bruised, and he had been shot three times in the chest. Walt's brother was convinced Manson was responsible, telephoned him, and said, "I know you done my brother in, and I'm going to kill you." He didn't; and that murder, too, remains unsolved.

Nor did Manson's arrest stop the murders. In one month alone Manson and his murderous Family had slaughtered nine people – Gary Hinman; Steve Parent; Jay Sebring; Abigail Folger; Wojiciech, or Voytck, Frykowski; Sharon Tate; Leno La Bianca; Rosemary La Bianca; and Donald Shea – and they went on and on. John Philip Haught (known as "Zero"), it was claimed, shot himself when playing Russian roulette. Linda Baldwin (or "Little Patty"), whose real name was Madaline Joan Cottage, said she had been lying on the bed next to him when it happened. The others, Bruce Davis, Cathy Gillies, and Susan Bartell ("Country Sue"), all told the officers they had heard the shot. They probably all lied. No one plays Russian roulette with a fully loaded gun; the case was clear of fingerprints; and there were no prints on the gun, either of the dead boy, or of anyone else. Further, a man contacted the police a

144

week later, claiming that he had been present when Zero was shot. Zero, he said, had not committed suicide. He had been murdered. He refused to give his name. His interrogator gave him twenty-five dollars to get to Marin County, in Northern California, and said there would be more if he returned to identify Zero's murderer. He never saw him again.

On November 16th, 1969, the body of a young girl was found dumped over an embankment at Mulholland and Bowmont Drive near Laurel Canyon, in almost the same spot where Marina Hake's body had been found. Brunette, in her late teens, five feet nine, weighing one hundred and fifteen pounds, she had been stabbed a hundred and fifty-seven times in the chest and throat. She was identified as Sherry Ann Cooper. In fact, she was not Sherry Ann Cooper, who had fled Barker Ranch at the same time as Barbara Hoyt, and was, fortunately, still alive. The victim, who had been dead less than a day, became Jane Doe 59, in police files. Her identity is still unknown. Was she present at the time of the murder, and then killed so that she could not talk? That murder is still unsolved.

On November 21st, 1969, the bodies of James Sharp, fifteen, and Doreen Gaul, nineteen, were found in an alley in downtown Los Angeles. The two teenagers had been killed elsewhere, with a long-bladed knife or bayonet, then dumped there. Each had been stabbed over fifty times. Again, the police believed that a Family member was involved; and, again, the murder remains unsolved. According to several sources, Doreen Gaul was a former girl-friend of a Manson Family member, Bruce Davis, who, like Manson, had been a Scientologist. Both James Sharp and Doreen Gaul were Scientologists. Davis's whereabouts at the time of the murders of James Sharp, Doreen Gaul and Jane Doe 59 were not known. He had disappeared shortly after being questioned in connection with the death of "Zero", that is, John Philip Haught. Both James Sharp and Doreen Gaul were Scientologists.

On December 1st, 1969, Jael Dean Pugh, the husband of a Family member known as Sandy Collins Good, was found with his throat slit in a hotel room in London. Local police decided the death was a suicide. On learning of this, the District Attorney from Inyo County, Frank Fowles, made official enquiries, specifically asking Interpol to check visas to determine whether one Bruce Davis was in England at the time. Scotland Yard replied: "It has been established that

Davis is recorded as embarking at London Airport for the United States of America on 25th April 1969, while holding United States passport 612 2568. At this time he gave his address as Dormer Cottage, Felbridge, Surrey. This address is owned by the Scientology Movement and houses followers of this organisation. The local police are unable to give any information concerning Davis but they understand that he has visited our country more recently than April 1969. However, this is not borne out by our official records."

Davis did not reappear until February, 1970. Then he was picked up at Spahn Ranch, questioned briefly, on Inyo County grand theft auto charges, then released. Indicted for the Hinman murder, he vanished again; reappearing in December 1970, after the mysterious disappearance of Ronald Hughes; and when he gave himself up he was accompanied by Family member, Brenda McCann.

Of three other murders, two occurred as late as 1972. On November 8th, 1972, a hiker near the Russian River resort community of Guerneville, in Northern California, saw a hand protruding from the ground. When police exhumed the body, it was found to be that of a young man wearing the dark blue tunic of a Marine dress uniform. He had been shot, and decapitated. James T. Willet, twenty-six, a former Marine, from Los Angeles County, had been murdered. When police saw his station wagon parked in front of a house at 720 West Flora Street, they were refused entry, broke in, arrested two men and two women, and confiscated a number of pistols and shotguns. Both women had the Manson Family sign – a cross – on their foreheads. They were Priscilla Cooper, aged twenty-one, and Nancy Pitman, also known as Brenda McCann, twenty. A third woman called, and was given a ride to the house, and the police also arrested Lynette Fromme (Squeaky), aged twenty-four, the leader of the Family in Manson's absence. The two men were Michael Monfort, twenty-four, and James Craig, thirty-three, both state prison escapees, wanted for a number of armed robberies in various parts of California. Both had "AB" tattooed on their left breasts – standing for the Aryan Brotherhood, described as "a cult of white prison inmates, dedicated largely to racism, but also involved in hoodlum activities, including murder contracts". The police also noticed freshly turned earth in the basement, obtained a search-warrant, dug, and exhumed the body of Lauren Willett, nineteen. She had been shot once in the head, not long after the identity of her slain husband had been revealed on news broadcasts. Questioned, Priscilla Cooper claimed that Laura Willett had killed herself "playing Russian roulette". The three women and two men were, however, charged with her murder. Due to go on trial in May 1973, on April 2nd four of the five entered guilty pleas. Michael Monfort got seven years to life in a state prison; James Craig got consecutive sentences of five years and two years, for being an accessory after the fact of murder, and for possessing an illegal weapon, that is, a sawn-off shotgun; and both girls were sent to a state prison for up to five years. Lynette Fromme, or Squeaky, was released for lack of sufficient evidence to link her to Lauren Willett's murder; and, once again, she went back to assume leadership of the Manson Family in his absence. Subsequently Monfort and an accomplice, William Goucher, twenty-three, pleaded guilty to the second-degree murder of James Willett, and were sent to a state prison for from five years to life. Craig pleaded guilty to being an accessory after the fact of the murder, and was given another prison term of up to five years. Motive? Unknown. But Lauren Willett was probably killed after learning of the murder of her husband from the news broadcasts to keep her from going to the police and revealing his intended destination.

Why was James Willett murdered? The official police theory is that he himself may have been about to inform the police about the robberies the group had committed. On the other hand, the Willetts may have known too much about another murder – that of Ronald Hughes, the defence attorney, killed during the trial itself.

The autopsy findings were: "Nature of death: undetermined. Cause of death: undetermined". However, one of the Manson girls, Sandra Good, admitted on film that when she and Mary Brunner learned of the Tate murders, while still in the Los Angeles County Gaol, they had decided to retaliate, and said that "Hughes was the first of the retaliation murders". To date, she said, they had killed "thirty-five to forty people".

So, determined to create a powerful world of hangers-on, prepared to obey his every whim, even to killing for him, Manson had surrounded himself with drop-outs, those with a deep hostility towards society and everything it stood for. By the use of drugs; by acting as a surrogate father to girls at odds with their fathers; by sex, he exercised an extraordinary control over his Family. He always took a smaller dose of LSD than the others, so that he could remain in command. He used repetition, too, constantly preaching and lecturing to the boys and girls in his power. "You can convince anybody of anything," he himself said in court, "if you just push it at them all of the time. They may not believe it a hundred per cent, but they still draw opinions from it, especially if they have no other information to draw their opinions from."

So, hammering at his isolated followers, cut off from the rest of society, and never seeing a newspaper, he created this extraordinary kingdom for himself – totally at odds with the world outside. He used sex, but he also used love: a strange love, but love, none the less, in their eyes; and he used fear. He created, in effect, a band of schizophrenics, encouraging their subconscious hatred, their submerged violence. They stole, they became prostitutes, they committed burglaries and armed robberies, and murder – all for him. He used religion, too, implying that *he* was Christ, coming to earth again. He had his twelve apostles – and he had his Judases, Sadie and Linda. He also used music, not only because he was a frustrated musician, but because music often engages young people more effectively than other devices. He used his superior intelligence – for he was older, brighter, more articulate, far cleverer, and more insidious than his followers. Even so, it is hard to understand how he could attain such a command over their minds that they would murder, willingly, if he ordered them to do so.

Charles Manson had been sentenced to death. But on February 18th, 1972, the California State Supreme Court announced that it had voted by a majority to abolish the death penalty in the State of California. So Manson escaped execution; and got life imprisonment instead. In October 1972 he was transferred to the maximum security adjustment centre at Folsom Prison in Northern California – "a prison within a prison", for "problem inmates", because of his "hostile and belligerent attitude". He lived in fear of his life even there, aware that convicts would be only too happy to stab him; for even they objected to his having killed a pregnant woman, and bore it against him.

So there we have a most horrible Phaeton in this bastard, showing great superstitiousness, that is, a predilection for occultism, Scientology and science fiction; with a strong

148

interest in religion, from Buddhism to Catholicism, leading, extraordinarily enough, to his claiming to be both Christ and Satan, in turns; a certain austerity, as when he was able to live for long periods on hardly anything, and when he pleaded to be allowed to remain in prison; recklessness of unbelievable proportions; an obsessive need for love, as evidenced in his determination to surround himself with the young people he called, interestingly enough, The Family; and a tremendous drive for power, though of a most undesirable kind. He lost the children of his first marriage to his divorced wife, but, it seems, was very fond of the child he delivered himself, biting its umbilical cord. That such a creature could attain such power, even over such drop-outs, is frightening.

As I finished this chapter, by coincidence, an interview with Manson in gaol was shown on British television – even before it was shown on American television. Jaunty, self-opinionated, conceited, and arrogant, there seems no change for the better in this abominable creature. It is to be hoped that he will never leave his prison.

CHAPTER 12

Letters from an Anonymous Phaeton

In this chapter I publish extracts from letters from a Phaeton who shall be nameless, but who has been corresponding with me for over eleven years, from the day when he first read a review of *The Fiery Chariot* in the *Sunday Express*, until my embarking on this book. They will illustrate the intensity of the will to succeed, against all the odds.

The first letter I received was the following, dated 20th December, 1970.

"20/12/70

"I was quite intrigued to read the review of your book, *The Fiery Chariot*, in the *Sunday Express* of 29th November. You see, I too had the same experience as Ramsay MacDonald, except that in my case I was shown a policeman, from the top of a bus. I was told too, 'That's him who was father to you'! I was then a very small boy, but the memory has lived with me all my life, and I am now a man of forty-six years.

"I can well understand the idea of the Phaeton Complex, and indeed, when I read of it, I suddenly acquired a far greater understanding of *myself* than I have ever known before. It has explained a whole host of things about myself, which formerly caused me to lie awake at nights, and wonder just what it was that made me drive myself on so. People such as I are driven by an inborn compulsion, to get to the top; to 'make it', and to leave the rest in no doubt that you *have* made it!

"I don't know whether this is a blessing or a curse, I only know for sure that *everything* in life is a challenge to us, and that we can rarely find contentment. I would say that it all springs from the fact that we all feel in some way inferior to our fellows; and indeed when the facts of one's birth are revealed, it is rammed once more into one's Consciousness that we started the great race of Life one pace behind the rest. *This* salient fact is the one that haunts us in everything we do. It make us arrogant, and hard to live with in our families. It makes us aggressive and domineering in our profession, and we show it as we strive to outdo our fellows. In victory, we can be the most generous of people, but in defeat the most bitter. Rarely can we find fault with ourselves, but always seek to blame the fault upon the odd circumstances of our birth. We would never admit this latter, but in our heart of hearts it is so. I, for one, get terribly frustrated if something I have set my mind on should elude me, and every side-swipe of Fate sets me to brooding, and planning afresh. All my life it has been this way, and one always laments about how it *might* have been if only one had had the advantage of a proper start. But, thank God, we are also born optimists. However Fate slaps us down, we are always ready to start all over again, and make bigger and better plans than we did before. I might add that, when we are successful, we are *jubilant*, and our benevolence knows no bounds! Oddly enough, it is only men that this applies to, for it is not quite so difficult for a woman. Girls get married, and their names change along with their circumstances. But boys are stuck with it, all their lives, and they feel it, oh so *deeply* they feel it. You would be truly surprised just how many times a boy can die, of sheer shame and embarrassment, as he tries to make his way through life, with this tag on him. It comes out in all kinds of ways, just when you begin thinking that it doesn't matter any more, and each time is worse than the last! *This*, then, is the basis of the Phaeton Complex, and the seed of the driving force behind such men of whom you have written.

"I hope that you don't mind my writing to you, but I am, in a small way, a Writer myself, and I think that it will please you to know that you have struck a very, very true note in what you have written, in *The Fiery Chariot*. And, also, you have awakened at least *one* man to the reason for his odd way of

151

living. My Good Wishes to you, and a Very Merry Xmas and New Year!

"PS: If you are ever up this way, it would be a rare pleasure to meet you, and to discuss this Phaeton Complex with you. I am sure that we would both find it most absorbing. I know I would!"

"1/10/72

"I was reading through your two old letters to me (which I cherish!), and I thought that a wee note might not be amiss. Just to let you know that your particular Phaeton is still battling on, against the odds. By all the rules, I ought to be able to take it easy, and sink into the comfortable rut of my local contemporaries. My fine house improves each summer, and my family are doing well. Life is reasonably good, all round. *But*, I feel like a mouse in a plastic bag, into which I dutifully hop every Monday at 7.30 a.m., and run around performing, until they let me out on Friday night, at 4 p.m. From then, until Monday, I can be *ME*!!! I have always hoped that I might have the chance to see you one day, but without any luck up to date. Is there no chance yet of your coming up this far North? There's always room, and a welcome, in our house, if you do. I am still writing my poems, and little stories; and have three chapters of a book done. But I don't have the chance to meet people, who could help me to find that vital first opening that I need, to get my work on the market. Oh, I have a library in my mind, yes; and enough material to keep a scriptwriter busy for years. But I need to *talk* to someone . . . *anyone* . . . who will listen to me, and be able to evaluate the worth of it all. I would be willing to come down to London, if only I can meet a producer/publisher/writer, who would be willing to just do that! I have to learn techniques, and I would be so willing, to work for *nothing* for a week, alongside any experienced writer, just to prove that I can do it. I *know* that this is somehow my natural bent, and I have to fight hard to find an opening for myself, somewhere. Time slips under one's feet, and another year goes by, and *still* the mouse hops around his little bag, with no hope of finding the exit he has so long looked for. Sure, one keeps on writing, and hoping. But even a circus elephant needs a bun, if he is to perform at his best! For a Phaeton, this is frustration to the *N'th* Degree, as *you* will understand. Above all else, we *must* be going forward, towards success and nothing less! (Reading that, I feel that you will be thinking, 'We *do* have a *right* one here!' But I think that you will also understand.) In short, I am *busting* to *create*, but haven't the very slightest chance to do so. Mrs Iremonger, as the first-ever chronicler of the Phaeton, do you, *please,* know of anyone who would listen/tape-record/read with me; or, in any other way, help me to find the break which I so desperately need? I will travel anywhere, to this end. I have a most comfortable home, a small and *admirable* Family, and my finances are quite sound. I have a job, which brings in a wage, so I am not wanting in that sense! My need is for mental stimulation, and *the* very necessary thing for a Phaeton, *that chance* to prove my ability to use the talents, that *we* are specially given, by a Providence that seeks always to redress the balance, but leaves it to us to find the way, and, in so doing, sows the seeds of our eternal frustration!! But Phaetons ever thrive, and strive, and battle on.

"In conclusion, my Good Wishes to you, and to your husband also!"

"27/3/76

"I thought that you might be interested to know that your particular Phaeton is still striving. As you have said, the drives from inside never let you rest and be content with the mediocre in life. It must be all, or nothing, against whatever odds that Fate might throw up. For example, not long ago, I took two "O" levels along with the kids in the local High School, just to prove to myself that I could do it. I am still writing, although the longed-for break still eludes me. However, I *know*, within myself, that it is just a matter of time. I know also that I was born to succeed, and that my particular hour has yet to be. When we are young, we rant against our fate, but as one grows older so one acquires wisdom, and insight, and one can almost reach out and grasp the plan. Almost, but not quite! I always liken it to passing down a hotel corridor, where one passes an open door without looking in. Only when we have passed it do we realise that within that door was the whole secret of Creation and the true source of Light. But, when we hasten to go back there, the door is shut, and we cannot discern *which* door it was anyway. I have often had this experience, when falling asleep, and have immediately awakened. But, like the door in the corridor, that tiny Psychic breakthrough is lost.

It is a strange fact, however, that I have this experience quite a lot, and each time it gets stronger, so one day I shall find the magic source! The main purpose of my letter, Ma'am, is to let you know that I shall be in London, from the 26th April, for about a week or so, and would very much like to meet and talk with you. I am not at all certain, yet, where I shall be staying, but am hoping that a friend of mine will be able to put me up in his flat, in Upper Berkeley Street.

"I am in London on business, which I am sure will be of great interest to one who can write a book like *The Fiery Chariot*! In the great tradition of the Phaetons, with their 'bubbling brains', I am also an Inventor, which may not surprise you, if it surprises others. I thought up a project, which involves literally re-creating the famous 'Cresta Bob-sleigh Run' in plastic. I got myself a partner and together we have secured the Patent Rights for it, in the UK. We have had a lot of publicity in the Scottish press, and indeed we are to be featured in next week's *People's Journal*. I have also been on the BBC, giving a wee talk about the project, and we have roused a lot of interest. The upshot of it all is that we have been invited to take part in an exhibition of Industrial Design from Scotland, which opens at the Design Centre in the Haymarket, on 26th April. I have made a rather splendid table model of the Sleigh Run, which we are to bring down with us, and which will be the centre-piece of our stand. So, your very own Phaeton will be all Kilted and Sporraned, and 'on parade', to try to sell our idea to any interested parties! The actual organisers of the Exhibition are quite thrilled with our unusual exhibit, and have told us that they will be bringing foreign and British business men and financiers to meet us. So you will gather that I am praying hard that we might be successful in our venture. From what we have learned so far, we could be on a 'winner', since there is a world-wide market for our scheme. The amount of money we could make quite frightens me! But, knowing what it was like to have nothing at all, in my childhood, I am willing to be frightened. It is a fact that, if we can sell the idea, neither I nor my partner will have any financial worries ever afterwards.

"If it comes off, *then* you will see the Phaeton take off, and rise like the Phoenix from the ashes! I have so many other plans, all waiting to be fulfilled, and, like I said, it is only a matter of Time. I don't know about other Phaetons, but this one is a visionary, and a Psychic, and possesses a strong sense of Destiny.

"I have a new collection of Verse, which I know will interest you, and which I will be bringing down with me anyway. And also I can bring along photographs of my family and I. My son, who is twenty-eight now, is presently a Sergeant in the Scots Guards, and is at Chelsea Bks. My daughter is twenty-two years old, and is to be married, on 24th April, when I shall have the great pleasure of wearing Highland Dress, and leading my daughter down the aisle behind a Black Watch piper. (Ah, what a comforting thought it is, to me, to know that they both have the right kind of Birth Certificate!!) I thank God that neither of my children will ever know the bitter recriminations, the railing against Fate, or the silent tears in the night, that haunt the young Phaeton from birth to manhood. The way, from darkness to the Light, is a long and lonely trail. But I see the Light, at last, in the far, far distance. Life gets better with each passing year.

"In conclusion, Ma'am, my Good Wishes to you and yours."

"1/5/76

"Many thanks for your very kind letter of 2nd April. Unfortunately, we have been informed (only a week before the event!!) that we have been 'pruned-out' from the Exhibition. Naturally I am bitterly disappointed about it, but there is nothing that we can do, since the organisers are at the London end, and the whole thing is in their hands. But, on reflection, this is the way life goes for a true Phaeton, you know. Life begins as a battle against the odds, and we have more than our share of pitfalls and barriers to battle against. So each time I meet a barrier, I just pick myself up, dust myself off, and get right back in there fighting!! This is my nature, and my destiny, and I know that I was born to win in the end. However, since we got the message from London, I have had a phone call from a reporter of the *Daily Mail*, who has somehow heard about this disappointment of ours. He has actually put me in touch with a firm in Southend, and they are sending one of their Reps up here to see me. So as one door closes, yet another one opens, and always there is light at the end of the tunnel!! Sometimes, I wish that I could tear out this creative/inventive streak from my system, and go through life being just another 'happy pudden'. But no chance! Phaetons aren't made that way, and

155

they struggle on, hard, to find fulfilment. Somehow, I believe that they all do. I am so very sorry that I will not now have the chance to meet you, but, who knows, perhaps it will come yet.

"In the meantime, I am enclosing a picture of my wife and I, which will at least give you an idea what I look like. We have quite a large house, with an acre round it, and my latest acquisition is a small pair of cannon, which grace my front doorstep! (Quite a difference from the poor terraces of the Lancashire mill town, where I was born, and where poverty was the rule rather than the exception.) I was thinking of you actually, last Saturday, when I took my daughter to Church for her wedding. In true Phaeton style, I combed Scotland for a carriage and pair, and succeeded in finding a lovely blue Brougham, with matching greys, from Kincardineshire. So you can imagine that the village was set right on its ear, when we drove to Church in style, and a Black Watch piper met us at the gates to pipe us to the Church door. I wore my Black Watch kilt, with dress jacket and buckled shoes; whilst my daughter looked radiant in her wedding gown, with her train carried by a kilted page. As we walked down the aisle, it crossed my mind how you would have loved to see it. We had a really great day, and rounded it off with a dance in the evening, to the Gordon Highlanders Band. Everything went so very well, and I was supremely happy.

"My wife and I are actually coming down to London, in June, for the Trooping, since my son is in the Scots Guards, so, if I may, I will phone you then, and perhaps we might meet. Or, if you ever fancy coming North for a visit, you would be most welcome to stay with us. Who knows, when you have had a long talk with me, you may very well have enough material for a follow-up to your *Fiery Chariot*!!!! I have led a very varied life indeed, and it has yet to be more varied still. I *know* this, instinctively, and am so impatient to 'take off'!

"Many thanks for your good wishes, I find your remarks very stimulating. My regards to you, and your husband."

"28/4/81

"Many thanks for your very welcome letter, and may I say how nice it was to be able to speak to you on the phone this evening. I have been thinking, during the course of the evening, over all the letters I have written to you in the past. I am so pleased that you find them informative, and that they have correctly conveyed something of the Phaeton, that you would perhaps not otherwise have been aware of. I find it so easy to communicate my thoughts in letter-form. Perhaps, when we met, you might have thought me rather diffident, and even somewhat 'shy', however, I do assure you that such is not the case! Although (like all Phaetons) I am something of an extrovert, you must take into consideration that our first meeting was somewhat brief, in view of the nature of the subject under discussion, which takes rather more time to 'get off the ground', and to get one's teeth into, before the discussion can really 'open up', and also, of course, we were complete and utter strangers too. Add to that the fact that my wife was present, which rather inhibited me. Although we have been married – and quite successfully! – for thirty-five years, I still feel that I cannot properly discuss the circumstances of my birth, nor truly explain to her what this Phaeton Complex is all about, since she finds it all rather difficult to understand, having never been in this position herself!! There again, few people would, and I never ever met anyone who *did*, until I read about you and met you. It was a revelation to me!! Although my knowledge of my origins is skimpy, I do remember being told by my Mother, when I was quite small, that my father was a policeman, who was already married and had a family. So, somewhere in the world, I have half-sisters and a half-brother. If my father is still living, he will of course be around eighty years old. I would have liked to meet him, and will forever wonder what he was like, but of course I wouldn't want to bring any distress or hurt to innocent people, who might not even know of my existence. But it is a very intriguing thought, that I have a half-brother, and half-sisters. (What a tremendous idea for a book, or a play, or even a TV film, of two such people meeting and falling in love, due to the unknown attraction that they have for each other!) Incidentally, without wishing to be thought too 'forward' I am sure that, in your research for *The Fiery Chariot*, and also your new book, you *must* have realised that *all* your Phaetons, without exception, are highly emotional, Psychic-sensitives, (to a *very* high degree!) and very highly sexed indeed. In the men, there is a marked tendency to fall in love with women rather older than themselves, especially when they are young; and, they find it difficult, indeed, to resist the age-old lure of a beautiful woman of any age! Perhaps it is in their nature to seek perpetual conquest of those by whom they were dominated in their youth, but the life of the Phaeton is a complex tapestry, into which is woven his many love affairs, some sad, some incredibly beautiful, but *all* of them most memorable. Look again at your Phaetons, Ma'am; look at them closely, there is much that you will learn yet!! Incidentally, too, they are very fond and adoring parents, passionately determined that their children should succeed in life; *and* can be excellent partners in a marriage too, providing the other partner is sufficiently wise enough to realise, and to understand in some measure, that they are married to an ever-boiling 'power-house' of energy that will not be stilled! For my part, I *know* that I have lived before (at least three lives, during one of which I served in a Highland Regiment in India!) and I am also made aware that I have not yet reached my zenith, in this life which I am presently living. That event is still to come, and it will not be too long now.

"There is so much more that I could tell you, but I see that time is passing me by, and I do have to get up early for work! I would much rather write, since I am in that 'Psychic' state when writing comes easily to me, but it is almost 2 a.m., and I have yet to take the dogs out, and to feed my two pet foxes!! In conclusion, Ma'am, my good wishes to you as always, and also to your husband. I hope all goes well for your publication day. I hope you find this letter as interesting as my other letters seem to have been, and that it might even open up new fields of thought, ere your manuscript is finished completely.

"May I also say that I have never opened up this Pandora's Box of a Phaeton's thoughts before, in my entire life, to anyone, as I have for you, and I find it all very stimulating indeed and, yes, satisfying too!"

"2/5/1981
"Thank you, very much indeed, for the copy of *The Fiery Chariot*, which I received this morning. I finished reading it, from cover to cover, at ten o'clock this evening. I am most impressed by your style of writing, and didn't find the book too difficult to understand, although I rather feel that Maryse Choisy seems to have taken a blanket coverage, in her statements on the Phaetons in general. Each of us are *quite* individual, so therefore no one theory can be applied to cover all cases. That would be just too much of a generalisation, I think.

158

However, I did find it all quite fascinating reading, although I doubt very much whether *I* could have lived alongside any of the men I read about. Really, what an odd collection!! I suppose, if I wished it, that I could find all kinds of Freudian cobwebs draping the obscure corners of my own mind. Thank God that I have never been well educated, and thus can only take Freud in wee doses. I think that if such as I were to delve too deeply into such realms, I would go completely potty altogether. As it is, I have a certain superficial knowledge of such matters; enough to engage in a discussion but still retain my balance in life. I wouldn't care to know much more. From my study of the book, I feel that the *true* Phaeton is the illegitimate, since the lack of that vital name, on his Birth Certificate, is *the* burning brand that drives him on, in every sense, to achieve the near-impossible. It colours every vestige of his life, from the first moment that he becomes aware that he is, in some way, different from his fellows. Those Phaetons who lose one, or both, parents in death are indeed subject to similar pressures, to succeed at all costs, and therefore are driven to strive harder, but they at least have a Certificate with their father's name upon it, a qualification that society expects, and indeed, in some cases, demands. The illegitimate (bastard is a word that I – naturally! deplore, and would never use), on the other hand, bears the *certain* knowledge, for life, that the man who fathered him didn't even care enough to enter his name in that blank space, and he feels robbed of his birthright. *This* is the special fuel which puts the Fiery Chariot on its blazing course, whether to glory or perdition, and it takes many, many years of living, till the Charioteer begins to gain control, at last. In my own case, I have driven my Chariot, like a ball-bearing careering down a long bagatelle table, cannoning off this obstruction and that, as fate placed them in my path, to the now-quieter waters of middle age, where I can drive with much more calmness and not a little more wisdom! But I am still driving on, still planning, still dreaming, still hoping, for what I am not quite sure any more. On the basis of creature comforts, and day-to-day living, I, as an ordinary working-class individual, can be *seen* to have it made, inasmuch as (a) I have a large and comfortable home, in generous grounds of an acre, in the rather middle-class section of our township. Moreover, it is my own property. (b) I have a steady job, in which I am the Head of my small Department, and the pay is not too bad, added to which I have now a generous army pension, so although I am in no way wealthy I do have sufficient funds to meet my needs. (c) I have fulfilled most of my ambitions, having travelled to many countries as a serving soldier, and having had enough adventure to satisfy even *my* boyhood dreams! I have met royalty, and tribesmen; dined with millionaires and hoboes; made friends with priests and – yes – prostitutes, as the whole gamut of the human race passed across my life-trail. I served my two Regiments with dedication and pride, in peace and war (even if I attained no great distinction, save that of Sergeant!) and can wear my medals with the secure knowledge that they were hard-earned. At regimental gatherings, my appearance is always warmly greeted, by all ranks, and I know that I belong there. (d) I have a very secure marriage, with a wonderful wife, who is a perfect (Aquarian) partner to my (Sagittarian-Fire sign) Phaeton make-up. I have two very splendid children, boy and girl, who are now grown-up and themselves married, and am also a grandfather. So my family is all that a man could wish for. Incidentally, my dream was that they should never, *ever*, know the poverty that I had known as a child, and I was fanatic about that, as they grew up. So they had a wonderful childhood, with travel and good army schools, and they never knew what it was to be short of anything in life at all, and *that* pleases me, intensely. They are both living very successful lives, in their own particular spheres. Both my wife and I are very popular members of our community, and are very well accepted here, although neither of us belong here originally.

"From the above, it will be seen that everything in life has worked out well for me. Naturally, as a Phaeton, I have had innumerable difficulties placed in my path, but I have managed to overcome most of them. It is a most definite *fact* that we who are true Phaetons *do* have the most incredible pitfalls placed in our way, as though we were given a deliberately hard row to hoe, on this long journey from birth to eternity! I am *quite* sure of this, and the story of my own personal strivings would make a book, on its own merits. But, of all things, the Phaeton is a born fighter, and will rise from the ashes of seeming disaster, to turn it into a triumph, in the end.

"But, to return to my own personal position, right here and now. If I did not bother to strive any further, I could comfortably sit on my backside, in this most pleasant situation, and grow old in comfort, pleasantly vegetating into old age; indeed, most men would be happy to do just that. But, I *can't!*!! Now, I want to become a serious writer; *not* for vainglory, *not* for the money either, since money is only a means to an end and not the end in itself. My purpose is to leave something behind me when I go; something of worth, to show that I was here and that I did not waste my time. I believe that each of us has something to offer our fellow men, and that the gift of writing was given to me. I have already produced two books, and have the capacity for much, much more. I feel that it would be wrong to pass from A to B, through this life, and leave no sign that I was ever here. But that is my own personal conviction.

"I note, in *The Fiery Chariot*, many references to Phaetons being somewhat obsessed with religion and the supernatural, etc. This, I think, stems from the fact that, when we suffer the constant bitter disappointments, and have our dearest, most idealistic plans frustrated, we tend to curse our Creator, for His total indifference to our struggles, *from birth*. Then, when suddenly, in the darkest hour of our despair, we see the gleam of light, and hear the sound of triumph once again, we hasten to made amends to Him, as the Chariot once more soars in splendour and our hearts are uplifted! Religion is a very personal thing with us, deep, deep down inside, although we may not show it much on the outside. The various religions of the human race amaze me, and I think that only the American Indians have the right approach, to the Great Spirit Life-Force, of which we are all a part of the whole. I became a spiritualist through my experiences as a soldier when, on many, many occasions, I came within a whisker of meeting my Creator face-to-face! I also saw a lot of good-living men die, which made *me* start to wonder just why a hell-raiser, such as I, should be allowed to survive. I could write a lot about that, but not here, since it would take too long.

"The kind of verse that I write is, believe it or not, sometimes *fed* to me from a Psychic source. This is *fact,* and I know it, and enjoy the experience; indeed, I think it a privilege to be so assisted by my friends in the other life. There is no magic about all this, since the other life exists side by side with this. I believe that we live seven lives, before we go on to another, greater dimension of spirituality. As far as the Organised Religions are concerned, I cannot really subscribe to any, fully,

161

and completely, although I did find the tour of the Holy Places, in Jerusalem, most moving. Whilst standing in the tiny room where Christ was imprisoned, beneath the house of the High Priest, and listening to a Dutch monk intoning prayers, *I* tried to reach out mentally to my Creator, and to ask 'Why *ME?*' and 'What *is* the answer to *my* problem?'. But if my Creator *was* listening, then He gave no sign at all, and *no* answers were forthcoming either, so I knew that I was on my own, and I'd just have to keep trying, and figure it all out as I went along. It *is* all working out too!!

"I am something of a philosopher, and try to be a deep-thinker, seeking in some way to stretch my mental capacity, in order further to understand the meaning of life, and *my* place in it all. I *do* know that I have a place, and a role to fulfil, since none of this complex life is by accident, there is a grand design. I know, too, that *my* tiny spark of intellect, the essential *ME*, within this flesh-and-bone frame, is the centre of *my* personal Universe, from where I can observe the antics of the rest of my kind. When you stop to consider the fact that if Jesus Christ *were* to come back amongst us again – as every Christian cleric tells us that He will – and if He should be so unwise as to land in the Falls Road area of Belfast, those for whom He suffered would immediately ask Him, 'Which foot dae ye kick with?', and then promptly shoot Him dead on the spot, since even *He* couldn't give an answer that would satisfy both sides!! (If you should be unfamiliar with that old quotation, it stems from the fact that Protestants are held to be Right Footers, and Catholics to be Left Footers, in the jargon of the bigoted!) It would be a better world without the organised religions, and certainly there would be less tormented people, worrying about the state of their souls. However, that is only my personal view.

"Amongst other things, I would dearly love to undergo regression hypnosis, to discover what and where I was in my previous lives. I find the subject fascinating. Also, I have a deep and abiding interest in flying saucers, and have had two experiences of seeing unexplainable things, up to now. I expect, in my lifetime, to have more, and would hope for some direct contact with these characters from elsewhere. It would be interesting, and I wouldn't be too afraid, since they couldn't be any worse than some of the clowns that we have on our own earth!! I read a great deal about these visitations, and the various theories that writers have about them.

162

"You know, Mrs Iremonger, it is a great pity that you and I couldn't have met for a few days, up here, where you could sit with a tape-recorder whilst we talked. I think that the resulting manuscript would be full of interest for you, in your study of the Phaeton, and could even lead to quite new avenues of thought opening up.

"I have tried, in this *monumental* letter, to cover all points of the compass, but I am sure that I must have overlooked *something*! Oh, *yes*, before it does escape me, let me mention that, in the book, there is much made about the Phaeton child being deprived of/searching for love. In my case, I was not short of maternal love, and indeed my dear mother did everything that she possibly could have done for me, and I was well brought up, as they say. Only as a teenager did I start to, in a way, 'withdraw'. This fact was, of course, the natural outcome of events, as I finally realised that everyone else in the neighbourhood knew more about my origins that I did myself, and *that* got under my skin, as nothing else ever did! At seventeen-and-a-half years I joined the Army and went off to Scotland, and have never lived in England since, nor have I ever felt the slightest pangs of 'homesickness' for the place I grew up in. When I walked through the gates of the Regimental Depot at Perth, the world opened up for me, and I took to the life as a duck takes to water! As you have said, the Phaeton will take tremendous risks to try and prove to himself that he is as good as, yes and even better, than his fellows. I have done that, many, many times, both on Active Service and in other ways, but still the urge is never quite satisfied, and one *must* find another challenge! In that statement lies the answer to the fact that I didn't rise above the rank of Sergeant (which I held *three* times!). My Phaeton brain, being what it is, would, after marshalling and considering the facts, drive me to challenge the opinions of my superiors, and to show, quite efficiently, why my version of events was the correct one. Also, when dealing with a Warrant Officer or a Commissioned rank, who had never been on Active Service and who sought to put me in my place, I would quickly point out that he was in no position to tell me how to do my job, since he had been in the Regiment for X number of years, and yet had never heard a shot fired in anger, etc. But that is all past history now; I merely mention it to show how the Phaeton quickly rises to the occasion. You would be amazed just how many men came to me when they needed advice, whether it be how to write a letter, or what defence to offer when up before the Commanding Officer!

"Amongst all the characters in the book, I can identify best with Lawrence of Arabia, because I too sometimes feel a distinct need to go well away from everyone, to seek peace of mind, and to recharge my batteries. I used to go up the Bush in Guiana, to a place where there was no one for miles, and there I would set up my tent and cook my meals on a small fire. It was utter bliss to me, and in the quiet of the Bush nights I could *feel* the silence all around me, and the spirit of all life seemed to reach out to me and gentle my soul. How I wish that I could go back there sometimes, but I can now get the same communion, sitting in my own garden in the quiet of a summer evening. What strange characters we Phaetons are! We are capable of the deepest spiritual feeling, and yet are also capable of the greatest excesses. If God did make us in His image, then He sure lent the same moulds to the Devil!! But, as Burns said, 'A man's a man for a' that'!!

"Well, Mrs Iremonger, I could go on for hours and hours, but I feel that I have said enough, and I am *quite* sure that you must be weary of this narrative by now. I have looked through the letters of mine that you sent to me, and they are innocuous enough, and may be used as you wish. Use them as you will, and this one also. *My* only purpose in all this is to help you to make a truly valid assessment of your Phaetons, and there is nothing like personal experience to help you in that. It has been of great assistance to me also to write all this, for I have never attempted such a task before, in explaining what it all means in my own life. I hope that my efforts are worthwhile, for you, and that my writings make sense to you. I do ask you, *please*, not to think that I have over-stressed anything, nor do I wish to seem in any way 'big-headed'!! I have tried very honestly to put the facts clearly, as they have applied in my own life. I can look back on my fifty-six years, and smile at it all, and really look forward now, with joy, to all that is to come. It really doesn't matter half as much now as it did in those days when I was a young and arrogant laddie! I thank my God for all that has happened to me and for the courage that I was given to endure the dark moments when they came to me.

"The Phaeton, like the Phoenix, rises from the ashes and is always willing to soar, seeking new challenges to conquer, and new fields always!!"

"28/5/81

"How very nice to be able to talk to you, the other night, even though 'Busby' does tend to put a strain on the phone bill. (My employers pay the rental, so that can't be bad!!) I was just thinking, last night, *how* time flies, doesn't it? It is ten years now since I first wrote to you, and at the time I never realised just how many words I *would* be writing to you, eventually. Please believe me when I say that, until fairly recently, I was rather reluctant to let myself go in my letters to you. I was just, somehow, afraid of creating the impression of my being boastful, or 'big-headed', and I didn't want that to happen. All that I have written has been truthful, *and* written with a certain sense of self-discovery also, since I have never in my life so opened up my innermost feelings to anyone, since I never before met anyone who could be expected to, even remotely, understand the complexity of my extraordinary character. When I first read that book review, in the *Sunday Express*, so long ago, it was as if a blinding light had suddenly shone into the deep, deep corners of my mind, wherein I keep my silent thoughts locked away. All the things about which I had long pondered, from boyhood, and which I had never even ventured to discuss with anyone else, *lit up* like neon signs on Broadway!! I *wasn't* the only one who thought like this!! I *wasn't* wrong, in my self-examinations, over the years, of the intricacies of my strange approach to life, and the sense of destiny in the warp and weft of it all. HERE was somebody who *knew*, and who could perhaps help *me* to understand the complex make-up that makes me, in some strange way, so different from my contemporaries. It was so tremendously exciting! Reading *The Fiery Chariot* through, I found, on every page, something applicable to myself. In a way, I found it comforting, too, that although the men I was reading about were poles apart from myself, each of us had something in common. The book is a revelation to me, and I would not have missed reading it for words! You know, Ma'am, even the event of *our* trails crossing, as they have done, is yet another aspect of the Phaeton Complex, wherein the fates conspire to draw the threads of life together, so that they produce yet another eventful star, in the star-dotted configuration of each individual Phaeton's life-pattern. This is the way *I* have *always* known it; and can even recognise the build-up as, in some cosmic fashion, events begin to shape themselves around me, and *every* sense within

165

me tells me that something (or someone) is about to enter my sphere of life, and that it will be yet another eventful star! It really is the oddest of feelings as I find myself mentally watching from the wings, like a complete outsider, as the jigsaw of life is re-adjusted to admit this special happening in my lifestyle. Countless times I have entered different premises, whether a restaurant, bar, barracks, etc. (or even on board ship!), both in this country and overseas, where I might not even have known one face; and yet, suddenly, I get *that* feeling within me. I have had some incredible experiences, in this way, and it still happens yet, and I guess that it always will. Things happen, and people happen, to me. That's the Phaeton! That's how it happened when I met the lady in Miami; we literally walked into each other, and before we even spoke to each other I *knew* that our trails were *meant* to cross, long, long ago, and that it was no accident. God, *how* I would love to look ahead of me! My whole life has been this way and, believe me, it can be *so* frustrating just wondering what *next* is waiting, around the corner, as the dominoes of my Phaeton life-style are shuffled by the unseen hands of the Architect of the Universe. We Phaetons are but puppets who dance upon our Master's Silver Strings; *but*, given the chance, *what* performances we *can* give, upon this splendid stage called life!

"Well, Ma'am, I feel that perhaps I have babbled on enough, maybe even too much, but I do get rather carried away, as you will know. I do so look forward to your book coming out, and I wish you every success with it. As I have so often said, if there is anything more that I can do to help further, please do not hesitate to call on me. And so, to bed!"

"30/5/81
"I have today been reading back over my notes of last night, to see if there is anything further that I might add. I could, of course, fill several books with my 'Life and Loves of a Phaeton' (in a *much* more romantic fashion than the late Frank Harris!) but I feel that it would not serve your purpose to relate too many tales of romantic 'scallywaggery' or of purple adventures! But two incidents from childhood spring to mind which I am sure will amuse you, both of which concern boys with whom I was great pals when I was about nine years old. Both boys were in the same situation as me, being both illegitimate, although their mothers were younger than mine. Altogether

there were about nine of us in our wee gang, and we all played together in the same area of streets, and went to the same school. One of the two was quite a smart lad, and his mother was quite a looker too. She was always dressed in the height of fashion, and appeared to have plenty of money (at least, for *our* part of the world!), at a time when everyone else was permanently skint. One heard the grown-ups muttering darkly that she was 'on the game', in Piccadilly, in Manchester, but no one ever seemed to be able to prove it. At all events, the wee fellow boasted to us of an amazing variety of 'Uncles' who came and went at all hours of the day and night, and invariably tipped him a bob or two. The same wee fellow, when his mother was out for the afternoon, usually on a Saturday, would invite the whole gang into his house, and spread out all his mother's underwear for us to gawk at. I never knew that ladies wore such splendid silks and satins, having always been under the firm impression that *all* women wore bloomers and whalebone corsets. The sight of all this eroticism was quite a landmark in a nine-year-old's education, and we all came out of his house with glazed eyes and hushed voices. Whenever she passed us at the street corner we all used to gaze up at her in awe, knowing that she wore green silk cami-knickers!! She must have often wondered just *why* we all should fall silent when she came on the scene, and why nine pairs of wee eyes should follow her with interest until she vanished into the house and the door slammed. Little did she know that, after the door shut, there was great discussion and a lot of guesswork, and finally nine wee kids were falling about in hysterics as the patter got wilder and wilder, and her own laddie was one of the wittiest! I often wonder what happened to him when he grew up, for he was quite a card as a youth, and a smart dresser too. The other chappie was a character and I would reckon that he too became a Phaeton. Certainly, *he* should have found his niche amongst the gnomes of Zurich, since he was able to make money at the age of nine! In the close-built houses of our kind of Coronation Street, where we all lived, the toilet was situated outside in the backyard, and was built side by side with the one next door, so one often heard conversations being held, quite loudly, between the occupants of each privy. It was all highly entertaining, and reputations were made (*and* lost!) through such discussions, which ranged from the health of the Monarch to who was living 'over-the-brush' with whom, and was it *true* that the strawberry-blonde at number 94 was having it off with the coalman, since she never appeared at the front door on a Friday night to pay for it, and *he* invariably went inside to get his dues!!! (Indeed, I remember one particular coalman who used to knock at the open door of a woman who was reputed to be 'a warm 'un'. She would call out to him, in sultry tones, 'Come in, Luv . . .' to which he would reply, 'Not bloody likely, just fling it out here and I'll catch it'!! You know, there just isn't the same *colour* in today's society, and I look back fondly on the education for life that my youth gave to me.) However, I digress too much and must return to my budding financier. Since the houses that we lived in were very old, and needed repointing, the mortar used to crumble between the old brickwork, and the floors were often covered in grit and sand particles. Our wee mate discovered that, by using a screwdriver, he could bore a hole through the mortar, and was thus able to observe the antics of the rather large lady who lived next door. It became well known to all the kids in the area, who cheerfully – nay, *desperately*! – queued up to pay a halfpenny in order to admire the descending bloomers and the *massive* blue-veined hams of the lady who was known to all and sundry as Big Nelly!! Many a time he stood the gang a bottle of Tizer soft drink out of his nefarious profits. I often wonder if, today, that same kid drives a Rolls Royce, or a Mercedes, and smokes only the finest Havana cigars! I always believe that urchins are born with the capacity to rule the world, and that their infinite, inborn cunning would leave the greatest of our diplomats gasping for words, whilst they, the urchins, went on to conquer! I told you that my life is a tapestry, rich in colour; and, added to that, is an inbuilt tape-recorder for a memory, which is surely God-given, since some day, when my star is in the ascendant and my chance comes really to *write*, I shall wish to produce such a book of these snippets from my childhood which are both comical and in essence charming. Although we lived in great poverty, we were not aware of being in any way deprived, since everyone we knew was in the same boat, and we lived and loved together through those rough times. We were not unhappy, it was just that sometimes we were happier than others, and we made the best of what we had. That's the trouble today, that people don't really appreciate what they have, and are not prepared to take less, at any price.

"I do hope that all my ramblings make sense to you, and that you see the pictures as I have painted them. That is my way, since I would rather describe myself as an artist who paints pictures with words than as a writer. I consider that a writer is someone who has at least a dozen books on a shelf, each with his name on the cover. This *is* my goal, eventually, so I keep striving. But, as a Phaeton, I am well used to planning things, with the very highest level of competence, only to find, at the *very* last minute, that the object of my aspirations is suddenly drawn out of my grasp. *This* can drive me to distraction, and I become hard to live with for a while, until I once more set to, to try again, *and* again, and *again*. In my mind, whatever be the quest, I set up my scheme/plan to accomplish, like a row of dominoes set on end, so that, when I judge the time to be ripe, I can tap the first one, and each section of my plan falls into place, as my mental dominoes ripple on to the final piece, and the end is achieved. When that happens, I feel an *immense* surge of pleasure that it should be so, as I orchestrated it to be. *Failure* is an anathema to me, and although I can understand and forgive it, in other people, I *cannot* do so in myself! Curious, but none the less true.

"So, *my* struggle takes *no* account of the rewards of success, but only in the very fact of the achievement in itself. I *am* different; I was *born* different; the shaping of my *life* is different from all those whom I have known, and I truly wonder what next awaits me, on the long trail. At least I have the satisfaction of knowing that, from here on, it is easier to bear than it used to be when I was young. I do not seek notoriety, nor world-wide fame, nor yet even riches; only the opportunity to use whatever talent I might have been given, for the benefit and the pleasure of those whose lives are brightened by my tales, and my pictures painted in words. When we are born, we bring nothing; when we die, we can take nothing with us. But it is a rare and splendid thing to be able to leave something *tangible* behind, to show that at least we *tried*, and the life we are given is not wasted in futility! I would love to be there, hovering in spirit, whilst my children – at last! – are able to go through all my many notes, and letters, and stories, etc, as they discover the many, many unknown strands that weave in and out of my life-story. Both my children have often told me that, in some way that they could never quite define, they found me to be different from the fathers of their friends and their cousins.

169

They found me to be a closer, warmer, helping person; and, as they grew older, we became very close friends, who enjoy each other's company, as we still do to this day. That is such a very comforting thing to know, and I feel that I have done my work, as a father, *successfully*, which, to a Phaeton, is *the* Great Accolade of all! My dear wife is the *rock* upon which solid foundation my entire dream of life is safely anchored; and whose love and patience, *and* understanding, of the odd personality of the man she married thirty-five years ago, is a never-ending source of comfort in moments of despair, and of joy in my small successes. A woman of infinite love and wisdom, and a partner beyond compare, in this strange caravanserai of life that I have brought her into. So, Ma'am, *here* is a Phaeton for your collection; well-loved, well-blessed, *but* still searching far out amongst the gods for *his* place amongst the stars, where *his* Fiery Chariot might at last come to rest, and the blazing trails that he once left across his particular canvas in life be left, to grow dim as the embers fade!

"Goodnight now, Ma'am, since it is the witching hour of midnight, and even the two dogs are fast asleep here beside me. The fire is low in the grate, and the house is silent and still, except for the Labrador snoring! Outside, the moon is shining over the quiet hills, tipping the peaks with silver, and one of my foxes – at this very moment! – has given a ringing call that echoes round the area. Whether it be a love-call to her mate, I know not; perhaps it's to remind *me* that they haven't been fed yet! I read back, through all that I have written, and remember the thousands of words that I have written to you before, and all this from a simple book review! What a revelation it all is to me. Somehow, from all this, my own view of my life has been rendered all the more interesting, and I have learned a lot about myself too.

"Well now, I really must close, and get to bed. If you don't mind, I would like you, *please,* to let me know what you think of this particular letter, and if it has been of any further help to you in the manuscript of your book. I *so* look forward to reading it, but I only ask that you treat my story – and me! – as a very human narrative, with all my faults (and any attributes that I might possess!), for to be dissected as a subject would hurt deeply, in true Phaeton fashion, of course. However, I *am* sure that you will take the greatest care possible to ensure that the publisher doesn't misquote. I always remember, in 1958,

170

how a reporter on the *Sunday Express* quite *wildly* distorted my remarks in a story about recruiting which he took from me. It cost me my promotion, and I never ever recovered my career from that moment on. That's one of the reasons that I didn't get beyond the rank of Sergeant (the Phaeton's luck again!). However, God is good, and life is full of promise!

"Walikum Salaam, God go with you.

"PS: May I say that I do look forward to our meeting, as I feel now that we know each other a lot better, and certainly you know far more about me, than you ever guessed you might do, from our *first* meeting! Why not think about coming up here, for a few days? It would be fun to have you as a guest in our home, and to introduce you to our dogs and foxes, and show you my museum. When you first see this house, you just *know* that it is a wee outpost of Empire, especially with the cannons at the door!"

This nameless Phaeton is a poet, too, and I publish here one of his poems, written in 1970.

"I Shall Love You

"And there shall be another place, another time . . .
And I shall truly love you!
My love for you is deep. My love is strong, and true, and pure.
And it shall hear your heart crying, in the long night.
Even through the veil, my love shall hear you.
Across the last great frontier, and far, far into the golden
   land,
My love will search for you, amongst the multitude . . .
And we two shall love, as we have never loved.
Your eyes are blind with tears: you sigh, and your heart is
   weeping . . .
Maybe, in eons long gone, we two were then lovers,
And held each other close, in the silent secret places,
Where the gods smiled and the air was ever-fragrant with
   our loving.
This great love; that was, that is, that cannot be, and yet shall
   forever be!
For it is written large, in the book of life, that
You and I exist to intertwine, and that our very souls shall be
   one.

171

O woman of beauty, woman of grace, come to me; love me,
   for
Without you there is no past, no present, and no future . . .
And I care not, though my spirit wander forever the empty
Lonely places of the everlasting night, if you are not there.
Without your love, the milk of life grows sour within me,
And my mortal heart cries out to God for succour.
Come to me, woman of wonder! Come to me, and take you
   this love I bring.
Take this love, this heart I offer humbly to you . . .
Cradle it tenderly, and keep it safely, deep in the hidden
   corners of your
Being, until the knowing hand of fate
Shall beckon, that you might draw it forth into the light . . .
And there shall be another time, another place . . .
And I shall truly love you!"

So there we have, in this anonymous Phaeton, all the
Phaeton characteristics – most notably, superstitiousness and
an intense interest in psychic phenomena, even to the extent of
believing that his verses were sent to him by psychic means; an
enormous love and concern for his children; a marked concern
with religion; and a never-ending search for love. It is, however, the insatiable determination to succeed, somehow, any-
how, one day, in some great ambition which is the most
notable feature in his character, a determination that he will
leave a name behind him for all men to admire. Let us wish him
luck.

"Orphans of the heart,
no less"

THOSE WHO HAD BEEN
ADOPTED, REJECTED, SEPARATED, OR
WERE THE VICTIMS OF DIVORCE OR
ILL-TREATMENT

Alan Ayckbourn, parents divorced when he was 5.

Honoré de Balzac, mother put him out to wet-nurse at birth, and did not visit him for 3 years. He had an obsession about her not loving him.

J.M. Barrie, mother lost her favourite son, David, and James never took his place. ("Nothing that happens after we are twelve matters very much.")

Aubrey Beardsley, sent at 11 to live with an aunt in Brighton.

Ludwig von Beethoven, drunken and cruel father, probably mentally unbalanced, who would, when he returned home late at night, pull the child out of bed and make him practise until dawn. Beethoven hated music and often longed to give it up.

Arnold Bennett, rejected by his father (see the autobiographical *Clayhanger*).

Thomas Carlyle, rejected by his father. ("His heart seemed as if walled in . . . it seemed as if an atmosphere of Fear repelled us from him. To me it was especially so.")

Raymond Chandler, his mother divorced his father when he was 8, and he never saw his father again.

Charlie Chaplin, his father an alcoholic, and his mother going insane. He never forgot his miserable childhood.

Clementine Churchill, wife of Winston Churchill, at 5 her parents parted for ever.

Winston Churchill, wrote that the love of a nanny for her charges is "the only disinterested affection in the world". He had a close relationship with Mrs Everest, nicknamed "Womany" by him. To his parents he wrote from Harrow:

175

"Please do do do do do do come down to see me. I have been disappointed so many times about your coming."

Noël Coward, domineering mother and ineffectual idler of a father who gave him no love.

Charles Dickens, put to work in a blacking factory for a period as a child.

Benjamin Disraeli, at odds with his mother.

Edward VIII, subsequently the Duke of Windsor, starved of love by his mother, Queen Mary.

George Eliot, clashed constantly with her father.

William Faulkner, subject to black depressions, diagnosed by a psychiatrist as caused by his mother's rejection of him.

Frederick the Great, subject to "that ultimate loneliness of heart that is both the strength and the curse of those for whom parental relationships have failed in infancy". (*Frederick the Great*, by Nancy Mitford.)

Vincent van Gogh, "They dread having me in the house as they would dread having a large savage dog. He runs into the room with muddy paws, he is rough, he is in everybody's way, he barks loudly. In short, he is a dirty beast. He might bark – he might go mad."

Franz Joseph Haydn, sent away from home when he was 6.

Victor Hugo, child of a broken marriage.

Henrik Ibsen, bankrupt and bullying father finally left home when he was 15.

Edmund Kean, deserted by his mother.

Charles Kingsley, had an unhappy childhood, with unloving parents.

Rudyard Kipling, sent to England from India, to dire experiences, and a sense of being betrayed by his adored parents.

Bernard Montgomery, had a wretched childhood, due to what he described as a clash of wills with his mother.

William Morris, poet and artist, tyrannical parents, bitterly resented by him as "an extreme form of emotional suffering".

Florence Nightingale, long at odds with her mother, and suffered from a psychotic illness.

Thomas Love Peacock, father disappeared when he was a child.

Alexander Sergeyevich Pushkin, parents gave him no love.

Odilon Redon, flower-painter, parents effectively abandoned him.

George Sand, parents gave her no love.

Bernard Shaw, in his own words, had "a devil of a childhood", ignored by both his father and his mother.

Percy Bysshe Shelley: "Passive obedience was inculcated and enforced in my childhood; I was required to love because it was my *duty* to love."

Madame de Staël, father left her as a child to her frozen-hearted mother.

Robert Louis Stevenson: "The children of lovers are orphans."

Talleyrand (Charles Maurice de Talleyrand-Périgord), suffered from a denial of love and justice in his early years. His biographer, Jean Orieux, was convinced that his ruthless ambition, coupled with sexual and financial depravity, were attempts to compensate for the misery of his early years.

William Makepeace Thackeray, mother married to another man after being told that her lover had been killed, married her lover on the death of her husband. Thackeray, the husband's child, was sent home to England from Calcutta, and never loved by his mother.

Titian (Tiziano Vecellio), left home at 9 to go to Venice.

Tito (Josip Broz), rejected by his father.

Anthony Trollope, never forgot his mother's not loving him, and his father's abandoning his family when forced to flee the country for debt.

Oscar Wilde, unhappy childhood with a mother who was unfaithful to her husband and indifferent to her son.

Godfrey Winn, his father left his mother whom he loved, and he hated him.

P.G. Wodehouse, treated with casual indifference by his mother.

CHAPTER 13

Charles Dickens (1812 – 1870)

Charles Dickens intensely disliked his mother.

This stemmed from a period when the family was so impoverished that he, a mere child, and a puny and sickly one at that, was put to work in a blacking warehouse. The six months he spent there was a period of anguish and humiliation which he never forgot.

Two weeks after Charles went to work, sticking labels on the pots of blacking, his family went into the Marshalsea Prison for a forty-pound debt of his father's. When, however, his father's mother died, his brother John inherited about two hundred and fifty pounds, and obtained his brother's release by paying the debt. The family returned to their home, and Charles's father visited his son at the blacking warehouse, to find that he, as he saw it, was being exhibited to the public view at a window. He wrote an insulting letter to the manager, who at once dismissed the boy. His mother, however, decided to mend matters, and did so next day, bringing home a request for him to return.

Charles Dickens wrote: "My father said I should go back no more, and should go to school. I do not write resentfully or angrily: for I know how all these things have worked together to make me what I am: but I never afterwards forgot, I never shall forget, I never can forget, that my mother was warm for my being sent back."

His father did rescue him, and sent him to school; but he could not pass the blacking warehouse without misery, and wrote, "My old way home by the borough made me cry after my eldest child could speak." The humiliation he had suffered never, in fact, left him, and neither did his dislike of his mother. He mentioned the blacking warehouse in no fewer than eleven of his books. As described by him in *David Copperfield*, it was a crazy, tumbledown old house, abutting on the river, and over-run by rats. "Its wainscoted rooms, and its rotten floors and staircase," he wrote, "and the old grey rats swarming down in the cellars, and the sound of their squeaking and scuffling coming up the stairs at all times, and the dirt and decay of the place rise up visibly before me." Later, too, he wrote, "My whole nature was so penetrated with the grief and humiliation of such considerations that even now, famous and caressed and happy, I often forget in my dreams that I have a dear wife and children, even that I am a man; and wander desolately back to that time of my life." He painted his mother as Mrs Nickleby, that inaccurate, voluble, foolish and unteachable woman. In 1844 he wrote to a friend: "Mrs Nickleby, sitting bodily before me in a solid chair, once asked me if I really believed there ever was such a woman."

Charles Dickens had an extreme reaction to bereavement. As a young man of twenty-three he married Catherine, or Kate, Hogarth. Her young sister Mary came to live with them in their tiny apartment, while Kate was expecting a baby, due at Christmas. It was a happy little household; but one night they heard a strange choking cry from Mary. The doctor was sent for, but she was beyond help. In an agony, Charles Dickens took the ring from her finger and slipped it on to his own little finger, where it remained until his death. The shock brought on a miscarriage for Kate, making the tragedy even worse. Dickens took on the mournful task of arranging the funeral in the new cemetery at Kensal Green, and he wrote a gentle epitaph for little Mary Hogarth: "Young, beautiful and good, God in his mercy numbered her among His angels at the early age of seventeen."

After the funeral he arranged for a rose-tree to be planted on the grave, then carried Kate off to the country. He himself was so stricken that he could not write his usual contributions for *Bentley's Miscellany*, and put a notice in the paper: "Since the last appearance of this work, the editor has to mourn the sudden death of a very dear young relative, to whom he was most affectionately attached, and whose society has been for a long time the chief solace of his labours" – not, one might think, the most tactful of notices as far as his wife was concerned. "Thank God she died in my arms," he wrote, "and the very last words she whispered were of me." Five years later he was writing to John Forster, his friend, "The desire to be buried next to her is as strong upon me now as it was five years ago, and I *know* (for I don't think there ever was love like that I bear her) that it will never diminish."

At the farm, where he had taken his wife, he sat in the rickety lean-to, with Forster and Daniel Maclise, and talked and talked of Mary. He never lost the sense of grief caused by her death; and in all the descriptions of death in his novels we find reminders of that suffering – most notably in those of Little Nell and of Paul Dombey. Only Rose Maylie in *Oliver Twist* was spared, for, as he wrote tenderly: "We need to be careful how we deal with those about us, when every death carries to some small circle of survivors thoughts of so much omitted and so little done, of so many things forgotten, and so many more which might have been repaired." Nor did he ever forget Mary. He would sit immobile in his study, mourning as if he could not be comforted. He would not even sit in the same part of the St James's Theatre, where he and Mary had occupied a box before her death, or sit in any part of the house from which that box could be seen.

In October 1841, Kate's younger brother, aged twenty, died, four years after his sister. Dickens had always wanted to be buried in Mary's grave, but now he had to abandon the idea, so that her brother could be buried there. "I don't think there ever was love like that I bear her!" he cried, and the uncomprehending doctor could only say that he had been overworking for years. Even when, years later, he stood by Niagara Falls, he recalled her: "What would I give if the dear girl whose ashes lie in Kensal Green had lived to come so far along with us – but she has been here many times, I doubt not, since her sweet face faded from my earthly sight."

Eventually Dickens began to identify little Georgina Hogarth, another sister of Kate's, with his lost Mary, seeing, as he put it, "the spirit of Mary shining out of Georgina". He bought a sketch of Georgina at the waterfall for between a hundred and a hundred and fifty guineas – a very large sum in those days.

Towards the close of 1850, he had two more shocks. First,

his father, who had been suffering from a disease of the bladder which he had not disclosed, collapsed, and was taken to hospital, to be operated on, without chloroform, in what Dickens called "the most terrible operation known to surgery". "He bore it," Dickens wrote, "with astonishing fortitude, and I saw him directly afterwards – his room a slaughter-house of blood. He was wonderfully cheerful and strong-hearted . . . I have been about, to get what is necessary for him, and write with such a shaking hand that I cannot write plainly . . . All this goes to my side directly, and I feel as if I had been struck there by a leaden bludgeon." John Dickens died on March 31st, and was buried in Highgate Cemetery, with his son's epitaph on his tombstone, referring to his "zealous, useful, cheerful spirit". His son might have painted him as Micawber, but he loved him, because his father had loved *him*.

Next, with his wife and Georgina away, came another shock. His five-months-old daughter, Dora, had always been sickly, and he had spent many hours at her bedside. Just before leaving home to preside at the dinner of the General Theatrical Fund, he ran up to the nursery to say good-night to the infant. Not long after, she had a convulsive fit, and died. The news was brought to the hall where he was, but it was kept from him until he had spoken. The shock was so great that his friend Mark Lemon, famous as the editor of *Punch*, had to sit up with him all night. The baby was buried in Highgate Cemetery a fortnight after her grandfather. Dickens sent Forster to Malvern with a letter from him to break the news as gently as possible to the child's mother. Once again Dickens had to arrange the funeral, and went to the lengths of asking the Queen's equerry to postpone his performance in *Not so Bad as We Seem* in the Great Exhibition from 1st May to a later date – 16th May. (It was then that Rosina Bulwer made the uncharitable remark, "Oh, Mr Dickens makes a habit of acting with a dead father in one pocket and a dead baby in the other.") The Queen, the Prince, and the dukes and duchesses all had to rearrange their engagements because of Charles Dickens's grief.

The death of his sister Fanny, of consumption, also hit him hard. She had been ill for some time, and he had spent many hours at her bedside, talking of their childhood days in Chatham, Rochester and the woods of Cobham. "Her death," as his distinguished biographer, Hesketh Pearson, commented, "affected him profoundly. This was all the more so as she left a young husband and family behind." In her memory he wrote *A Child's Dream of a Star,* published in the second number of *Household Words*.

The year 1863 brought more grief for Charles Dickens. First Augustus Egg, his partner and friend, died, in Algiers. Then his mother, Mrs John Dickens, died, in London. Worst of all, his son, Walter Landor Dickens, died, in India, on the last day of the year. Charles Dickens did not hear of it until February, by which time another son, Francis Jeffrey Dickens, was more than half-way to Bengal. To all these events he reacted with grief – even to his mother's death.

His reaction to the death of Thackeray, on Christmas Eve, 1863, at only fifty-two, was perhaps strangest of all. Dickens went to Thackeray's funeral although he had not been at all friendly with him during his lifetime. The funeral took place at Kensal Green on December 30th, 1863, and an observer, watching him, said that, "he had a look of bereavement on his face which was indescribable". When everyone else had left the graveside he still stood there, as if rooted to the spot, watching every spadeful of earth thrown upon it. Then, walking away with friends, he began to talk, but soon his voice quavered, and, shaking hands with everyone, he went off, rapidly, alone. The death, even of a mere acquaintance, clearly upset him profoundly – possibly the thought of the annihilation of another author, with whom he could identify, was particularly upsetting.

In 1866 another bereavement hit him hard – that of Jane Carlyle, wife of Thomas Carlyle. Her death, famous in literary annals, took place suddenly. She had picked up her pet dog, which had been run over in Hyde Park, and had climbed into her brougham to drive home with it. When the coachman looked into the carriage he found her dead, with her dog on her knees. Dickens mourned her deeply. "None of the writing women," he exclaimed, "came near her at all!"

Then again, in 1870, his old friend, the painter Daniel Maclise, died, to his deep distress.

Dickens searched for love all his life. His first love was Maria Beadnell, and he never got over his disappointment at not marrying her. He was only seventeen, but he fell madly in love with her. It was not reciprocated. Maria was a flirt, and he was merely an amusement for her. When they were both over forty he would write to her: "It is a matter of perfect certainty to me that I began to fight my way out of poverty and obscurity, with one perpetual idea of you." He would write, too, many years later: "My entire devotion to you, and the wasted tenderness of those hard years which I have ever since half loved, half dreaded to recall, made so deep an impression on me that I refer to it a habit of suppression which now belongs to me, which I know is no part of my original nature, but which makes me chary of showing my affections, even to my children, except when they are very young." (Queen Victoria, whose father died when she was eight months old, was another Phaeton who did not show affection to her children, except when they were very young.)

Charles Dickens's marriage was not a success, and he always sought love elsewhere. In 1858 he fell in love with Ellen Ternan, a young actress, twenty-seven years younger than he, being eighteen to his forty-five, and, as so often in these cases, a Phaeton herself, her father having died insane when she was seven years old. By then he and his wife had been legally separated. The liaison was to last for twelve years and a son would be born of it. His daughter Kate wrote: "More tragic and far-reaching was the association of Charles Dickens and Ellen Ternan and their resultant son than that of Nelson and Lady Hamilton and their daughter. My father was like a madman. Nothing could surpass the misery and unhappiness of our life." For twelve years, at any rate, Dickens believed that he had found the love he had always sought.

Ellen herself was not in love with him, and the thought of intimacy with him repelled her. She kept him at bay for a long time, but eventually gave way, the combination of his fame and his cash overcoming her scruples in the end. She became his mistress, almost certainly in 1863. Dickens was fully aware that she did not love him, but took a house for her in 1867, when she was expecting his child, and kept her in great comfort in Camberwell, spending part of every week with her. She suffered from remorse, and was always reproaching herself. It all made him very wretched. As his physician, Thomas Wright, put it: "He imagined that he had entered into a new life, and that it would be roses, roses all the way. He forgot that roses have thorns. He thought he was in front of the supremest felicity ever enjoyed by mortal man. He wasn't." He suffered abominably from jealousy, and, in Bradley Headstone, painted that passion most poignantly.

He left Ellen one thousand pounds, free of legacy duty, in his will, an unwelcome piece of publicity for her. Her story had a happy ending, however, for in 1876 she married, perhaps surprisingly, a clergyman, the Reverend George Wharton Robinson, with whom she lived until 1914. (The clergy often figure interestingly in these cases. Nelson's illegitimate daughter, Horatia, also married a clergyman.)

Dickens was fascinated by magic, superstitition and the occult. When he was in America in 1866 he was deeply moved by the tale of Abraham Lincoln's premonition of his death. "Gentlemen, something very extraordinary is going to happen, and that very soon," Lincoln is supposed to have said; and when the Attorney General asked, "Something good, sir, I hope?" he replied very gravely, "I don't know, I don't know. But it will happen, and shortly, too." The Attorney General then asked him whether he had received any information not disclosed to them, and he replied, "No, but I have had a dream. And I have now had the same dream three times." Each time, he said, the dream had preceded a disaster to the Federal cause. "I am on a great broad rolling river," he said, "and I am in a boat – and I drift – and I drift – but this is not business! Let us proceed to business, gentlemen." Abraham Lincoln was shot that night. It was a story that greatly impressed Charles Dickens.

Later Dickens became interested in mesmerism, as a result of meeting the Reverend Chauncey Hare Townshend, poet and scholar, who had studied it at Antwerp. The reverend gentleman had brought out an account of what he claimed to have witnessed, entitled *Facts in Mesmerism*, which sought to prove that somnambulism could be induced, that spirit demonstrably dominated matter, and that the mind was merely a source of power. Dickens became fascinated by the conversation of Townshend and his friend Dr John Elliotson, and took lessons in the art of animal magnetism. He was delighted to find that he could send people to sleep, and make them wake up again. Soon he was even more involved in Dr Elliotson's experiments, which were causing dissension at University College Hospital, where he carried out minor operations under the anaesthesia induced by his so-called magnetic powers. Dickens refused to be magnetised himself, but frequently practised on his wife Kate, and her sister, and on others who had no objection. He never went in for spiritualism, but he experimented with the psychograph owned by Bührer, an instrument which was said to write at the dictation of the foreign count who was alleged to materialise in Bührer's rooms.

Later Dickens also practised table-turning with the famous Miss Coutts. After Mary Hogarth's death he was very interested in dreams, and liked to recount his dream about a Miss Napier, who visited him in a scarlet opera-cloak. Two days later a friend came to visit him, with a lady. "This lady is very desirous of being introduced to you," he said. "Not Miss Napier?" Dickens asked. "Yes, Miss Napier," the friend replied; and there, in a scarlet opera cloak, was Miss Napier.

Charles Dickens was religious. He impressed on Edward Bulwer Lytton the truth and beauty of the Christian religion, and what he called "the wholesome practice of private prayers", which, he said, he himself "had never abandoned".

In America he was impressed by the American Unitarians, and especially by Dr Channing, their leading pastor. As he himself belonged to no specific church, he decided that he might do worse than join the London Association at the Essex Street Chapel on his return. The definition of their religion by W.J. Fox, the well-known preacher, politician, and author of the day, would present no difficulty for him: "Belief in God the Father, and in the humanity and divine message of Jesus of Nazareth." To him it was, Dickens said, "the religion that has sympathy for men of every creed and ventures to pass judgment on none". On returning from America he attended the Essex Street meetings, and then paid for pews for himself and his family at the chapel in Little Portland Street, the minister of which was to become a trusted friend. He found, in fact, great relish in the discovery of Unitarianism.

He wrote a little book for his children on the New Testament. As he put it, "I have always striven in my writings to express veneration for the life and lessons of Our Saviour; because I feel it; and because I rewrote that history for my children – every one of whom knew it from having it repeated to them – long before they could read, and almost as soon as they could speak."

The congregation he considered most important, expressing a vigorous preference for "the packed Protestant churches of the New World, with their attentive, intelligent congregations, and their well-lit, well-polished interiors". He was scathing about the Cathedrals in Italy, though he made a point of visiting them, and he was strongly anti-Catholic, considering the rituals both soporific and tawdry, and part of a dead past. Nor did he care for the Pope, complaining that in Holy Week he was "carried about like a Guy Fawkes", and objecting to "the Washing of the Feet", and the slow Good Friday "knee shuffle" up the Scala Santa, calling it "ridiculous and unpleasant in its unmeaning degradation". Dickens always mourned the decay of Christian feeling, and believed it responsible for much oppressive and avoidable misery. So he set great store on the spirit of Christmas – to him it was Christianity in action, and he preached it with all his might. When he came to make his will he closed it with the words: "I commit my soul to the mercy of God through our Lord and Saviour Jesus Christ, and I exhort my dear children humbly to try to guide themselves by the teaching of the New Testament in its broad spirit, and to put no faith in any man's narrow construction of its letter here and there."

It may seem strange to speak of the engaging sentimentalist, Charles Dickens, one whose very name conjures up the picture of cosy firesides, the joys of home, and glowing Christmases, as a man of isolation and reserve, but such was the case. It was not only that he was incapable of showing affection, except, of course, to his children when young. Periodically he went off alone, on the acceptable excuse of gathering material, but stayed away very much longer than was necessary. When hard at work he refused to dine out more than once a week, for, as he said, "I have always given my work the first place in my life." His family considered him "a terror to the household" at such times. But, more than this, the man of good cheer was austere in his personal habits. There were no excesses in his home. He ate and drank very little – no champagne, and never any whisky. He drank madeira, but extremely sparingly. He did not smoke when on tour, refused all wine at meals (and cigars afterwards), from the time when, as he called it, his readings "set in".

His ambition had taken various forms. He had begun by wanting to be an actor. Then he had wanted to be a Member of Parliament, but was only offered a Scottish seat, and turned it down. Then he had tried to be made a police magistrate in

London, thus getting a regular stipend, and applied to a leading member of the Government, but was turned down. His highly successful career as an author was fourth choice.

Charles Dickens suffered from ill-health all his life. The sickly, undersized child, suffering from spasmodic attacks, was unable to play with the other boys at school; the young man suffered from rheumatism, headaches, dizziness and physical lassitude; the man from pains in his side, attacks of sickness when emotionally upset; fistula (as he believed, from too much sitting at his desk), for which he underwent an operation; colds so severe that they made him deaf, hoarse, red-nosed and fractious; recurrent attacks of his childhood pains in the side; a weak kidney; neuralgia; lumbago, and, at various times, frost-bite, heart-disease, gout, and, in the end, haemorrhage – which killed him. Recklessly, he went to America, where he refused to recognise the symptoms of heart-disease, gout, and catarrh in the later stages. His difficulty in breathing, insomnia, and fainting fits, took a severe toll of his health.

He had the Phaeton's interest in storms, too, and, as early as 1839, in his own words, staggered down to the pier at Broadstairs to watch one, actually creeping under the lee of a large boat to do so, and returned home "wet through".

Determined to maintain his privacy, on September 3rd, 1860, he burnt all his private papers and correspondence at Gad's Hill. For the rest of his life he destroyed every letter which did not deal with future matters as soon as he had finished with it – a loss to posterity.

Like most Phaetons, Dickens had an interest in Sir Walter Scott and his works. When, in June 1841, he visited Scotland to receive the freedom of the city, he made a point of visiting Abbotsford, where Scott had lived for twenty-seven years, and was deeply moved by the sight of his pathetic relics.

Dickens could be reckless. Once he abandoned a safe job on the *Daily News*, letting down those who had trusted him to back them. The break-up of his marriage was courting disaster in the puritanical Victorian society – a disaster which never came, for Queen Victoria herself received him and presented him with her own *Journal of Our Life in the Highlands*, requesting a set of his works, which she received, handsomely bound. It was rash, too, and nearly disastrous, to journey to the United States in such a poor state of health.

So there we have the typical Phaeton pattern once again: a man of abnormal sensitivity, isolation and reserve, demonstrating an extreme reaction to bereavement, extreme religious concern, obsessive need for love, a determination to achieve total support, showing intense devotion to his children when young, with recklessness and superstitiousness notable features of his character. He was interested in storms, and in Sir Walter Scott. Here was a man, too, who, from a very low stratum of a highly stratified society, with no education and no culture, through talent and determination rose to the very pinnacle of public esteem.

He was actually buried in Westminster Abbey. Bagehot wrote: "No other Englishman had attained such a hold on the vast populace."

He had always intended to rise to great heights, for he had supreme confidence in himself, and had long since decided to climb as high as he could. But even he might have been surprised to find how far the puny, sickly child in the blacking factory had risen.

CHAPTER 14

Robert Louis Stevenson
(1850 – 1894)

Robert Louis Stevenson considered himself starved of love. "The children of lovers," he wrote in a touching phrase, "are orphans."

All his life he sought a mother to give him what he believed he had lost in affection, always falling in love with women as unlike his mother as possible – and swarthy, where she was very fair. He had, he said, no happy memories of his childhood. Yet his mother certainly had no guilt about her relationship with her child. A wife and mother at barely twenty, she kept a series of small almanac books, one for each year, in which she noted the progress of her baby son as soon as he could walk. Yet Robert Louis Stevenson felt deprived, and if he felt deprived he was deprived. She was a sick woman, suffering from the weakness of the chest which he inherited, and could not give him all the attention he desired; and she was spoiled by her thirty-year-old husband.

His nurse, Alison Cunningham, known to him as Cummy, was his first mother-substitute. Often she sat up with him at night when he could not sleep, reading to him, or telling him stories, giving him the security that he craved. To her, in gratitude, he dedicated his *A Child's Garden of Verses*, published in 1885, with a touching poem.

For the long nights you lay awake
And watched for my unworthy sake;
For your most comfortable hand
That led me through the uneven land . . .
My second Mother, my first Wife,
The angel of my infant life –
From the sick child, now well and old,
Take, nurse, the little book you hold.

Like all Phaetons, Stevenson had an extreme reaction to
bereavement. In 1883 he lost his friend, James Walter Ferrier,
probably from the effects of alcoholism. Stevenson was
terribly distressed by his death, writing that Ferrier had
believed in himself profoundly, but that he had never believed
in others, and saying that he had learned more, in some ways,
from Ferrier than from any other man he had ever met. "He,
strange to think," he wrote, "was the best gentleman, in all
kinder senses, that I ever knew." He had had a "fine, kind,
open dignity of manner", yet had ended up as "such a tem-
poral wreck". Stevenson mourned him, and all his oddities,
such as his "romantic affection" for pharmacies. To him his
death, in the words of James Pope Hennessy, his biographer,
"seemed to undermine the earth". "All my friends," he wrote,
"have lost one thickness of reality since that one passed."

His father's death also had a terrible effect on him, despite
his feeling of neglect by the lovers, and his once writing, "I
think I never feel so lonely as when I am too much with my
father and mother, and I am ashamed of the feeling, which
makes matters worse." When he was summoned to his father's
death-bed he found a changed man, whom he described in a
poem written after his death.

Once more I saw him. In the lofty room
Where oft with lights and company his tongue
Was trump to honest laughter, sat attired
A something in his likeness. "Look!" said one,
Unkindly kind. "Look up, it is your boy!"
And the dread changeling gazed on me in vain.

After his father's death he was haunted by what he called
"ugly images of sickness, decline and impaired reason", but
they passed away with time. "He now haunts me, strangely

190

enough, in two guises," he wrote, "as a man of fifty, lying on a hillside and carving mottoes on a stick, strong and well; and as a young man, running down the sands into the sea near North Berwick, myself *aetat* eleven, somewhat horrified at finding him so beautiful when stripped."

Years later, he was to write a memoir of his old friend, Fleeming Jenkin, who had died suddenly, in Edinburgh, in June 1885, of blood-poisoning, after a trivial operation on his foot. It was written at his widow's request, but is full of poignant sincerity.

From early childhood Stevenson was passionately interested in religion, encouraged by his mother, and used to preach from a home-made pulpit. He described himself later as "piping and snivelling over the Bible, and saying nothing without adding, 'If I am spared'." He would repeat psalms, or the story of the Shunammite's son, weep over Christ's agony on the cross, and chant impromptu verses of a religious nature, some of which his parents preserved – what he called his "Songstries". By the age of fifteen, however, he was professing agnosticism, and he and his friend, Bob Stevenson, were deriding every tenet their parents held sacrosanct. He was still an agnostic at thirty-five, admitting that he could not believe in an after-life. Life to him was a pilgrimage, from nothing to nowhere. He wrote:

> For who would gravely set his face
> To go to this or t'other place?
> There's nothing under Heaven so blue
> That's fairly worth the travelling to.
> On every hand the roads begin,
> And people walk with zeal therein,
> But wheresoe'er the highways tend,
> Be sure there's nothing at the end.

To his father his agnosticism was painful – he regarded it as atheism. "A poor end to my tenderness," he wrote to him, "I have worked for you, and gone out of my way for you, and the end of it is that I find you in opposition to the Lord Jesus Christ. I would ten times sooner have seen you lying in your grave than that you should be shaking the faith of other young men and bringing such ruin on other houses as you have brought already upon this. I had thought to have

191

someone to help me when I was old." His father prayed for him at family worship, and Stevenson was divided between pity for him and ridicule. Yet at the end of his life he formulated a philosophy indistinguishable from that of the Sermon on the Mount – what Lloyd Osbourne later described as Christianity without Christ.

Always superstitious, as a child at his grandmother's manse Stevenson fancied that he could see the souls of the dead peeping through the chinks of the churchyard wall, and he christened the path that led to it "The Witches' Walk". Then, the story of *The Strange Case of Dr Jekyll and Mr Hyde,* which came to him in one of the nightmares he was always subject to, was a remarkable instance of "magic" being used for fictional purposes.

He was reckless, too. Perhaps the most reckless act of his life was setting off to join his inamorata, Fanny Osbourne, ten years older than he, in America, without a word to his parents – an escapade which seriously affected his health, and may have led to the severe deterioration which was to develop from then on. With no money, he had to live on practically nothing – hardly any breakfast, a fifty-cent lunch, and a cup of coffee and a roll at six o'clock, the asceticism of the Phaeton taken a great deal too far. In no time he had his first haemorrhage from the lungs, and for the rest of his life lived under the threat of sudden death. In Fanny, however, he had found the mother he was looking for, and one as unlike his own, very fair, mother as could be. Of her he wrote:

> The hue of heather honey
> The hue of honey bees,
> Shall tinge her golden shoulder,
> Shall tinge her tawny knees.
>
> Dark as a wayside gypsy,
> Lithe as a hedgewood hare,
> She moves a glowing shadow
> Through the sunshine of the fair;
> And golden hue and orange,
> Bosom and hand and head,
> She blooms, a tiger lily,
> In the snowdrift of the bed.

192

Tiger and tiger lily
She plays a double part,
All woman in the body,
And all the man at heart.
She shall be brave and tender,
She shall be soft and high,
She to lie in my bosom,
And *he* to fight and die.

Yet this reckless act was exceeded by far by the plan he conceived of going to Ireland in 1887, specifically in order to get himself and his family murdered by the resentful farmers who were murdering British people living in farms rented from their former landlords – such a murder of a distinguished literary man would, he was convinced, create a furore, and "arrest the whole civilised world". Only the illness of his father prevented his putting the plan into action.

All his life he fell in love with older women, from Mrs Sitwell, twelve years older than he, to Mrs Fanny Osbourne, ten years older. He wrote to them both as to a mother, telling Mrs Sitwell that he longed to sit down with his head on her knees and have a long talk and feel her smoothing his hair. "It is not a bit like what I feel for my mother *here*," he wrote to her. "But I think it must be what one *ought* to feel for a mother." Then he added, doubtless in order to reassure Mrs Sitwell of her erotic appeal, "That's a lie; nobody loves a mere mother as I love you, madonna." Despite that, this is a clear plea for a substitute mother. He even called her, first, madonna, and then, Mother of my Soul.

All his life Robert Louis Stevenson tried to buy love. As soon as he had any money he spent it on his friends. When he married Fanny Osbourne, he took on the financial support of her daughter, and her alcoholic and unfaithful husband Joe Strong, quite unnecessarily. As a result he had to abandon his plan to send her son, Lloyd Osbourne, to Cambridge – a more rewarding objective.

The rest of the story is sad, and all too well known. The recklessness of marrying a woman who, as he knew, had suffered a full-scale mental collapse, was brought home to him very clearly in Vailima, Samoa. Fanny, badly deteriorated, was quarrelling with her daughter and her son-in-law, and with her mother-in-law; Joe Strong was drunken and disloyal; and

Stevenson was subjected to intolerable strain. It was all made infinitely worse when his wife had another mental collapse, and had to be held down on her bed to prevent her running away.

Soon Stevenson was far closer to his wife's daughter, Belle, than to her, and his wife was showing her age – now she was over fifty, getting heavy and grizzled, and said to resemble an old lioness. Belle was only thirty-two, and even swarthier than her mother. She was, in those last, sad days, most certainly closer to him than her mother was. By the spring of 1893 he was admitting the difficulties of his situation: "Fanny is not well, and we are miserably anxious. I may as well say now that for nearly eighteen months there has been something wrong; I could not write of it; but it was very trying and painful – and mostly fell on me. Now we are face to face with the question: what next? . . . it's anxious . . . I am stupid and tired and have done little even to my proofs."

The doctor pronounced no danger to her life, but certainly a danger of insanity. He struggled on, trying to write against odds. The woman who had once saved his life, for she had married him believing that she would be his widow in a few months, was now his greatest trial. To Lloyd Osbourne he revealed his tortured soul and the moments when he earnestly longed for death. Lloyd even caught him gazing up at the green corner of Mount Vaea, which he had chosen as the site for his tomb. He wrote to Mrs Sitwell that the gods did not love him, and he was meant to die young. And now, at the end of his life, he wrote his *Vailima Prayers,* written by him for reading aloud to his family and Samoan household, and which would be reprinted in Great Britain and the United States of America.

On December 3rd, 1894, he seemed well and resilient. At noon he stopped work. Shortly after five o'clock Belle heard Fanny calling for hot water and, suspecting nothing amiss, walked calmly downstairs. Louis, in the great hall, was slumped back in a big red armchair, unconscious and breathing stertorously, while Fanny and his mother rubbed his hands, and the native boy brought hot water for his feet. Belle rushed over to her brother's cottage, and he galloped to Apia for the doctor. The end, when it came, was sudden. Robert Louis Stevenson, recovered, played a card game to distract Fanny, then fetched wine from the cellar, and began to help her make mayonnaise for supper, putting in oil drop by drop with a steady hand. All at once he cried out, and then asked Fanny, "Do I look strange?" He had had a cerebral haemorrhage. He fell to his knees and never regained consciousness. He died at ten minutes past eight that evening – he was only forty-four.

The path to the top of Mount Vaea, his chosen resting-place, the making of which had always been superstitiously deferred by Lloyd Osbourne, had to be rapidly cut. Ninety Europeans and sixty Samoans climbed to the top, but Louis's wife, his mother, and his stepdaughter watched the coffin disappear into the trees from the verandah of the house.

On his tomb he is remembered by the verses he had written for it:

> Under the wide and starry sky
> Dig the grave and let me lie.
> Glad did I live and gladly die
> And I laid me down with a will.
>
> This be the verse you grave for me:
> "Here he lies where he longed to be;
> Home is the sailor, home from the sea,
> And the hunter home from the hill."

Interestingly, when his stepfather died, Lloyd Osbourne, a Phaeton himself, collapsed, and became so gravely ill that those about him feared he would die from grief. Robert Louis Stevenson had succeeded in fulfilling one of the most difficult of relationships, that of stepfather, with surprising success.

Whatever one thinks, too, of Fanny Stevenson, one should remember that it is to her that we owe the remarkable *Dr Jekyll and Mr Hyde* in its final form. It was she who objected, to his anger, to the story as Robert Louis Stevenson originally produced it. To his credit, he decided that she was right, and rewrote it.

So, once again, we have the Phaeton characteristics – an extreme reaction to bereavement; extreme religious concern; superstitiousness; recklessness; and a never-ending search for love.

CHAPTER 15

Bernard Montgomery (1887 – 1976)

Bernard Montgomery had a wretched childhood. He himself said of it: "Certainly I can say that my own childhood was unhappy. This was due to a clash of wills between my mother and myself. My early life was a series of battles, from which my mother invariably emerged the victor." His mother in fact was his enemy, and he never forgave her for it. It is a significant fact that Marlborough, Wellington and Montgomery were all unhappy in their childhoods.

His mother was only fourteen when she became engaged to Henry Montgomery, one of the curates of her father, Dr Farrar (author of *Eric, or Little by Little*) when he was Canon of Westminster, and Rector of St Margaret's, Westminster. She married Henry at sixteen, when he was thirty-four. She was a dominant personality. She had nine children, and seems to have been a good mother to the others, but never got on with Bernard, or his sister and friend, Una. Bernard Montgomery himself admitted that he was a difficult child, but how much was the cause, and how much the effect, of his mother's lack of love for him, it is not, of course, possible to say.

Perhaps it was because of his mother that Montgomery seemed to have had no use for women, indeed to have detested them, until his own happy marriage. He may be said to have loved only three people in his life – his father, the Bishop; his wife, Betty; and his son, David. Because his mother rejected him, he did not love her – indeed, he hated her. As late as the First World War a reconciliation might have been effected; but when he sent her presents she gave them away. To one present of a coat he even attached a note, "This is not to be given away to the Belgians – it is to be worn by you."

Montgomery had an extreme reation to bereavement as is later shown by his reaction to the death of his wife. In January 1926 he had met Betty Carver, at Lenk, in the Bernese Oberland, on a skiing holiday. She was the widow of an army officer who had been killed at Gallipoli, and the mother of two small sons. Though not beautiful, this dark-haired, heavy-featured woman had a face that radiated kindness and intelligence. She was regarded as a little eccentric, and was an amateur painter, living in a house at Chiswick let to her by A.P. Herbert, after she had fled from the oppressive atmosphere of her in-laws' home. It took two visits to Lenk before Montgomery made up his mind, but, once decided, he moved without hesitation. On 27th July, 1927, they were married in Chiswick parish church. A complete transformation in his whole existence then took place.

Montgomery had a deep, and total, love of this woman, and had little or no control over that emotion. Until he met Betty Carver no woman had got close to him; he had had no small talk; and he had avoided emotional relationships. He had been, in fact, deeply, and, apparently irreversibly, immature. Now everything changed. Later he would write in his memoirs that it had seemed to him impossible that such love and affection could exist. At last he had the friendship, the loyalty, the understanding, and the approval, that he had always lacked; and he entered a new, enchanting world. Of course, being Montgomery, he assumed the role of commanding officer in the marriage, treating his wife as a delightful, but incompetent, subordinate.

They went abroad twice together, once to Alexandria, on duty, and then on holiday to Japan. By then they had a son, David, and returned with him to England in 1937. Montgomery was given command of a brigade in Portsmouth, and moved into a large army house near by. He immediately began to organise the installation of books, carpets and souvenirs.

In the summer, with the house nearly ready, Montgomery took his brigade on manoeuvres for the first time, and Betty and David went to Burnham-on-Sea for a holiday. Suddenly tragedy struck. On the beach one day at Burnham, Betty was taken ill. She remembered being bitten on the leg by an insect.

At first there was no concern, but as she felt weak and faint, and was rather run down, she was taken into the local cottage hospital for observation, and Montgomery was informed. By the time he arrived at the hospital it was obvious that something was seriously wrong. Betty's leg was swollen, and the infection was spreading fast. After an amputation, and weeks of pain, she died, on 19th October, 1937. The last voice she heard before she died was that of her husband reading to her:

> The Lord is my shepherd, I shall not want,
> He maketh me to lie down in green pastures,
> He leadeth me beside the still waters.

Montgomery's reaction was bitter, and extreme. He retired to the big house near Portsmouth, covered the furniture, closed many of the rooms, and began a period in which he worked obsessively, never went out, and never discussed his wife's death with anyone. In his memoirs he wrote: "I was utterly defeated. I began to search my mind for anything I had done wrong, that I should have been dealt such a shattering blow. I could not understand it; my soul cried out in anguish against this apparent injustice; all the spirit was knocked out of me. I had no one to love except David, and he was away at school."

Montgomery had not allowed David to visit his mother in hospital from his prep-school at Hindhead, saying that he could not bring himself to let the boy see her suffering. Nor did he allow his son to see his mother buried, since the funeral was in term-time. He undoubtedly did what he thought was right, but the impact of the death on a vulnerable boy must have been shattering.

After his wife's death Montgomery spent a few holidays with his son, and recalled that they were happy times, on the whole. But soon he had to leave his son. He refused his sister Winsome's offer to take him; and left him in the care of friends in Portsmouth – yet another Phaeton.

Twenty-five years later, Montgomery was still suffering from the death of his wife. After her death no other woman ever interested him, and in 1961, in the epilogue to his book, *The Path to Leadership*, he inserted a remarkable passage, in which he described a dream he had had. The figure of his dead father had appeared to him in the garden of his house in

Hampshire. After they had talked to one another for a while the old man smiled and moved away down the garden path.

"Then," wrote Montgomery, "something seemed to happen in the garden and I longed to see what it could be. There was a slight breeze, and a stir, too, among the shrubs – not like the whispering of leaves in the wind, but more human, as though they murmured in their own language. And I thought I saw figures of people, shadowy figures which I could not see clearly. Was my wife, my darling Betty, in the garden? I hurried down the grass paths between the beds, along the river bank, through the orchard, but I could not see her – and I knew that I must wait yet awhile."

The cold and unemotional Montgomery had given his heart to his wife, warmly and for ever. After her death he was totally inaccessible to any other woman. The barriers he had erected during his five months of desolation in 1937 would never again come down.

Montgomery's isolation and reserve were a byword, and the asceticism of his life from his earliest years was extreme. He was obsessed with physical fitness. He always smoked and drank very little, and in later life became so antipathetic to smoking that no soldier was allowed to smoke in his presence without his express permission. He was ruthless in punishing anyone whose efficiency was impaired by alcohol. He had no hobbies. The legend that at his lectures there were fifteen-minute intervals for coughing still lives. He made himself very unpopular by banishing officers' wives, who used to travel with their husbands. Women, as we know, had no place in his life until he married. Love-affairs were for others; for him only success, and the power it brought, mattered.

He was reckless, too. The story of his racing on his Indian cavalry charger, Probyn, on which he hunted with the Peshawar Vale Hounds, in a point-to-point, is a classic example. Probyn was a baggage horse which he had bought for a mere eight pounds. He trained fanatically, and when the race began found his starting price satisfyingly high. Then he fell off. Undeterred, he remounted and charged after the field. Soon he was leading in the race. Then he lost his stirrups, and, having galloped past the winning-post well ahead of his rivals, fell off again just as he was being declared the winner.

Less acceptable was the episode of his early years at Sandhurst, when he arranged that an unfortunate young cadet should be pinned from the front with a bayonet while Montgomery set fire to his shirt-tails. The cadet was badly burned and went to hospital. He did not reveal Montgomery's name, but his superiors found out, and reduced him to the lowest rank, that of gentleman-cadet, and he had to stay on for an extra six months before being allowed to graduate.

Montgomery, however, made up for such an escapade many times over, and gained great kudos with his troops, by refusing, possibly foolishly, to take cover during air-attacks as the Alam Halfa offensive began; and, later, at Mareth, he simply went on talking to a fellow-officer, totally unmoved by a shell-burst nearby.

Incidentally, it was at Ypres, where Adolf Hitler, also a Phaeton, but by bereavement, not rejection, gained his own medal for a certain reckless courage, that Bernard Montgomery also demonstrated, at the age of twenty-six, in 1914, courage with a distinct element of recklessness in it. Drawing his sword, and shouting "Follow me!" he charged at a trench. Confronted by a trench full of German soldiers, he realised that one of them was about to fire his rifle at the sword-brandishing subaltern. "An immediate decision was clearly vital," Montgomery later wrote. "I hurled myself through the air at the German, and kicked him as hard as I could in the lower part of the stomach; the blow was well aimed at a tender spot. I had read much about the value of surprise in war. There is no doubt that the German was surprised and it must have seemed to him a new form of war; he fell to the ground in great pain and I took my first prisoner!"

At the end of that day Montgomery lay in the mud and the rain, protected only by the body of a dead comrade, the Germans shooting continuously at them. Brought back to camp, he was so ill that a grave was dug for him. The result of the exploit in the end was the award of the Distinguished Service Order – and a citation: "Conspicuous gallant leading on 13th October, when he turned the enemy out of their trenches with the bayonet. He was severely wounded."

Another example of recklessness was his issuing a pamphlet on venereal disease, which caused outrage and dismay in the vestries of the Royal Armies' Chaplains' Department. Even Montgomery was frightened by the result of this premature flirtation with the permissive society, which nearly got him into very serious trouble. He actually wrote in the pamphlet,

"My view is that if a man wants to have a woman, let him do so by all means; but he must use his common sense and take the necessary precautions against infection – otherwise he becomes a casualty by his own neglect, and this is helping the enemy. Our job is to help him by providing the necessary means: he should be able to buy French Letters in the unit shop, and E. T. [Early Treatment] rooms must be available for use."

This led to trouble, and it was only thanks to General Alan Brooke that he was saved. For once the arrogant Montgomery kissed the rod, and, frightened by what he had done, thanked Brooke humbly.

Another example of recklessness was his decision to let Clarence Football Field, on Southsea Common, to a fairground promoter for a bank holiday fair. The man offered a thousand pounds, but Montgomery demanded fifteen hundred pounds, and got it. The City Council refused to agree to a fair on the common, but when Montgomery offered the Mayor five hundred pounds he persuaded the Council to agree. Montgomery gave the Mayor his five hundred pounds, and spent the rest on the garrison welfare services. If the story is accurate, and he himself said that it was, he deliberately contravened army regulations, and bribed an elected member of a municipal council. The War Office failed to appreciate his attitude, but was prepared to overlook it if he handed over the fifteen hundred pounds at once. He said that he could not, as he had spent it. His career hung perilously in the balance, but he was saved, probably by Wavell, and he moved ebulliently on to his next appointment.

Montgomery was, perhaps unexpectedly, superstitious. In May 1939 he became seriously ill, in Palestine – so weak that it seemed he might be dying. The doctors found a patch on his lung and suspected tuberculosis, but no treatment did any good. He had a powerful conviction that if he could get to England he would recover speedily. So he persuaded the doctors to send him home. In the summer of 1939 he was carried aboard a P.&O. liner at Port Said, with two nursing sisters and two nursing orderlies. He seemed desperately ill. Yet a few days later the helpless stretcher-case was able to appear on deck, and he walked off the ship at Tilbury, and went direct to the Millbank Hospital, in London, to be told that he was in perfect health and the patch on his lung had disappeared. Whether his illness had been psychosomatic or not, he was now well, and where he wished to be. He was able to nag those in power at the War Office, and a week before the declaration of war he was appointed to the command of the Third Division. Soon he was able to go to France with the British Expeditionary Force, and he was on the threshold of his greatest triumphs. It was on 8th July, 1942, that he would receive a telephone call to the effect that General Gott, who had been selected to lead the Eighth Army, had been killed in an air-crash, shot down by a German fighter-plane, and that he was to take his place.

As a young man, religion meant a great deal to Montgomery, and it was always a matter of concern to him. At one time, so shaken was he by what was happening in the First World War that, to his father's distress, he announced that he was an agnostic. When the war was over, however, in the early 'twenties, he was fascinated by a book by Guy Thorne, an Edwardian melodrama called *When it was Dark*, which gave him what he was seeking. This story of a Jew who tried to prove that the resurrection never took place had a certain success, and, to Montgomery, this meant that "the brute in man was awake, unchained and loose, cruelty and lust reared their heads". Now, again, he was convinced that Christianity had the rights of it, and started going to communion again.

From then on, he was safe in the harbour of the Anglican church once more. When he was in Jerusalem he took the opportunity to explore the sacred places of the Holy Land, and to strengthen his commitment to the Lord Mighty in Battle, whose aid he was to invoke with utter confidence. The intensity of his religious feeling was deepened by the death of his father, at the age of eighty-nine. His father had always, sometimes against the evidence, had confidence in his son, believing him to be destined for great things. Montgomery's love for his father was deep, and lasting, and he mourned him sincerely, if not with the agony occasioned by his wife's death – it was, we recall, his father, as well as his wife, who visited him in his dream. That father had written in his book, *A Generation of Montgomerys*, "Carry on, my dearest children, the holy traditions of Godliness and humility, and steady labour and true piety, so that the name of Montgomery, as it has borne no stain in the past, may receive no injury when it is chiefly in your keeping." It was an exhortation that Bernard Montgomery took very seriously.

The Battle of El Alamein, and the campaign in the Western Desert which followed it, made Montgomery one of the heroes who will never be forgotten.

In conclusion, I can do no better than quote his distinguished biographer, Lord Chalfont.

"What did make the Field-Marshal tick? How did he overcome the ostensibly paralysing deficiencies of character and personality to become a national hero and a legend in his own time, a man whose name has become a household word in many of the countries of the world? . . . His relationship with his mother, who denied him the attention and the tenderness which he obviously craved, is almost certainly the key to the strange character which lay behind the piercingly clear blue eyes and the high-pitched didactic voice. This relationship, with its crippling failure of understanding, conditioned much of his later development."

I would take issue with only one word in that paragraph. I would say not "almost certainly", but "certainly".

CHAPTER 16

It was of some interest to me that, after the publication of *The Fiery Chariot*, a large number of Members of Parliament approached my husband, then a Member of Parliament himself, to say that they recognised themselves in the characteristics outlined. One said that he had a sense of *déjà vu*.

It was with some interest, too, that I observed that China's premier, Hua Guo-Feng, in the first televised interview broadcast from Peking to the West since the revolution, chose to say, as his very first words, that he had lost his father at the age of six. One might not have assumed that that was the most important thing he had wished to convey to the West!

Divorce, with the statistics rising steadily, constantly increases disturbance in childhood. Dr Margaret White, a Croydon juvenile court magistrate, claims that more than eight in ten of the children appearing before her come from broken homes – the effects are severe, and long-lasting. Frequently, as was observed in a recent article in *The Reader's Digest*, divorce "hits them [children] nearly as hard as the death of a parent, leaving them grieving. Five-year-old Timothy told a social worker that, when his father left, it was 'like having a tummy-ache, only worse – it hurt all over'. Many erupt into anger, like four-year-old Trevor, who flew into a rage when told his father was leaving, thumped both parents in turn, then lapsed into stony silence."

A remarkable example of this very form of behaviour was evinced by Hermann Göring. In the spring of 1893 Fanny Göring weaned her three-month-old son, and left Germany to rejoin her husband and the rest of her family in Haiti. It was three years before they returned to Germany. During that time Hermann was left with a family in the Bavarian town of Fürth, and was brought up with the two young daughters of the house. They would afterwards remember him as a child given to fits of tears and tantrums, which were invariably followed by gifts and gestures of affection. "It is the cruellest thing that can happen to a child to be torn from his mother in his formative years," Hermann Göring was to say, many years later.

His older sister Olga remembered that when Herr and Frau Göring eventually returned from the Caribbean, and Hermann was taken to the railroad station to meet them, the three-year-old Hermann deliberately turned his back as the train steamed up to the platform. When his mother took him in her arms and embraced him, he responded by beating her about the face and chest, and then bursting into tears. He completely ignored the stranger who was his father. His devotion to food – he was plump even as a young German pilot – was probably an attempt to compensate for this deprivation.

It has been maintained that divorce affects the children's own marriages. According to the Head of Counselling at the National Marriage Guidance Council, a surprisingly high proportion of those who come to them for help with their marriages are themselves the children of divorced parents. Divorce, say some, has been made too easy since 1969. Since then the divorce rate has nearly doubled, to an annual 144,000, one for every three marriages, involving more than 160,000 children under sixteen each year. In England and Wales today, it is sobering to note, there are perhaps one million children of divorced parents. If the present rate continues, there could be more than two and a half million by 1990.

The shock to a child can be very severe. Children under four often regress to an even younger age, and become more dependent. Those between six and twelve may have guilty feelings about the break-up, asking whether it was because they were "naughty" that a parent went. When a father leaves, the child may become very nervous that the mother too may go.

Another stress is the conflict between the parents. The child longs for the parents to get back together, and hates being dragged into a battle between the two. It is vital that divorce should not, as far as possible, deprive children of their father and mother, even though the parents may no longer be husband and wife.

What of bereavement over my arbitrarily chosen fifteen years? One can find many bereaved over that age who clearly show the Phaeton characteristics. However, in this book I restrict myself to those under fifteen.

Again, what of other cultures, in which the Western nuclear family is not the norm? There was a story told when I lived in the Pacific that the missionaries had to rewrite the Bible to translate God-the-Father into God-the-Mother's-Brother, since among certain Polynesian peoples the head of the family was the mother's brother, and the physical father had no important role. It raises the questions as to whether the death of the mother's brother would have the same devastating effect as the death of a father in our Western-type family.

Thirdly, what of earlier ages, where parent-child relationships were very different: for example, in the fourteenth century, as portrayed by Barbara Tuchman in *A Distant Mirror*? Such queries are not easily resolved.

So there we are. There is no doubt that, whether by death, or by such shocks as separation, rejection, divorce and so on, children are very vulnerable to the loss of a parent or parents. It is, unhappily, one of the facts of life over which one has no control; but perhaps understanding a little about the effects may help those concerned to comprehend and cope rather better than if there were no such awareness.

ABBREVIATED BIBLIOGRAPHY

General

Mary D. Ainsworth, see under World Health Organisation
R.G. Andry, *Delinquency and Parental Pathology* (Methuen)
 1960
—— *Parental and Maternal Roles and Delinquency* (Methuen)
 1962 (See also under World Health Organisation)
John Bowlby, *Child Care and the Growth of Love*. Based by
 permission of the World Health Organisation on the report
 Maternal Care and Mental Health by John Bowlby, M.D.,
 abridged and edited by Margery Fry (Penguin) 1965.
Felix Brown, "Depression and Childhood Bereavement"
 (Journal of Mental Science, 1961, pages 107 and 754–777)
Maryse Choisy, *Le Complexe de Phaéton* (Psyché No. 48, pub-
 lished by Psyché, 19 rue Monsieur, Paris VII) 1950
—— *Moïse* (Editions du Mont Blanc, Geneva) 1966
J. and J.F. Egelson, *Parents Without Partners, a guide for divorced,
 widowed, or separated parents* (E.P. Dutton, New York) 1961
George E. Gardner, "Separation of the Parents and the
 Emotional Life of the Child" in *Readings in Child and
 Adolescent Psychology*, edited by Lester D. and Alice Crow
 (Longmans, London and New York) 1961
Robert D. Harlow, see under World Health Organisation
S. Lebovici, see under World Health Organisation
Susan Isaacs, see under New Education Fellowship
Peter Marris, *Widows and Their Familes* (Routledge & Kegan
 Paul) 1958

207

John McCord (et al), "Some Effects of Paternal Absence on
Male Children" (Journal of Abnormal and Social Psychol-
ogy, 1962, pages 64(5), 361–369)
Margaret Mead, see under World Health Organisation
New Education Fellowship (1 Park Crescent, London W1),
*Problems of Child Development – a Contribution to the Under-
standing of Children's Needs,* 1948, containing *inter alia* the
following papers:-
Susan Isaacs, *Fatherless Children*
Joan Rivière, *The Bereaved Wife*
Ella Freeman Sharpe, *What a Father Means to a Child*
Everett Ostrovsky, *Father to the Child: Case Studies of the
Experience of a Male Teacher* (G.P. Putnam, New York) 1959
Ovid, *Metamorphoses,* with an English translation by Frank
Justus Miller (2 volumes, The Loeb Classical Library) 1916
Dane G. Prugh, see under World Health Organisation
Joan Rivière, see under New Education Fellowship
Michael Rutter, *Children of Sick Parents* (Oxford University
Press) 1966
Ella Freeman Sharpe, see under New Education Fellowship.
Virginia Wimperis, *The Unmarried Mother and Her Child* (Allen
& Unwin) 1960
Sula Wolff, *Children Under Stress* (Penguin) 1969
Barbara Wootton, see under World Health Organisation
World Health Organisation, Geneva, *Public Health Papers, No.
14, Deprivation of Maternal Care – a Reassessment of its Effects,*
containing the following papers:-
Dane G. Prugh and Robert G. Harlow, *"Masked Deprivation"
in Infants and Young Children*
R.G. Andry, *Paternal and Maternal Roles in Delinquency*
Margaret Mead, *A Cultural Anthropologist's Approach to
Maternal Deprivation*
S. Lebovici, *The Concept of Maternal Deprivation: a Review of
Research*
Mary D. Ainsworth, *The Effects of Maternal Deprivation: a
Review of Findings and Controversy in the Context of Research
Strategy*
Margaret Wynn, *Fatherless Families. A Study of Families Deprived
of a Father by Death, Divorce, Separation or Desertion before or
after Marriage* (Michael Joseph) 1964

Chapter 3   Adolf Hitler

Adolf Hitler, *Hitler's War Directives* (1939–45) edited by H.R. Trevor-Roper (Pan Books) 1966

Adolf Hitler, *Mein Kampf* translated by Ralph Manheim with an introduction by D.C. Watt (Hutchinson) 1972

Walter C. Langer, *The Mind of Adolf Hitler (The Secret Wartime Report)*, Foreword by William L. Langer, Afterword by Robert G.L. Waite (Secker & Warburg) 1972

William L. Shirer, *The Rise and Fall of the Third Reich* (Secker & Warburg) 1960

H.R. Trevor-Roper, *Hitler's Table-Talk, 1941–1944. His Private Conversation* (Weidenfeld & Nicolson) 1953

H.R. Trevor-Roper, *The Last Days of Hitler* (Macmillan) 1960, (Pan Books) 1968

Chapter 4   Mary Shelley

Jane Dunn, *Moon in Eclipse* (Weidenfeld & Nicolson) 1978

Rosalie Glynn Grylls, *Mary Shelley, a Biography* (Oxford University Press) 1941

Elizabeth Nitchie, *Mary Shelley, Author of Frankenstein* (Rutgers University Press, New Brunswick) 1953

Mary Shelley, *Collected Tales and Stories* edited by Charles E. Robinson (John Hopkins University Press) 1976

Mary Shelley, *Frankenstein, or the Modern Prometheus* Everyman's Library, No. 616 (Dent), (Oxford University Press) 1980

Chapter 5   George Gordon, Lord Byron

Leslie Marchand, *Byron,* 3 volumes (Alfred H. Knopf, New York and John Murray) 1957

Chapter 6   Horatio Nelson

Geoffrey Bennett, *Nelson the Commander* (Batsford) 1972

Ernle Bradford, *Nelson the Essential Hero* (Macmillan) 1977

Tom Pocock, *Nelson and His World* (Thames & Hudson) 1968

David Walder, *Nelson* (Weidenfeld & Nicolson) 1975
Oliver Warner, *Nelson* (Hamish Hamilton) 1978

Chapter 7   Augustus John

Michael Holroyd, *Augustus John, a Biography, Vol. I, The Years of Innocence* (Heinemann) 1974
Michael Holroyd, *Augustus John, a Biography, Vol. II. The Years of Experience* (Heinemann) 1975

Chapter 8   Marilyn Monroe

Truman Capote, *Music for Chameleons* (Hamish Hamilton) 1981 (Copyright 1980)
Fred Lawrence Guiles, *Norma Jean* (Mayflower) 1974
Norman Mailer, *Of Women and their Elegance* (Hodder & Stoughton) 1980

Chapter 9   Ignace Jan Paderewski

Rom Landau, *Paderewski* (Ivor Nicholson & Watson) 1934
Alfred Nossig, *Ignace Jan Paderewski* (Leipzig) 1901
Ignace Jan Paderewski and Mary Lawton, *The Paderewski Memoirs* (Collins) 1939
Charles Phillips, *Paderewski, the Story of a Modern Immortal* (Macmillan) 1934

Chapter 10   Aristotle Onassis

John Ardoin and Gerald Fitzgerald, *Callas* (Thames & Hudson) 1974
Stephen Birmingham, *Jacqueline Bouvier Kennedy Onassis* (Gollancz) 1978
Frank Brady, *Onassis, an Extravagant Life* (Circus Books, Futura) 1978
Willi Frischauer, *Onassis* (Bodley Head) 1968
Stelios Galatopoulos, *Callas, La Divina* (Cunningham Bass) 1963

Kitty Kelley, *Jackie-Oh!* (Granada) 1978
Arianna Stassinopoulos, *Maria, Beyond the Callas Legend* (Weidenfeld & Nicolson) 1980

Chapter 11   Charles Manson

William Bolitho, *Murder for Profit* (Elek) 1962
Vincent Bugliosi with Curt Gentry, *The Manson Murders, an Investigation into Motive* (Bodley Head) 1975
Ed Sanders, *The Family* (Hart-Davies) 1972

Chapter 13   Charles Dickens

Hesketh Pearson, *Dickens, the Outstanding Genius of English Literature* (Macmillan) 1949
Una Pope-Hennessey, *Charles Dickens* (Chatto & Windus) 1945

Chapter 14   Robert Louis Stevenson

James Pope-Hennessey, *Robert Louis Stevenson* (Cape) 1974

Chapter 15   Bernard Montgomery

Alun Chalfont, *Montgomery of Alamein* (Weidenfeld & Nicolson) 1976
R.W. Clark, *Montgomery of Alamein* (Phoenix House) 1960
Professor Norman F. Dixon, MBE, *On the Psychology of Military Incompetence* (Futura) 1979
Ronald Lewin, *Montgomery as Military Commander* (Batsford) 1971